"This textbook is a timely, comprehensive and essential read for all clinicians facilitating group psychotherapy. The co-editors Drs. Collins-Greene, Riva, Lefforge and all the contributors of this volume artfully and compellingly illustrate the latest advances in best practices, skills, and competencies of efficient multiculturally informed supervision. The editors have compiled chapters from leading experts in the field and from different theoretical approaches. I highly recommend this book which provides replete practical and clinical frameworks for optimizing supervision outcomes and advancing ethical competency-based training and research in group psychotherapy."
— **Leonardo M. Leiderman**, PsyD, ABPP, FAACP, CGP, AGPA-F, *Director, Neurofeedback and Psychological Services, PC, President, American Group Psychotherapy Association*

"With the recent designation of Group Psychology and Group Psychotherapy as a Recognized Specialty by the American Psychological Association, this book is timely and needed. Collins-Greene, Riva, and Lefforge have assembled renown group psychotherapists with extensive experience in the supervision of group psychotherapy to create an in-depth resource on the supervision of group psychotherapy covering everything from the history and models of group psychotherapy supervision, specific competencies for supervisors, ethical issues, and multicultural considerations. This book should be required reading in psychotherapy supervision practicum students and anyone engaged in (or considering engaging in) the practice of supervision of group psychotherapy."
— **Joe Miles**, PhD, *Professor and Director of Clinical Training, Counseling Psychology PhD Program*

"This comprehensive manual fills a critical gap in the supervision literature by providing essential guidance for training group psychotherapy supervisors and consultants. The authors expertly integrate foundational principles with contemporary approaches, covering crucial areas from supervisory competencies, methods, ethical considerations, and Justice, Equity, Diversity, and Inclusion perspectives."
— **Jane E. Atieno Okech**, PhD, NCC, *Editor of the* Journal for Specialists in Group Work, *Vice Provost for Faculty Affairs, and Professor of Counselor Education and Supervision, University of Vermont*

I0038767

Supervision of Group Psychotherapy

Supervision of Group Psychotherapy: A Training Manual is a new essential resource for training supervisors of group psychotherapy.

This manual provides updated general standards and guidelines for supervising group therapy, including those that are unique to various training sites such as private practice, hospitals, mental health agencies, and academic training centers, across disciplines such as social work, counseling, psychology, and psychiatry. The manual includes historical perspectives and foundations, research, theory, ethics, and applied knowledge of group psychotherapy supervision. Integrating theoretical, clinical, and research perspectives, it offers a thorough analysis of the dynamic interplay among supervisor, therapist, and group—key elements in shaping effective supervisors as well as group therapists. It can also be used for supervisors training practitioners to become Certified Group Psychotherapists (CGPs).

Filled with concepts considered core knowledge for any group supervisor-in-training, this manual provides the gold standard for group therapy supervision.

Michelle A. Collins-Greene, PhD, ABGP, CGP, AGPA-F, consults, supervises, and mentors group psychotherapists nationally. In her private practice in New Haven, CT, and Port Washington, NY, she leads several psychotherapy groups. She has extensive experience creating supervision groups in hospital and community mental health centers.

Maria T. Riva, PhD, is Emerita Professor of Counselling Psychology at Morgridge College of Education, University of Denver. She publishes on supervision, group supervision, and group psychotherapy topics with a recent APA-spotlighted article coauthored with Randi Smith, PhD.

Noelle L. Lefforge, PhD, ABPP, CGP, AGPA-F, is a professor and Clinical Director at the University of Denver's Graduate School of Professional Psychology. She has published group psychotherapy education and training guidelines in training and education in professional psychology that are shaping the future of supervision of group psychotherapy.

AGPA Group Therapy Training and Practice Series
Series Editors: Les R. Greene and Rebecca MacNair-Semands

The American Group Psychotherapy Association (AGPA) is the foremost professional association dedicated to the field of group psychotherapy, operating through a tri-partite structure: AGPA, a professional and educational organization; the Group Foundation for Advancing Mental Health, its philanthropic arm; and the International Board for Certification of Group Psychotherapists, a standard setting and certifying body. This multidisciplinary association has approximately 3,000 members, including psychiatrists, psychologists, social workers, nurses, clinical mental health counselors, marriage and family therapists, pastoral counselors, occupational therapists and creative arts therapists, many of whom have been recognized as specialists through the CGP credential. The association has 26 local and regional societies located across the country. Its members are experienced mental health professionals who lead psychotherapy groups and various non-clinical groups. Many are organizational specialists who work with businesses, not-for-profit organizations, communities and other "natural" groups to help them improve their functioning.

The goal of the AGPA Group Therapy Training and Practice Series is to produce the highest quality publications to aid the practitioners and students in updating and improving their knowledge, professional competence and skills with current and new developments in methods, practice, theory, and research in the group psychotherapy field. Books in this series are the only curriculum guide and resource for a variety of courses credentialed by the International Board for Certification of Group Psychotherapists. While this is the series' original and primary purpose, the texts are also useful in a variety of other settings including as a resource for students and clinicians interested in learning more about group psychotherapy, as a text in academic courses, or as part of a training curriculum in a practicum or internship training experience.

For more information about this series, please visit https://www.routledge.com/AGPA-Group-Therapy-Training-and-Practice-Series/book-series/AGPA.

Books in this Series:

Group Psychotherapy Assessment and Practice: A Measurement-Based Care Approach, *by Martyn Whittingham and Rebecca MacNair-Semands*

Group Psychotherapy with Children: Core Principles for Effective Practice, *by Tony L. Sheppard and Zachary J. Thieneman*

Supervision of Group Psychotherapy: A Training Manual, *Edited by Michelle A. Collins-Greene, Maria T. Riva, and Noelle L. Lefforge*

Supervision of Group Psychotherapy

A Training Manual

Edited by Michelle A. Collins-Greene,
Maria T. Riva, and Noelle L. Lefforge

Routledge
Taylor & Francis Group

NEW YORK AND LONDON

Designed cover image: Getty Images

First published 2026
by Routledge
605 Third Avenue, New York, NY 10158

and by Routledge
4 Park Square, Milton Park, Abingdon, Oxon, OX14 4RN

Routledge is an imprint of the Taylor & Francis Group, an informa business

For Product Safety Concerns and Information please contact our EU representative
GPSR@taylorandfrancis.com. Taylor & Francis Verlag GmbH, Kaufingerstraße 24,
80331 München, Germany.

Trademark notice: Product or corporate names may be trademarks or registered trademarks,
and are used only for identification and explanation without intent to infringe.

ISBN: 9781032531595 (hbk)
ISBN: 9781032531588 (pbk)
ISBN: 9781003410621 (ebk)

DOI: 10.4324/9781003410621

Typeset in Optima
by Newgen Publishing UK

Supervision of Group Psychotherapy

A Training Manual

Edited by Michelle A. Collins-Greene,
Maria T. Riva, and Noelle L. Lefforge

Routledge
Taylor & Francis Group

NEW YORK AND LONDON

Designed cover image: Getty Images

First published 2026
by Routledge
605 Third Avenue, New York, NY 10158

and by Routledge
4 Park Square, Milton Park, Abingdon, Oxon, OX14 4RN

Routledge is an imprint of the Taylor & Francis Group, an informa business

For Product Safety Concerns and Information please contact our EU representative
GPSR@taylorandfrancis.com. Taylor & Francis Verlag GmbH, Kaufingerstraße 24,
80331 München, Germany.

ISBN: 9781032531595 (hbk)
ISBN: 9781032531588 (pbk)
ISBN: 9781003410621 (ebk)

DOI: 10.4324/9781003410621

Typeset in Optima
by Newgen Publishing UK

Michelle dedicates this book to Harold Bernard, and her husband, Les Greene, and to all the "quiet" supervisors that came before, to come, and within us all.

Maria—For my husband, Bruce Janson, who was incredibly supportive throughout the writing of this manual. Thank you.

Noelle—To my husband, Andrew Cummings, for making it possible.

Contents

About the Editors

Michelle A. Collins-Greene, PhD, ABPP, CGP, AGPA-F, is board-certified in group psycho-therapy, a certified group psychotherapist, and is a fellow of the AGPA. She serves on the Executive Committee of AGPA, is a board member of the International Board for Certification of Group Psychotherapists, a past chair of the Affiliate Society Assembly of AGPA, and a past president of the Eastern Group Psychotherapy Society. She holds a PhD from the Derner Institute of Advanced Psychological Studies at Adelphi University, has a certificate in psycho-analysis and psychotherapy from the Postdoctoral Program at Adelphi, and served as presi-dent of the Adelphi Society for Psychoanalysis and Psychotherapy. As half-time faculty at the Derner Institute of Advanced Psychological Studies, she has supervised graduate students in groups. At Columbia-Presbyterian she supervised interns and externs in a training program that she developed. She maintains a private practice in New York and Connecticut where she conducts group psychotherapy and provides supervision to group psychotherapists.

Maria T. Riva, PhD, is an emerita professor in the Department of Counseling Psychology at Morgridge College of Education, University of Denver. She coedited the *Handbook of Group Counseling and Psychotherapy* (2004, 2014), coauthored a chapter in the *Oxford Handbook of Applied Psychological Ethics* (2018) entitled "Ethical Considerations in Group Psychotherapy," and published several other group-related articles, including the coau-thored 2024 article in *Psychotherapy* that was spotlighted by APA, entitled "Beyond the Dyad: Broadening the APA Supervision Guidelines to Include Group Supervision." She is a fellow of the American Psychological Association (Division 49) and the Association for Specialists in Group Work. She is a past president of APA Division 49: Society of Group Psychology and Group Psychotherapy, and a past chair of the Council of Counseling Psychology Training Programs. She is on the editorial board of several journals, including *Group Dynamics: Theory, Research, and Practice* and the *International Journal of Group Psychotherapy*.

Noelle L. Lefforge, PhD, ABPP, CGP, AGPA-F, is a professor, Associate Dean, and Clinical Services Director in the PsyD program at the University of Denver's Graduate School of Professional Psychology (GSPP). Dr. Lefforge is board-certified in group psychotherapy and Fellow of the Society of Group Psychology and Group Psychotherapy (APA Division 49), the AGPA, and the American Board of Group Psychology (ABGP). She has published on responding to microaggressions in the *International Journal of Group Psychotherapy*, on the specialized practice of group psychotherapy in the *American Journal of Psychotherapy*, and most recently on the education and training guidelines for group psychotherapy in *Training and Education in Professional Psychology*. She is also Associate Editor for the *International Journal of Group Psychotherapy*.

Contributors

Nina W. Brown, EDD, is a professor and eminent scholar emerti at Old Dominion University in Norfolk, VA, a distinguished fellow of the AGPA, a fellow of the American Psychological Association, and the author of over 40 books on group therapy and narcissism.

Susan P. Gantt, PhD, ABPP, is Chair of the Systems-Centered Training and Research Institute; emeritus faculty at Emory University School of Medicine in the Department of Psychiatry and Behavioral Sciences, where she has taught and supervised group psychotherapy and coordinated group training for residents and psychology interns for 29 years; and is a faculty member in Emory University Psychoanalytic Institute where she teaches systems-centered group therapy.

Scott Giacomucci, DSW, LCSW, BCD, CGP, FAAETS, TEP, is Director/Founder of the Phoenix Center for Experiential Trauma Therapy in Pennsylvania and an adjunct professor and research associate at Bryn Mawr College Graduate School of Social Work. He is the author of *Social Work, Sociometry, & Psychodrama* (2021), *Trauma-Informed Principles in Group Therapy, Psychodrama, and Organizations* (2023), along with multiple research studies, articles, and book chapters. Scott has served two elected terms on the Executive Council of the American Society of Group Psychotherapy and Psychodrama (ASGPP), co-chairs the Research Committee, co-founded the Sociatry and Social Justice Committee, and is Co-Chief-Editor of the *Journal of Psychodrama, Sociometry, & Group Psychotherapy*.

Les R. Greene, PhD, a past president of the AGPA, holds a clinical faculty appointment in the Department of Psychiatry at Yale University School of Medicine where he has supervised residents in individual, couple, group, and milieu therapies for over four decades. He currently serves as coeditor of the "AGPA Group Therapy Training and Practice Series."

Francis J. Kaklauskas, PsyD, has led multiple groups for the past 35 years. He has published and presented extensively on the pragmatic integration of group theory, clinical experience, and research. Currently, he serves as Director of Counselor Training at Naropa University, as well as leads several training and supervision groups through the Collective for Psychological Wellness in Boulder, CO.

J. Joana Kyei, PsyD, is a licensed clinical psychologist in Ghana and the Commonwealth of Pennsylvania. She holds a PsyD in clinical psychology from Rutgers University, and her clinical and research interests include group dynamics, clinical supervision, trauma, and the intersection of culture and mental health. She is currently Lead Counsellor at the Ghana Institute of Management and Public Administration's Counseling Unit and oversees the peer counselors' training program.

Molyn Leszcz is a professor at the Department of Psychiatry, University of Toronto. He served as president of the AGPA from 2020 to 2022. Dr. Leszcz also served as psychiatrist-in-chief at Sinai Health System, 2006–2017; clinical vice chair for the Department of Psychiatry, University of Toronto, 2010–2017; and interim chair for the Department of Psychiatry, University of Toronto, 2014–2015. Dr. Leszcz has been the recipient of a number of education and teaching awards at the University of Toronto, where he supervises residents in group psychotherapy.

Stephanie McLaughlin, PhD, ABPP, is a board-certified clinical psychologist. She completed a fellowship in group psychotherapy at the University of Las Vegas and has presented and written on a variety of group psychotherapy topics at conferences and training settings. She was a former associate editor (2020–2023) of the *International Journal of Group Psychotherapy* and a former chair of the Supervision and Training Special Interest Group of the AGPA. She has extensive clinical experience in group therapy, including serving as group psychotherapy coordinator and supervisor at in-patient hospitals and community mental health centers. She currently works at a women's clinic in Bend, OR, as their behavioral health consultant where she focuses on perinatal mental health.

Leah M. Niehaus, LCSW, CGP, is a licensed clinical social worker who has been in private practice for 21 years and is Founder and Clinical Director of The Wellness Collective, a group practice she established eight years ago in Hermosa Beach, CA. She is a CAMFT-certified clinical supervisor and CGP who provides clinical supervision to associates in her practice as well as to other clinicians gaining clinical hours toward licensure. Niehaus leads two supervisor consultation groups and has developed comprehensive clinical supervision guides and best practices for onboarding associates in private practice. She has presented on clinical supervision at AGPA conferences, been featured on podcasts discussing supervision practices, and was recognized by the City of Hermosa Beach as "Best of Clinical Social Work 2023."

Michele D. Ribeiro, EdD, ABPP, CGP, AGPA-F, is a board-certified, licensed psychologist and group psychotherapist at the Western University of Health Sciences, College of Osteopathic Medicine of the Pacific, and is adjunct faculty for the Oregon State University and Zanzibar University in Tanzania. She is a fellow with the American Psychological Association and the AGPA, serves as the APA Council Representative and President-Elect for Division 49 (The Society of Group Psychology and Group Psychotherapy), and is Co-Chair Designate for the AGPA annual conference. She has also published two (co) edited books entitled *The College Counselor's Guide to Group Psychotherapy* (2018) and *Examining Social Identities and Diversity Issues in Group Therapy*: *Knocking at the Boundaries* (2020) and two digital seminars (2019) entitled *Yoga for Trauma* and *Yoga & Mindfulness Therapy* through PESI Inc.

Rita M. Rivera, PsyD, CGP is a licensed clinical psychologist at Yale University. She also holds credentials as a CGP by the International Board for Certification of Group Psychotherapists and is a Certified Trauma Professional (CTP) by the International Association of Trauma Professionals (IATP), a Certified Brain Injury Specialist (CBIS) by the Brain Injury Association of America (BIAA), and a certified crisis worker by the American Association of Suicidology (AAS). Dr. Rivera has clinical and research experience working with multicultural and multilingual individuals, immigrant populations, college students, patients with neurological conditions, and trauma survivors in the United States and Latin America. Her interests include anxiety and depressive disorders, trauma, neurocognitive presentations, and cross-cultural adjustment. Currently, Dr. Rivera serves on the boards of the International Council of Psychologists (ICP), the American Academy of Clinical Psychology (AACP), the APA's Society of Group Psychology and Group Psychotherapy (Division 49), and the Connecticut Psychological Association (CPA).

Tony L. Sheppard, PsyD, CGP, ABPP, AGPA-F, is Founder and Director of Groupworks Psychological Services in Louisville, KY. Dr. Sheppard has worked, taught, and supervised in the field of group psychotherapy for over 20 years. He teaches group psychotherapy in the School of Professional Psychology at Spalding University and has supervised graduate students in group work with children and adolescents throughout his career.

Kun Wang, MS, is a doctoral candidate in counseling psychology at the University of Iowa. His broad research goal is to advance knowledge of what makes individual and group psychotherapy work and the cultural factors that hinder or enrich the psychotherapy experience of culturally diverse clients. Additionally, his scholarship addresses how cultural dynamics influence supervision and training practices, particularly focusing on multicultural responsiveness and cultural humility to enhance therapeutic effectiveness and trainee development in diverse clinical contexts.

Ellen L. Wright, PhD, is a founder and faculty member at the Center for Group Studies in New York City and a supervising and training analyst at the Philadelphia School of Psychoanalysis and the Institute of Contemporary Psychoanalysis in Los Angeles. She provides training and supervision in weekly, biweekly, and intensive formats to mental health providers nationally and internationally.

Salaheddine Ziadeh, MA, PsyM, PsyD, is a clinical psychologist with special expertise in group psychotherapy and multicultural training. He holds a doctorate in clinical psychology from Rutgers University and a master's degree in psychology from New York University and is a graduate of the doctoral training program at Montefiore Medical Center of the Albert Einstein College of Medicine in New York. He has two decades of postdoctoral experience in a variety of settings and roles—including psychotherapy, education, consultation, training, and supervision—half of which has been overseas. With a special affinity for international and multidisciplinary work, fluency in several world languages, and broad cultural exposure, Dr. Ziadeh has successfully trained and supervised treatment providers in various parts of the world (e.g., Bangladesh, Lebanon, Peru, Tanzania). His contributions to the field of global mental health involve published research in addition to training and supervision, including cultural adaptation as well as acceptability, feasibility, and dissemination studies.

Preface

Michelle A. Collins-Greene

Many group therapy supervisors have found themselves learning on the job even after an advanced career in conducting group psychotherapy. What they most likely also learned is that group psychotherapy supervision requires expertise above and beyond academic training and experience as a group psychotherapist, and even beyond having been in supervision oneself. Few supervisors have had any formal training, which is provided by this manual. Even if one already supervises, they will find standards, ideas, and theories in this manual to expand and inform their supervision expertise. If you have been given your first group psychotherapy supervisory role, you will certainly want to peruse this manual to gain confidence and knowledge. The manual is also useful for those who would like to train supervisors in group supervision.

This training manual was written to update Bernard and Spitz's 2006 *Training in Group Psychotherapy Supervision*. Their manual was a first of its kind for the training of group supervisors, and since then there has been no new published programs to teach group psychotherapy supervision. The first manual was organized into four "modules": an "Overview," the "Supervisory Relationship," the "Content of Supervision," and "Special Considerations." The current manual is organized simply in seven chapters.

The initial chapters will review relevant historical, theoretical, and in-practice contributions to current concepts about group supervision. We also discuss the competencies and credentialing needed to become a group psychotherapy supervisor, including institutional credentialing, as well as necessary experiential training and teaching experience. Current models of supervision will be covered in a chapter on contemporary supervision by senior group therapy supervisors.

Within chapters on group psychotherapy supervisor skills, the manual covers the supervisory relationship, multiculturalism and diversity, ethical and legal issues, evaluation and monitoring of outcomes of supervision, and the usefulness of relevant research. The relational processes of supervision will be emphasized in all of these topics.

Finally, we cover telehealth and supervision along with future directions of group psychotherapy supervision. Future directions will include necessary research and standard settings regarding process and outcome, as well as applied innovations offered by technology.

As with all psychotherapy, the creative process of integrating knowledge, personal skill, and even personality, plus adhering to ethical standards with the intention of promoting the mental health of our patients and clients should not be lost. No prescriptive manual will substitute for that creativity and integrational expertise necessary to become a truly good supervisor. We do hope that this manual will highlight the attention necessary to the complexity of group process and human interaction that supervision and group leadership require. Becoming a good supervisor, and a good group psychotherapy leader, has historically been through many years of experiential learning. This manual will make suggestions and guide-lines for that experiential learning. Supervisory training requires not just the use of a manual but also the personal interaction of the supervisor trainer and the supervisor-in-training and a reflection of those interactions.

Supervision has long been an essential component of becoming a group therapist. This manual will serve as guideposts for training of supervisors of group psychotherapy in order to promote more competent and confident group psychotherapists. Our intention is that this manual will be useful to current supervisors, supervisors-in-training and trainers of supervisors.

Acknowledgments

As editors, first we would like to thank and are very grateful to the AGPA and its leadership, Angela Stephens, CEO, and the International Board for Group Psychotherapy Certification, who have continuously supported this project. The AGPA's Science to Service Task Force has guided this project forward, and we thank the co-chairs, Rebecca MacNair-Semands and Les Greene. We are grateful to Elizabeth Olsen and Joe Miles who reviewed the work within this manual, providing their expertise and ideas. We want to acknowledge the work of additional authors and co-authors of specific chapters: Stevie McLaughlin, Molyn Leszcz, Nina Brown, Ellen Wright, Leah Niehaus, Susan Gantt, Scott Giacomucci, Francis Kaklauskas, Tony Sheppard, Les Greene, Michele Ribeiro, Kun Wang, Joana Kyei, Salaheddine Ziadeh, and Rita Rivera.

It is with gratitude that we express our deepest appreciation toward our group members, group leaders, supervisors, mentors, teachers, and friends who are deeply imbedded in each of these chapters. Our heartfelt thank-you to you and to our primary groups, our partners, and our children who picked up the slack and allowed us space and time for writing.

We hope this manual provides beneficial information to supervisors and supervisees of group psychotherapy. We also hope that the manual deepens the knowledge and appreciation of the importance of group psychotherapy supervision.

Michelle A. Collins-Greene
I would like to acknowledge all the supervisors and supervisees who have contributed to my knowledge and experiences of group supervision. Their voices are present in this manual, and I appreciate their openness, graciousness, and willingness to learn from me, as well as all I have learned from them. My current supervision group has been a source of joy and inspiration. I would also like to thank my husband, Les Greene, who has served many roles—a patient and insightful editor, emotional support, colleague, and coauthor. I could never have completed this without the work and friendship of my coeditors and authors Maria Riva and Noelle Lefforge. Maria was tirelessly supportive and indispensable through our multiple drafts and edits. Michele Ribeiro and her team filled in with an original chapter on multicultural supervision, for which I am grateful. Lastly, I would like to thank the late Harold Bernard for his collegial support and encouragement to write, and Ronnie Levine for the many years of excellent group therapy experience.

Maria T. Riva
I want to acknowledge the many group researchers, practitioners, students, and clients who have influenced my love of group psychotherapy for over 35 years. During that time, I have made many friends and colleagues who also are passionate about group dynamics. I am

honored to continue to be included in projects on group psychotherapy and supervision of groups, and as the field has matured, so has my appreciation for the power of group therapy and the need for competent supervision. I want to thank the reviewers of this manual, including Drs. Joe Miles, Elizabeth Olson, Les Greene, and Michelle Collins-Greene who provided their generous and thoughtful comments that substantially improved my writing. Thank you also to my family for their continued support of my group psychotherapy musings even in my "retirement."

Noelle L. Lefforge

I would like to acknowledge the group psychotherapy supervisors who were instrumental in developing my foundations as a group psychotherapist, including Dr. Denise Kagan and Dr. Lynn Northrop, as well as those who are a never-ending source of learning and support, including Dr. Nina Brown, Dr. Gary Burlingame, Dr. Lorraine Wodiska, Dr. Molyn Leszcz, Dr. Cheri Marmarosh, Dr. Amy Nitza, Dr. Martyn Whittingham, Fran Weiss, and Dr. Josh Gross. I would also like to acknowledge all those who have been open to learning through my supervision. They make supervision worthwhile by extending the reach of group psychotherapy. There are far too many to name beyond those who I trained as postdoctoral fellows: Dr. Amelia Black, Dr. Stacy Graves, Dr. Stephanie McLaughlin, and Dr. Claudia Mejia.

> "Just as ripples spread out when a single pebble is dropped into water, the actions of individuals can have far-reaching effects."
>
> —Dalai Lama

Introduction

Goals, Definitions, and Chapter Overviews

Michelle A. Collins-Greene

Goals of the Manual and Functions of Supervision of Group Psychotherapy

The goal of training supervisors and consultants of group psychotherapy is to enhance competency, confidence, and well-being of those who supervise group leaders, which in turn provides the same for group psychotherapy leaders and their group members. Both beginning and experienced supervisors will benefit from the comprehensive overview of the components of supervision of group therapy in this manual. This manual includes the latest theory and research, competency-based models and best practices for group therapy supervisors, and a chapter on how current seasoned supervisors practice in their settings. While mostly addressing the basic functions and foundations of supervision of group therapy, it is intended to be applicable across a range of settings, in accordance with those settings, and in accordance with organizational, institutional, and legal guidelines. Some specialized group treatments, such as for eating disorders, substance abuse, psychosis, and severe personality disorders, require additional knowledge beyond the scope of this manual. However, every supervisor of group therapy will find the fundamentals of supervision here, on which to build further knowledge where needed.

There are many functions of supervision. This manual will make explicit some of the different skills and knowledge needed to become a skillful group therapy supervisor. Supervision of group has been described as the "third eye" by Meg Sharp (1995) and as "super vision" that takes a "quantum leap" in skills, communication, ability to detect interactions beyond words and systems of interaction (Hardy & Bobes, 2017). Both these depictions recognize supervision of group therapy as providing extraordinary vision of a complex process. If individual therapy can be viewed and interpreted from many angles, group therapy is even more complex. Supervision of group offers many more opportunities for interpretation of process than does supervision of individual therapy—such as of the group-as-a-whole and of all the individuals' dynamics in relation to the group and to the therapist. The group process creates a myriad of possible interventions at many different levels. For a beginning group therapist, a supervisor can help harness and contain the infinite possibilities and provide an anchor; for an experienced group therapist, a consultant can offer new ways to view the group and the leader's interventions. In either case, the supervisor offers an opportunity to inform and elevate the treatment process while providing an anchor and a safe haven of support.

Another function of the supervisor is to further the development of the group leader insofar as their clinical skills, identity, and confidence as a professional, and to nurture their interest in the work of group therapy (Lonergan, 1985; Klein, et al. 2011). A skillful supervisor can

DOI: 10.4324/9781003410621-1

capitalize on a group therapist's strengths, along with shoring up therapeutic vulnerabilities, and promote the group leader's capacity for self-reflection. While this is often a very personal process for the supervisee, an adept supervisor respects the leader's boundaries and focuses on aspects of their personality that have to do with their functioning as a group leader. This is related to one of the functions of the supervisor, which is to provide a safe environment for the supervisee to explore the relationship with the supervisor and co-supervisees and, most strategically, to identify those dynamics that are parallel to the supervisee's group processes. All these functions require a supervisor who is astute to the dynamics and functioning of the interpersonal relationship with each supervisee and—in group supervision of group therapy—of the climate of the supervision group and interrelationships among members. And the supervisor has a role and responsibility in addressing racist, sexist, classist, heterosexist, and otherwise biased or oppressive comments and microaggressions. This includes in making sure antiracist and biased enactments are monitored, addressed, and accounted for whether between supervisor and supervisee, within the group supervision, or in the group leader's psychotherapy group. These are sensitive issues the supervisor of group therapy is responsible to meet head-on by facilitating discussion of these difficult situations.

Adding to their functions is for the supervisor to be updated and ready to explore the relevance of research and new theories of group therapy and group leadership. The supervisee(s) and supervisor collaboratively discuss ways that new research can be incorporated and how new theories can be incorporated into each individual supervisee's work and professional development.

A final function is an evaluative, gatekeeping function, particularly in university and certification capacities, which require knowledge of standards, competencies, and best practices. While this best proceeds in a collaborative manner, the hierarchy of the relationship and methods of evaluation needs to be acknowledged and made clear and transparent. To help ameliorate negative aspects of a hierarchical relationship, mutual feedback can be encouraged, along with the fostering of a multicultural orientation (Kivlighan & Chapman, 2018) characterized by cultural humility and the willingness of the supervisor and supervisee to address issues related to the sociocultural identities of the supervisor and supervisee(s) as relevant to both the supervision and the supervisee's group itself. Many of these functions will be covered in depth by the chapters of this manual.

Definitions, Terms, and Roles

This manual is specifically meant for trainers of supervisors and consultants of group psychotherapy leaders and for supervisors-in-training. The roles to define are *trainer of supervisors-in-training, supervisor-in-training, consultant,* and *client* and *patient.* The processes to define are *supervision* and *consultation, group therapy, group counseling* and *group work,* and *supervision* of individual versus group.

There does exist a hierarchy of power and responsibility in role delineations: The *trainer of supervisors-in-training* is "the person responsible for preparing supervisors-in-training to assume supervisory responsibilities [and] must have a great deal of experience both in conducting groups and in supervising them. The trainer needs a thorough knowledge base about all the elements that constitute a complete group psychotherapy experience, from pregroup considerations through termination. In addition, the trainer needs to have good teaching skills and an ability to tolerate and accept different approaches to group psychotherapy supervision" (Bernard & Spitz, 2006, p. 10). In short, the trainer needs to model all the attributes and qualities of a good supervisor.

The *supervisor-in-training* already has a good knowledge base and many clinical hours of conducting group psychotherapy and may only have supervisory experience for individual therapy. Experience doing group psychotherapy and conducting individual supervision might be advantageous, but it's not necessarily sufficient for conducting supervision of group therapy. Perhaps they have found this out as they were shuffled into a supervisory position for group work by an agency or institution only to discover that individual and group supervision of group psychotherapy are much more complicated than they realized.

The qualities a supervisor-in-training strives for are an expanded knowledge base about multiple foci of group therapy and the supporting research (Bernard & Spitz, 2006). Further, the qualities for which the supervisor-in-training strives for are a refinement of interpersonal group skills, such as avoiding acting all-knowing with one right way and an ability to acknowledge power and identity differentials and be able to support the supervisee's unique personality, therapy style, and skills. The supervisor-in-training learns to refine balancing constructive criticism and support, including their timing, in order to maintain a safe and secure space for work. The teaching ability of a good supervisor is not rote didactics but an understanding of the individual supervisee's level of development, learning style, and growing ability to use and give feedback. Supervisors become adept at recognizing the nuance and multiplicity of clinical scenarios and dilemmas in actual clinical practice. And finally, a supervisor internalizes ethical procedures for the profession of group psychotherapy and its various settings and, as such, provides a model for the supervisee.

"Supervision" and "consultation" are often used interchangeably, and their functions overlap. In general, supervision is more regulated, carries more responsibility to the clients and supervisee, has a hierarchical structure in terms of evaluation, knowledge, and organizational position, and its purpose is to guide the supervisee to a higher level of licensure or certification. "Consultation" is more often a collaborative agreement between colleagues, is less regulated and less hierarchical (though the consultant may have more clinical experience), and aims to expand perspectives and reflections of the group process. The skills required of a supervisor of group therapy are also desirable components of a consultant. Sometimes the distinction between their actual functions depends only on the requirements of the setting. The goal of this manual is to provide more formal training to "supervise" group therapy, though most of its contents would apply to consultation as well.

Similarly, the difference between a "patient" and a "client" is hierarchical arrangement and implies the degree of responsibility on the part of group therapist for the welfare of each. A patient generally indicates a degree of mental health challenge and dependence on the expertise of the therapist, whereas a client indicates more independence and a more equal balance of power between therapist and client.

The differences between "group psychotherapy," "group counseling," and "group work" can often be vague, and perhaps there are more similarities than differences. Group psychotherapy comes from the tradition of a medical model and treatment of an individual's mental health in the group. Group counseling, though similar to group psychotherapy in the treatment of individuals in the group, is usually more supportive, problem-focused, and psychoeducational than traditions of group psychotherapy that are more psychodynamic. Group work comes from the social work tradition of treating social issues that affect individuals and the group as a whole.

Supervision of individual therapy and group therapy has many commonalities—the importance of supervisory alliance, allegiance to ethics, appreciation of boundaries, multicultural awareness, and assessment of the client. The differences are the many foci needing attention in group psychotherapy. Bernard and Spitz (2006) identified "1.) The simultaneous unfolding of individual, sub-group, and group-as-a-whole phenomena; 2.) The possibility of group forces running rampant and career out of control; 3.) The choices that must be made about what is focused on at any point in time; 4.) When to intervene and when to let the group process continue to unfold; and 5.) How to deal with difficulties and challenges before they become unmanageable" (p. 12).

What the Chapters Cover

The first chapter is "History and Foundations of Supervision of Group Therapy," in which foundations, roots, and socially situated supervision of group therapy are explored. This chapter reviews the evolution of group supervision over the last century, from undefined mentorship and apprenticeship models, with spontaneous boundaries and roles, leading to today's emerging standardized profession with various theoretical orientations. The second chapter, "Group Therapy Supervision: Qualifications, Competencies, Tasks, and Methods," is core to the manual. It covers the steps required in becoming a credentialed supervisor of group therapy and the general concepts and theoretical orientations of group therapy that supervisors will address with their supervisees. The concepts, skills, and core competencies that group therapists acquire and improve upon during supervision are delineated here. Among these are the three foci of group therapy—the individual in the group, subgrouping, and the group-as-a-whole. A crucial role of supervision is guiding the supervisee toward their own sense of when to intervene in the group process, when to let it unfold, and at what level of process to intervene. The supervisor assists the group leader in identifying and dealing with difficult challenges (e.g., scapegoating, attacking, silence, monopolizing, group think, antigroup, unconscious roles, and antitherapeutic processes) before these become unmanageable. Finally, this chapter gives an overview of the various methods the supervisee can use to present material to the supervisor, and the creative ways to make use of them given the resources available to the group leader in their setting. The supervisory processes, materials, and methods for presenting clinical data include didactic methods, role-playing, experiential methods, modeling therapy techniques, audio/video recordings, process notes, reporting from memory, case conference, live supervision, and co-led supervision. Chapter 3, "Contemporary Approaches," contains a collection of short essays from seasoned current supervisors from various settings and with various theoretical orientations to demonstrate contemporary methods of supervising group psychotherapy.

Chapter 4, "The Group Supervisory Relationship in Group Psychotherapy Supervision," explores how to cultivate a productive supervisor–supervisee relationship that facilitates the supervisory task of promoting the clinical skills of the group psychotherapist in a way that improves the treatment process. The importance of a good supervisory relationship is highlighted for new therapists-in-training, which may have different nuances than for group leaders who have completed advanced training in group therapy and are seeking consultation. The chapter includes several developmental models of supervision and the supervisory relationship, timing of different supervision techniques, and the supervision contract. Setting the right climate for supervision (i.e., an open and collaborative atmosphere that ensures confidentiality, clarity around evaluative and power dimensions, and encouragement of the different ways that clinicians have of working) is paramount. In this context transference, countertransference, parallel processes, and mutual feedback enhance the supervisory work and the group leader's learning. Only in a supportive, nonjudgmental climate can challenges to the supervisory process,—such as authority conflicts, anxieties about groups, personalities of the supervisor/supervisee dyad, rupture and repair in supervision, cultural biases, and competency issues—be addressed.

Chapter 5, "Multiculturism and Diversity in Group Psychotherapy Supervision," addresses how multicultural competence and humility in supervision involve in-depth training and experience in cultivating multicultural awareness and managing subtle and not-so-subtle enactments of bias and microaggressions and discrimination. The supervisor and supervisee alike promote awareness of cultural/social/ethnic identities as they emerge in group while keeping in mind individual differences, personalities, defenses, and strengths. The supervisor must make it apparent that they are open to exploring these issues as an invitation to allow them to emerge in the group process. In parallel, the supervisee must become comfortable inviting open discussion and processing of multicultural issues in their group.

In Chapter 6, "Ethical Guidelines for the Supervisory Process," legal and liability issues for the supervisor regarding their supervisee's practice, ethical guidelines produced by the various group therapy disciplines and organizations, the standard ethical practices of providing confidentiality, contracts, managing crisis, and reducing harm to patients and supervisees alike are all covered. Even with the many standard and legal ethical guidelines, the supervisor of group psychotherapy is in a position having to use "super vision" (Hardy & Bobes, 2017) judgement when clinical and ethical dilemmas present themselves. These sticky situations, and some possible ways of handling them, complete this chapter.

Chapter 7, "Research–Supervision Relationship," reviews research that is relevant to group therapy supervision. It supplies the supervisor-in-training with the necessary methods of evaluation and monitoring process and outcomes. It covers research into the efficacy, efficiency of group psychotherapy, as well its equivalence in outcome to other treatment methods. Studies informing group psychotherapy processes and supervision of groups are reviewed.

In Conclusion

Historically, supervisors have held numerous roles for the supervisee with varying boundary settings. Supervisory functions have been among colleagues, mentors, and past therapists, professors, and sometimes even friends. Today, more best practices and research about supervision have contributed to the professional, systemized practice of supervision of group psychotherapy. For example, it's now important for the supervisor and supervisee to have an open and collaborative understanding of the relationship and its boundaries at the outset, the supervisee's and group leader's role in the supervision, and to agree to the parameters and norms of the supervision process. Supervisees best learn if they can collaboratively create an alliance with the supervisor where they feel comfortable sharing the full range of therapeutic challenges generated by the group and within themselves. It is helpful if the supervisee is open about their transferences to the supervisor, and countertransferences to the individuals in their group, as well as the group-as-a-whole. This makes the exploration of parallel process a valuable tool in supervision.

Hopefully this training manual will contribute to the professionalization of supervision of group in general (Alonso, 1985), and to the supervisor of group psychotherapy in particular. At the very least it promises to provide to a prospective supervisor, and even a practicing supervisor, a thorough foundation in the elements and processes of supervision of group therapy.

A final distinction needs to be made between the necessary components of training a group therapist and supervisor. All the components of training include a firm didactic base of group psychotherapy (which is largely provided by the *Core Principles* of Group Psychotherapy by Kaklauskus and Greene (2020), a group experience of some kind, being a member of a therapy group and/or training group, and lastly what this manual takes up is the supervision of actual clinical work. This manual does not address the training group experience that is considered different from the supervision of groups where actual group work is presented and is the focus of discussion. When personal issues, transference and countertransference, unconscious enactments, parallel process, and quality of interactions between supervision group members are addressed in supervision, it is for the purpose of furthering the leader's competence of conducting group psychotherapy, as distinguished from the group leader's own personal therapy, albeit that may also be a byproduct.

This manual is essentially a didactic foundation for supervisors. It is also recommended that supervisors of group psychotherapy group together, or even individually; engage in supervision of supervision when possible; and join professional organizations where they can share experiences and learnings from their actual ongoing work as supervisors (Alonso, 1985).

References

Alonso, A. (1985). *The quiet profession: Supervisors of psychotherapy.* Macmillan.

Bernard, H. S. & Spitz, H. I. (2006). *Training in group supervision.* American Group Psychotherapy Association.

Hardy, K. V. & Bobes, T. (2017). *Promoting cultural sensitivity in supervision.* Routledge.

Kaklauskus, F. J. & Greene, L. R. (2020). *Core principles of group psychotherapy.* Routledge.

Kivlighan III. D. M. & Chapman, N. A. (2018) *Extending the multicultural orientation (MCO) framework to group psychotherapy: A clinical illustration.* Psychotherapy, *55*(1) 39–44.

Klein, R. H., Bernard, H. S., Schermer, V. L. (2011) On Becoming a Psychotherapist: The Personal and Professional Journey, Oxford.

Lonergan, E. C. (1985). *Group intervention: How to begin and maintain groups in medical and psychiatric settings.* Jason Aronson.

Sharpe, M. (Ed.) (1995). *The third eye: Supervision of analytic groups.* Routledge.

Chapter 1

History and Foundations of Supervision of Group Psychotherapy

Michelle A. Collins-Greene

Understanding the evolution of supervision of group psychotherapy sheds light on the necessary complexity of the profession. The practice of supervision itself is the vehicle of transmitting learnings of history and foundations to new generations.

(Alonso, 1985)

Introduction

Most of today's components of supervisory competencies and best practices of professional supervision of group psychotherapy have roots in historical practices of group therapy. In this chapter the foundations of supervision of group therapy and its legitimization as a science by the medical profession are discussed as they evolved throughout history. The development of group therapy and supervision has been embedded in, and shaped by, historical eras of European medical advances in neurology, American religious movements and education, medicine and science, social service movements, professionalism, world wars, and periodic struggles toward social equality. Personalities and backgrounds of several group therapy pioneers were shaped by these historical eras, and in turn they shaped the foundations of theory and practice of group psychotherapy through their supervision and training.

As late as 1985, Anne Alonso wrote a book dedicated to the professionalization of supervision remarking on its historical invisibility. She noted that supervision is "sparsely documented" (p. 4) in comparison to psychotherapy. To unearth the antecedents of professional supervision of group psychotherapy, two threads of historical development since the 1900s are followed—that of the professionalization of group therapy through its innovators, and the supervisory practices of psychotherapy. These two intertwining, mutually supporting historical threads have led to today's professional practice of supervision of group therapy. The invisible supervisors of group therapists are tracked, along with their mentoring and supervision influences of next generations. And finally, how the elements of supervision of group psychotherapy became systematized and professional are followed.

Ancient Antecedents of Supervision and Group Psychotherapy

Preceding the 20th century, what might be gleaned as supervisory functions existed and can be traced as far back as the Middle Ages with "apprenticeships" in the trades (Wikipedia, n.d.a.), a practice which continues to be a foundational model of supervision in the health

DOI: 10.4324/9781003410621-2

professions. Under the guidance of a master craftsman or professional (akin to a "super-visor"), a member of the younger generation received on-the-job training. Often the master was repaid by employment of the new professional for a period of time, as seen in our internships and externships of today. The senior person and trainee often worked side by side, the master serving both as an example of how the work is done and as a guide while overseeing the trainee's work in progress. Remarkably, current practices of supervision of psychotherapy resemble the ancient apprenticeship model where the supervisor is both a model and a guide of the novice's in-vivo work. Despite this foundational model of supervision, the systemization and professional recognition of supervision would not start to come about until the 1970s.

Similar to supervision, the history of professional group psychotherapy typically traces its origins to the middle of the past century (Scheidlinger, 2000), while the use of groups to heal goes much further back in time. Meiers (1945), a first historian of group psychotherapy, ventured that group therapy has "a long past" of unrecorded roots in ancient cultures, "and a short history" of professional recognition (p. 3). Meiers stated that the long past includes "the history of cults and religion, of folklore, folk tales and poetry, of Egyptian, Greek, Oriental, East Indian, Chinese, Polynesian and … American Indian medicine" (p. 261). Bloom (1997) and Lex (1979) echo this view, noting that our ancestors and original peoples gathered in healing groups with rituals and rites to overcome collective traumas, a practice that continues to this day. Kaklauskas and Greene (2020) similarly note that "the practice of people getting together to learn, grow, and support one another is timeless" (p. 3).

Meier's (1945) "short history" proffers that group therapy as a formal discipline was initiated barely a century ago, in the 1930s, when Moreno "coined it" as "group therapy," and his work was recognized by the American Psychiatric Association. That recognition reflected the necessity in those days and, still today, of legitimization by the medical establishment. However, the trajectory of group therapy as an independent, professional treatment modality has been fraught with cultural and political vagaries. For example, the editor of Meier's 1945 historical review article of group psychotherapy found it necessary to add a cautionary note to readers that "group therapy" was not yet considered a profession in its own right.

Supervision, albeit in the form of mentorship, apprenticeship, consultation, and oversight of groups, had to have occurred from the beginnings of group therapy, even if in an ad hoc informal basis, and unclearly defined. In its broadest sense, supervision is that aspect of training that provides witness, reflection, and feedback to what actually happens between therapist and patient(s) and group. It also includes an evolutionary function of theory and practice going forward through the training of new group therapists. Original forms of supervision were mentoring to help the therapist to develop a professional identity, invariably in the context of a personal relationship, as well as an educative function. That is, the supervisory relationship has served throughout history not only an educative function but one that facilitates professional identity and personal growth as a group therapist (Klein et al., 2011).

Social Roots of Group Psychotherapy, Consultation, and Supervision

Saul Scheidlinger (2000) delineated several "eras" in the history of group psychotherapy, each characterized by specific sociocultural and sociopolitical circumstances. He identified the iconic figures in each era who contributed to the development of group therapy. Scheidlinger's classification is adopted not only to review the developments of group therapy over time, but also to uncover supervision processes and supervisors of those times.

The Precursors (1905–1930)

Scheidlinger (2000) named this first era "Group Psychotherapy's Precursors (1905–1930)" since group therapy was in an experimental phase, and not yet considered a scientific formal profession, much less including any formal training and supervision. The "precursors" were essentially innovative pioneers, both American and European intellectuals trained in the medical tradition of psychiatric neurology. They consulted and mentored between colleagues and protégées, sometimes even via mail and steamboat travel between Vienna and America (cf. Hale, 1971).

Antisemitism throughout Europe and Russia led many of the original pioneers of group therapy to emigrate to the US and England. Medical and neurological advances were being made in Vienna's and Germany's universities. Freud's development of psychoanalysis attracted many of the intellectuals interested in neurological psychiatry. American pioneers of psychiatry went to Vienna to learn Freud's craft. At the same time the empirical, experimentalist schools of thought in philosophy and psychology evolved to attract still others. America was the frontier that offered innovation and the fertile grounds for group psychotherapy. Supervision in the form of mentoring relationships occurred in universities where the medical and psychiatric practitioners earned their degrees.

The American setting was the "gilded age" of the early 1900s, when America became a world power in industry, communication, science and medicine. This had a two-pronged outcome that would set the stage for the development of group therapy. On the one hand, it offered Americans and European immigrants hope and a new start especially after ravages of European wars and antisemitism. On the other hand, it also resulted in a very rich class and an impoverished working class that sorely needed medical and psychiatric services. Another aspect of American culture was the proliferation of religious orientations which were largely behind the founding of universities in America (Van Schoor, 2000). Medical doctors, often with religious affiliations themselves, joined with pastors and home visitors to provide services for the sick, mentally ill and needy. However, the American Zeitgeist increasingly favored scientific grounding and professionalism over lay workers.

The first documentation of therapeutic groups was recorded in 1905, when Joseph Hersey Pratt (1872–1956), an American doctor, partially trained in Europe, organized groups for his tuberculosis patients that lived in tenements. Pratt called it the "Home Sanatorium Method" initially, expecting that a clean, open air, friendly environment would play a role in a cure of the devastating spread of Tuberculosis at the time. He came to realize that the 76% improvement rate (Pratt, 1908) among his consumption patients had to do with the weekly group work, that included his large class lectures, the patients' weekly journal writing, and the relationships developed between patients in which they often gave each other encouragement (Ambrose, 2011). Pratt renamed it the "class method."

Pratt's mentors for his group experiment were William Osler (1849–1919), his teacher at Johns Hopkins Medical School in Baltimore in 1896, and his good friend Reverend Dr. Elwood Worcester (1862–1940) at the Episcopal Church in Boston (Pinney, 1978b). Pratt shared a lifelong collegial and personal relationship with Osler whose paper "The home care of consumption" influenced Pratt's first experiment in group therapy. Osler, a philosopher of life himself, was interested in Pratt's both professional and personal growth as he wrote to him frequently and encouraged him: "One element you have not laid stress upon— your own personality" (Ambrose, 2011 p. 46). In turn, Pratt wrote about Osler being a great clinical teacher, a humorist and humanist, and a valued mentor and friend (Ambrose, 2011).

For the pioneers of group therapy, supervision often entailed a lifelong mentoring relationship with interest in the whole person, in addition to the technical aspects of the work.

The less recognized consultant of Pratt was Worcester, whose preaching style and methods Pratt adopted through his regular attendance to the Emmanuel Church (Pinney, 1978b). In turn, adopting Pratt's protocol for tuberculosis patients, Worcester was arguably the first to treat mentally ill patients in small groups. He combined religion and science by collaborating with doctors such as Pratt, and conducted groups of 10–12 emotionally disturbed patients, not the large classroom groups that Pratt conducted. Worcester documented in 1908 that these groups had been successful. Worcester sought scientific legitimacy by bringing in neurologists to lecture and supervise the groups to make sure they were being run in accordance with the medical standards and understanding of mental illness at the time. Worcester wrote:

> We determined to begin similar to the Tuberculosis Class work among the nervously and morally diseased. As a preliminary step we consulted several of the leading neurologists of New England to ascertain, first, whether such a project, undertaken with proper safeguards, would meet with their approval, and secondly, whether they would be willing to cooperate with us in it. A favorable response being given to these questions, our work began on a very stormy evening in November, when Dr. James J. Putnam [an American psychoanalytic physician who had studied with Freud's group in Vienna] presided at the preliminary meeting and gave the first address. Thus, from the beginning our work has been closely associated with very able physicians and we have done nothing without their cooperation and advice. Had this assistance been withheld, we should not have proceeded further. As we are attempting to establish no new dogma, and as our motives are entirely disinterested, our single desire is to give each patient the best opportunity of life and health which our means allow.
>
> (In Pinney, 1978b, p. 111)

Through his supervising and mentoring influence, Worcester inspired Alcoholics Anonymous, and the Emmanuel movement. Courtenay Baylor in 1912 joined Worcester's staff and began running groups for alcoholics. He was a layperson, claiming no medical training, but adopted the values of compassion and understanding underlying anxieties that spurred alcoholism, along with the small group framework of Worcester's groups. Later he came to influence one of his students, William Wilson (1895–1971), the founder of Alcoholics Anonymous. These were some of the first groups led by lay people not under the supervision of MDs, and under religious auspices (emmanuelboston.org).

Practices and theories of group therapy up until the 1930s reflected the mix of, and sometimes a tension between, the inspirational oration (derived from pastors) and scientific justifications (derived from MD's status and training; see Thomas's historical review, 1943). Over time the universities became more secular and the faith in religious institutions was largely replaced by faith in higher university education—though originally founded by religious institutions (Van Schoor, 2000). Science and materialism won over faith and mysticism in the professional development of group therapy and hence its supervision.

As science began to dominate the medical field over religious faith, religious and moral treatments for the mentally ill came under question. Worcester was later demonized in several news articles of the time—accusing him of meddling in areas that had been given over to science (Pinney, 1978b). Though his contributions to the beginning of group psychotherapy, along with his supervisory consultations, have been all but erased in the group therapy literature, he had significant influence on Pratt's procedures, proliferated group treatment with the mentally ill, planted the seeds of Alcoholics Anonymous, and made an impact in religious communities through the Emmanuel Movement that adopted his method of group classes.

The MDs that were brought in by Pratt and Worcestor to supervise, consult and lead their groups had trained with Freud. Though Freud (1856–1939) did not practice or even believe in any sort of group therapy, he influenced, mentored, and even supervised almost all who did. Freud did not see group as a therapeutic vehicle. In *Group Psychology and Analysis of the Ego* (Freud, 1965) he purported that individuals lost their sense of self and threw ego functioning to the wind in favor of following the mass group and idealized leader. He understood that belonging to a group gave them a sense of belonging to something bigger than themselves. However, Freud valued the development of ego functioning of the individual as leading to mental health and he pathologized regression and primitive impulsivity that the group seemed to incite.

Notwithstanding his own criticisms of group, Freud began his Wednesday evening group in 1902, a format that could be considered the first supervision group (Frawley, 2001; Smith & Gallop, 2024). He included seven of his closest male colleagues, friends, and his own physician. As leader/mentor/supervisor, Freud's abiding intention was to promulgate his psychoanalytic theory by teaching and supervising protégées and having them set up psychoanalytic institutes where others would be taught his psychoanalytic theories. Those who might be treated or supervised by Freud were called "disciples" (not supervisees). His supervision was at times quite intrusive by taking over a case and dictating procedure. Yet despite this clear hierarchy, there was an element of collaboration and mutual consultation through letter writing, reading each other's works, sometimes adding comments, praises or critiques that began between these members. As portrayed by Gay (2006), here is one of the best recorded descriptions of how the supervision group ran:

> Max Graf, a Viennese musicologist and father of "Little Hans," who had first encountered Freud in 1900 and joined the Wednesday group soon after its initial inception, described the ritual and atmosphere of the early meetings of the society: "The gatherings followed a definite ritual. First, one of the members would present a paper [the appointed member was drawn from an urn (Schwartz, 1999)]. Then, black coffee and cakes were served; cigars and cigarettes were on the table and were consumed in great quantities. After a social quarter of an hour, the discussion would begin. The last and decisive word was always spoken by Freud himself. There was the atmosphere of the foundation of a religion in that room. Freud himself was its new prophet who made the heretofore prevailing methods of psychological investigation appear superficial." The papers were often theoretical with presentations of a case.
>
> (Gay, 2006, pp. 174–175)

Of note, Freud's group ran for 36 years with changing membership, up to 150 "supervisees" (Schwarz, 1999; Smith & Gallop, 2024). From those 150 undeniably came most of the innovators of psychotherapy, as well as of group psychotherapy and supervision; and, the theories were transplanted to America by European neurologist immigrants and Americans traveling to Vienna in the first third of the 20th century.

Freud had his style of authoritarian leadership of these groups and accepted little competition. Unlike group supervision practiced today, there was no attention paid by Freud to boundaries, or power and authority issues in the supervisory relationship (Smith & Gallop,

2024). Because of the boundaryless personal nature of Freud's analyses (he analyzed his own daughter, went on skiing trips with patients, and analyzed most of his "disciples") the boundary between supervision and personal analysis of his supervisees was blurred such that supervision from a psychoanalytic viewpoint continues to include the exploration of trainee's personality, and transferences and counter-transferences of the analyst. Freud qualified his protégées by insisting they be analyzed, if not by him, by one of his disciples. Current psychoanalytic supervisors warn of this intrusion into the supervisee's personal life, except when warranted with regard to treatment of the client(s) (McWilliams, 2021).

To give status and recognition to psychoanalysis as a profession, Freud promoted among his devotees the formation of analytic societies and training institutes. That supervision became requisite in these training institutes was the work of Max Eitington (1881–1943), an original member of Freud's group. The idea first came to him when it was noted by Freud's protégées (specifically Hans Sachs) who were conducting training analyses, that supervision cases were constantly being discussed in their personal analysis. Eitingon was the founder of supervision as a specific training method, that is, the discussion and focus was on the therapist's cases, and not just on the therapist's dynamics. As the founder of psychoanalytic supervision, his unique life story merits telling giving insight as to how he was led to create supervisory training. As were most of Freud's group, Eitingon was of Jewish descent, born to a well off orthodox Jewish family with two brothers and a sister (Watkins, 2013). In 1891, his family was expelled from Russia in a wave of antisemitism (put into law and imposed by the royal government of Nicholas II), when Max was only 10 years old. They again moved to Leipzig, Germany at age 12. Apparently, the displacements were so disturbing to him that he developed a stutter which impeded his ability to graduate from high school. He later took courses to qualify to enter college and then earned a medical degree in Leipzig, the then world center of medical science, where he studied with Bleuler and Jung, who introduced him to Freud. Max first visited Freud in 1907. He was analyzed by Freud, with what was then called a "training analysis," which seemed like a rather casual analysis and supervisory consultation since it was during evening walks over a few months. However, Eitingon was impressed and thought to make personal analysis an essential part of training. Because of his challenged years as a student, he was inherently interested in educational methods which he employed as a lifetime pursuit in the service of psychoanalysis. To institutionalize the teaching of psychoanalysis, and having the ability to do so because he was financed by his father who had been successful in international fur trade, Eitingon helped to establish psychoanalytic institutes in Budapest, Vienna, and Berlin, becoming president of the Berlin Psychoanalytic Polyclinic, 1920–1933, and finally settling and forming an Institute in Palestine (now Israel). "The polyclinic [in Berlin] was the first center in the world for treating patients with the Freudian psychoanalytic method and the first training institute for young analysts. The clinic trained candidates from all over the world to address the mental and social problems of postwar Europe. The training curriculum lasted two years, then three, and comprised three separate tracks: theory, personal analysis, and supervised analysis" (Encyclopedia.com, n.d.; Michelle Moreau Ricaud, n.d.). Eitingon had separated out supervision from personal analysis (Smith & Gallop, 2024). For the first time, he made supervision of cases essential to training. It was even named the "Eitingon Method." Eitingon's system of psychoanalytic education and supervision continues today not only in individual psychoanalytic training programs, but also in group therapy training programs consisting of didactic seminars, personal training analysis, and the clinical supervision he originated (Watkins, 2013). A current day example is the Eastern Group Psychotherapy Society's training program.

Pratt and Eitingon represent two poles of sociocultural philosophy about human psychology: Pratt represented the more American positivist, belief in willpower side of human aspiration (Ambrose, 2013) and Eitingon represented the darker forces of the unconscious, rooted in repressed or dissociated trauma. The dialectic between these two worldviews has reached through the century to today's tension between the psychoanalytic and cognitive-behavioral approaches. Despite some nuanced differences in theory, there has always been two camps of psychotherapy and group psychotherapy, the psychoanalytic, and the cognitive-behavioral, which is carried through to supervision and training. Though not mutually exclusive, cognitive-behavioral supervision emphasizes the competent application of technique while the psychodynamic focuses on the person of the therapist and the relationship dynamics of therapist to patient(s), and therapist to supervisor.

The first US-born person to study psychoanalysis in Vienna (Drury & Tudor, 2022) with Freud, Trigant Burrow (1875–1950) brought psychoanalysis to America and founded the American Psychoanalytic Association (APA) in 1911 with eight others to train and supervise in psychoanalytic methods. At a New York theater performance in 1909 Burrow had met Freud and Jung on their way to the landmark Clark conference in Worcester. Inspired, he immediately moved his whole family to Vienna to study with them for a year. Jung was his main teacher and mentor (Pertegato & Pertegato, 2018.

Though trained in Vienna, and taken by psychoanalysis, Burrow also became interested in the social effects on the individual, which was contrary to Freudian intrapsychic determinants of human behavior, and which led him to ideas about group therapy (Burrow, 1992). While mentored by Jung and Freud, he applied their principles to group interactions, which proved to be too far afield from their individualist, intrapsychic psychology.

Pertegato and Pertegato (2018) regarded Burrow as the "forgotten pioneer" of group therapy despite his prolific writings and experimentations with group psychotherapy, and despite his mentoring many future group psychotherapists. There was a reason for this that had to do with his mentors that originally supervised his work. In essence he was before his time and out of step with the momentum of orthodox Freudian psychiatry in those early decades. During this precursor era, Burrow emerged as a forerunner of seeing the individual within his socio-biological context (Van Schoor, 2000), a notion that Freud largely avoided.

Burrow practiced as a psychoanalyst as early as 1911 up until 1927 in the US while using psychoanalytic methods in group analysis with a focus on such notions as identification with, and internalization of early objects, and the centrality of group members' relationships to each other, a forerunner of Object Relations Theory. He reduced the authority of the therapist by deferring to the group process. He believed group was an opportunity for the individual to be authentic in a social situation. With this experience, he wrote most of his papers on the group method in the latter part of the 1920s. His first book on the subject was *Social Images versus Reality* (Burrow, 1924) where he talked about group-as-a-whole and projections of transferences onto group members and the leader.

Burrow's integration of psychoanalytic methods with group therapy did not impress Freud. In 1913, when Jung and Freud broke off, Freud invited Burrow to come be analyzed by him, but Burrow declined. At the outbreak of WWI in 2017, Burrow offered Freud refuge at his home in America, and had continued to send his manuscripts to Freud, but Freud disregarded them as not well thought out.

The APA, which Burrow helped start, elected him president in 1924 and 1925, but expelled him from it in 1932 because of his emphasis on group life. He was irrevocably alienated from psychoanalytic training institutions when he started groups in the Adirondacks called "Joy of Life" to study how social issues affected the life of small groups (Burrow, 1992). As were many of the group therapy pioneers, Burrow was an independent thinker, but later ended up paying for it, specifically for differing from his mentors in writing about and promoting group psychotherapy. Freud no longer supported Burrow, mostly on the basis of their theoretical disagreements about instincts and the role of social upbringing, but perhaps also largely because Burrow declined to be analyzed by him and Burrow's affiliation with Jung. This was an example of a mentor/supervisor (Freud) expelling a supervisee from his realm for not conforming to the mentor's image. The separation individuation of a supervisee from their mentor may not always run smoothly (Pertegato & Pertegato, 2018). Nevertheless, Burrow had impact on group therapists to come such as Franz Alexander, Nathan Ackerman, Carl Rogers, and Eric Berne (Drury & Tudor, 2022). It's said that Harry Stack Sullivan read Burrow and based much of his interpersonal theory on Burrow without giving him credit (Drury & Tudor, 2022).

The Role of Social Work's "Group Work" in American Precursors

While there was proliferation of psychoanalysis in Vienna along with Eitingon's supervision methods, and the establishment of the APA in 1900s America, psychiatry was joining hands with social work through supervision. Together they started to take seriously the environment's impact on physical and mental health, thus moving beyond an exclusive focus on the intrapsychic or individual which had become typical of Freudian treatment.

In context, America at the turn of the century was at a height of prosperity as it expanced its industrial revolution. Great wealth was amassed by innovators of transportation and factories, while a poorer working and immigrant class evolved. It was in this economic social setting that the Mental Hygiene Movement, including the increasing prominence of social work, began. The mentally ill had been holed up in sanatoriums designed to isolate them from society. The sanatoriums were run by "superintendents"—a primitive form of administrative supervision of lay workers. Mental illness was largely believed to be genetically and biologically of origin with little hope of cure, behaviorally or medically. So, in a sense, the 1900s started a new age of hope for the mentally ill, and as such was part of the American Progressive Era (Sicherman, 1980). Clifford Beers (1876–1943) led the way. He had been hospitalized with bipolar and recovered and in 1909 started the establishment of the National Committee for Mental Hygiene (NCMH) with the mutual collaboration of medical, psychiatric, and social work leaders of the time, including the MDs, Adolph Meyer, William H. Welch, William James, and social workers, Jane Addams, and Julia Lathrop. Social workers who were still considered "lay workers" pioneered the majority of group work.

Social workers were originally called "friendly visitors," and came from a tradition that started as far back as the 1600s in Europe and came to the US in the 1800s. They were sponsored by the church, then the governments when the church was unable to fill the need. From its inception these friendly visitors were primarily women who visited the impoverished. They worked on a volunteer basis with churches, charitable organizations, hospitals, government agencies, schools and in "settlement housing," housing projects that offered community services mostly for immigrants. They organized groups in their natural settings—children in a playground, tenants in settlement housing, and patients in hospitals. The therapeutic aspects of group work were deeply imbedded in everyday activities such as creative handicrafts and artwork, singing, club participation and discussion, and being a functioning member of a democratically operating association (Bogardus, 1939). Giacomucci (2021, chapter 2) formulated that "the group work of Social Work was founded in values of democracy, social functioning, mutual aid (the group heals itself) where the leader is simply a guide, the true benefits are from the group helping itself, group cohesion, conflict resolution, interpersonal communication, the group is treated as a whole, not individually ... It was cognitively focused ... have roots in Moreno's group activities—theatre, dance, expressive, nonverbal, art" (p. 20). This democratic value of group work, credited to these early American social workers would influence future methods of group therapy and supervision alike.

Among social workers that achieved recognition for training and supervising were Mary Richmond (1861–1928), the "mother of social work," along with Jane Addams (1860–1935). In 1920 they saw "group work" as "the future of social treatment" (Richmond, 1930). These social work groups started with investment in changing social conditions and helping those that suffered from them. This marriage of psychiatry and social work created a challenge for the supervisory relationship as psychiatrists who supervised were immersed in psychoanalytic theory which viewed mental health strictly from an intrapsychic perspective while social workers "group work" addressed real life social problems. Gradually, however, the social workers running these groups incorporated psychological perspectives from psychiatry into their group work. As a consequence, social work gained prestige and a road to professional recognition as an independent discipline. Both case work and group work, and both intrapsychic and social determinants became important in the therapeutic process of group therapy according to Gertrude Wilson (1956). Thus, group psychotherapy came to be shaped in 1920s America by two powerful forces: the psychoanalytic, individual pathology-based practice of psychiatry and neurology, and the social work movement.

The Pioneers/Founders (1930–1940), the Second Era of Group Psychotherapy: Supervision as Mentorship

WWI, 1917–1920, had brought awareness of the trauma that came from war and human discord, and then the Great Depression, 1929 negatively impacted personality, adjustment to society, and individual well-being. Those that pioneered group therapy had direct experience of the danger of groups. It was recognized that groups could become unsafe and hazardous, especially when one group of people is pitted against another or even when an individual within a group is scapegoated (Barlow, 2013; Freud, 1965; LeBon, 1903). They also understood that groups can also be healing, if conducted in a way that brought out the best in people supporting, advising, self-reflecting, and helping each other, with a benevolent, trained group leader. As a sign of resilience, many of those who are now regarded as the pioneers of group therapy emerged in the aftermath of WWI, particularly the Europeans. Their histories underscore how their war time experiences significantly influenced their desire to promote human beings getting along better, and peacefully, through groups. In America, psychiatry, social work, religion and education continued to converge to motivate pioneers of group therapy.

An American mid-Westerner minister, cousin of Buffalo Bill (who popularized Western American cowboy culture), Cody Marsh (1883–1949) was an example of religion merging with psychiatry. Originally a minister, he retrained to become a psychiatrist and is best known for his quote: "By the crowd they have been broken; by the crowd they shall be healed." He held: "The chief problems both in the etiology and treatment of mental illness are social rather than mental" (Marsh, 1931; 1933). He believed this to be true even in the treatment of psychotic patients. His treatment was to form a model hospital environment with therapeutic groups at all levels of personnel and inpatient community. Marsh could perhaps be the first to start what was later known as the "therapeutic community." He worked with inpatients in groups in a cognitive-behavioral manner and often gave lectures about mental illness and encouraged adaptive behavioral functioning, for example by simply attending and showing up on time (Barton, 1987). He conducted discussion groups with staff, family members, and community pastors to create more compassion toward patients, and he mixed groups with healthy and mentally ill (Durkin et al., 1971). By 1931, at Worcester State Hospital, he was gaining cooperative participation in "a large group" (Barton, 1987), in which one can imagine he combined his skills as an inspirational minister and scientifically informed psychiatrist. His group methods widely varied and often consisted of therapeutic activities such as singing and psychoeducational lectures.

The supervision he might have done is undocumented, though in his therapeutic communities he trained and oversaw staff as well as patients. The therapeutic community model in which he engaged was a foundational group treatment and training method that became popular again in 1970s and 1980s in inpatient and residential mental health care. An American of religious background and firm in his belief of social effects on mental health, Marsh was untouched by Freudian psychoanalytic theory, unlike the American Burrow who had tried to integrate group therapy with psychoanalysis, and the contemporary Paul Ferdinand Schilder (1886–1940), who tried to integrate many facets of biology with psychoanalysis with group.

Schilder came to America from Vienna in 1930. He was quoted as saying "You know, America is so big and there are so many different opportunities here. If you fall down in one place, you get up in another—so different from the limited opportunities in Europe. There, once you are checkmated, you are through. Not so in America" (Adler, 1965).

Born into a Jewish family in Vienna, Austria Schilder had lost his father, a silk trader, at age four. Consequently, his mother was his strongest advocate and supporter. He married an accomplished psychiatrist Lauretta Bender and they had a mutually consulting and mentoring relationship on their many psychiatric projects. He was an avid student and prolific writer and in Vienna had mentors in both philosophy and biomedicine. With determination, he completed his doctorate in medicine while serving in WWI as a medical assistant, then later completed an additional doctorate in philosophy. He became a member of Freud's Viennese Psychoanalytic Society in 1919, was promoted to professor in 1925, and appointed to head the Viennese Psychoanalytic Society's new clinic dedicated to the treatment of psychosis in 1929 (Wikipedia, n.d.b.) where he undoubtedly supervised, but this is undocumented. In his efforts to integrate biomedical psychiatry and psychoanalysis in Vienna, Schilder seemed to displease both and soon emigrated to the US. In America he became lecturer at Johns Hopkins in Baltimore, worked at Bellevue hospital and was a professor at New York University (Parker, 1985, Chapter 1).

Freud, one of Schilder's original mentors and supervisors later scolded him in 1936 that he had never been analyzed, and that he worked in "too wide dimensions" (Galdston, 1985, Chapter 4), undoubtedly referring to his pan-theoretical tendencies to integrate biology, neurology, psychoanalysis and sociology. Schilder had differed from Freud on several theoretical counts, questioning his drive theory and the death instinct, and claimed himself to be more of a phenomenologist, future oriented psychologist, than the fateful regressiveness inherent in Freud's theories. He did not denounce psychoanalysis; however, he had in common with Burrow that he declined the invitation of being analyzed by Freud, and did not adhere to orthodox psychoanalytic thought, incorporated social environment in his theories, and like Burrow was barred from the APA.

"Schilder would have to be recognized as the first to conduct psychoanalytic group psychotherapy" (Pinney, 1978a, p. 133). In 1935 he was doing group therapy with adult psychotic patients at Bellevue on an experimental basis (Shaskan & Roller, 1985). He framed patients' unconscious and irrational beliefs as their "ideologies" which he would bring into the group to discuss (Ettin, 1989; Pinney, 1978a; Schilder, 1936; Shaskan & Roller, 1985).

His theory of "ideologies" which he referred to as the conscious manifestations of often unconscious learning of values and truisms from a person's larger society, family, and within their own personal mind and experience of the world. He said that sometimes the "ideologies" from different frames of reference would contradict themselves, but the person usually held onto them regardless (Schilder, 1936). Group therapy was the vehicle where these ideologies would become evident and played out and thus having the possibility of transformation. Additionally, Schilder used psychoanalytic concepts of repression, resistance, and transference between members and with the group therapist. For this, he is often credited as an originator of psychoanalytic group therapy (Shaskan & Roller, 1985).

It was said that Schilder walked the streets of New York preoccupied in his own mind and paid little attention to traffic. Schilder was fatally hit by a motor car as he crossed the street in New York in 1940, which cut short his contributions to group therapy (Bender, 1985, chapter 3; Foulkes, 1985, Chapter 7).

As his student, colleague and supervisee, Alexandra Adler (1965), in her eulogy, mused: "My contact with him left many unforgettable memories; it stimulated constructive thinking and revealed to me his leadership as a teacher. Everyone who worked with him came under the influence of his personality and many developed a deep abiding loyalty to him" (p. 848). No other references to his supervisory processes reached documentation.

Four more noted European Jewish émigrés had significant roles in group therapy and began supervisory practices between the wars. Three immigrated to the US and one to England. Wender and Foulkes continued in the Freudian psychoanalytic tradition, and Low and Lewin were of the empirical schools of thought. All would have significant supervisory influences on future group leaders.

Louis Wender (1890–1966) came to the US in 1900 from Lithuania with his family to escape antisemitism, received his medical degree at L.I. College Medical School, and later returned to Vienna to pursue psychoanalytic training with Freud's group. He attended Freud's lectures and was analyzed and supervised by an unidentified colleague of Freud's. Afterwards, in the US, he worked with William Alanson White, the founder of the White Institute along with interpersonalists Erich Fromm, Freida Fromm Reichman, Harry Stack Sullivan, The Rioches, and Clara Thompson. The institute was started to offer alternative training to the strict Freudian psychoanalysis of the APA. By its emphasis on interpersonal psychology and social aspects of psychological development, the Interpersonalists offered a theoretical steppingstone to group psychotherapy that would still include intrapsychic conflict.

According to some, Wender was the first small group therapist for mentally ill in America (Thomas, 1943; Scheidlinger, 2000) because he had the medical and psychoanalytic credentials. He worked at Hillside Hospital, Pinewood Sanatorium, when it first started in Upstate New York with inpatient populations, and later with outpatient populations in the 1930s. Wender (1945) described his 15 years (1930–1945) of conducting group psychotherapy there. He organized patients into small groups (compared to the "class size" of Pratt's groups) of six to eight patients and met with them twice weekly. He had a more optimistic perspective than did Freud on the regressive nature of groups, in that he used regressive libidinal drives (the instinctual drive for attachment) for the patients in the group to begin to connect with each other, and eventually rework healthier, happier relationships. They would overcome emotional interpersonal "fixations" that were developed and repeated in the trauma of their early family lives. Wender believed that the role of the therapist in the group was to put patients at ease to elicit spontaneous, unselfconscious participation by all in the group. Making the unconscious conscious was for individual work, which he also advised as a corollary to group therapy ("combined individual and group treatment").

It only seems reasonable that Wender supervised and taught other group therapists, but again his supervisory functions, and with whom, are invisible to history. Wender had a long career and worked in New York until his death at age 76.

Abraham Low (1891–1954) though trained as a psychoanalyst, adopted Americanism entirely. Born in Poland, attended school in France, served in the Medical Corps in the Austrian Army, and as many others would, completed his MD in Vienna. He immigrated to the US in 1920, in order to pursue more career opportunities. He did work at first as a qualified psychoanalyst 1921–1925 in New York but apparently received much criticism from his colleagues, most likely because he diverged from the orthodox Freudian methods prevailing at the time. He then became a professor at Illinois Medical School, and subsequently director of the Neuropsychological Institute. In 1927 he became an American citizen and spent the rest of his life and career in Chicago developing a self-help method that fought for patient's rights and the destigmatization of patients. His methods were similar to Pratt's with psychoeducation, aphorisms, affirmations, and the endorsing of will power (Low, 1943, 1984). The use of groups was for members to give each other support, allow each other to express themselves, and remind each other of positive affirmations.

Although Low did not have a systematic method of supervision that was documented, he supervised staff of State Hospitals and treated severely mentally ill (recoveryinternational. org; Wikipedia, n.d.c.). As part of that work, he conducted trainings in his group method with staff, and in an egalitarian mode with patients, could be viewed as a mode of supervision. Thirty-six of his recovered, devoted ex-patients started "Recovery" in 1937 which was a group treatment model where patients helped and supported each other. His historical influence was in founding Recovery International (Recovery International, n.d.), using cognitive-behavioral methods, which his daughter has carried on and still exists today. In 1943 he published *The Techniques of Self-Help in Psychiatric Aftercare* in three volumes: *Volume I: Recovery's Self-Help Techniques, History and Description*, now titled *Mental Illness, Stigma and Self-Help*; *Volume II: Group Psychotherapy*; *Volume III: Lectures to Relatives of Former Patients*, now titled *Peace versus Power in the Family* (see sites.neoninspire.com).

Of all the group therapists, Kurt Lewin's (1890–1947) theory and research was most directly influenced by his experiences of war, discrimination and antisemitism. He would have the most profound influence on one branch of group therapy supervision, namely training leaders, professionals and organizations to lead groups that could productively communicate in order to improve society.

Lewin was born in a peaceful small town in Germany which is now part of Poland. His father had leadership qualities, and for a short time, was president of the local synagogue, ran a small general store in town and they owned a small farm a few miles outside of town. Kurt had an older sister and two younger brothers. When he and his younger brother served together in WWI, Kurt was wounded and hospitalized, but his younger brother Fritz was killed in action. In 1933, when Hitler took over governance of Germany, Lewin moved his family to the US. Unfortunately, when WWII broke out, he was unable to get his mother a passport and she was killed in a concentration camp. Lewin was deeply affected by his losses and antisemitism, social prejudice and injustice. He turned his studies from experimental research to apply them to social justice, while keeping a scientific basis and explanation for his theories.

Lewin's mentors in Berlin were Carl Stumpt who was an experimentalist (Perlina, 2015) and Narziss Ach who studied habits and stimulus response as moderators of will power. Though his studies were interrupted by WWI, Lewin was able to receive his doctorate and a position as university lecturer in 1921 in Germany. During his stay in Berlin, he was in close contact with Berlin Gestalt psychologists, Max Wertheimer, Wolfgang Köhler, and Kurt Koffka—who founded the journal *Psychologische Forschung* together with Kurt Goldstein and Hans Walter Gruhle in 1921 (Glatzer, 1971).

His main contributions to group theory and training were conflict resolution, social bias and prejudice retraining, and productive communication. Additional significant fundamentals for group therapy that he developed were the idea that the group-as-a-whole was more than a sum of its parts and could be studied as such. This was applied to the study of prejudice which he believed was more of a cultural phenomenon than an individual personality one. This differed from the psychoanalytic approach where the individual psychology of each person in the group was the focus. He also did preliminary work of showing that groups, and the group-as-a-whole, could be studied scientifically with a mathematical formula suggesting that behavior is a function of the interaction between the person's personality and their environment. Lewin was the innovator of what we now call the "three-legged stool" to represent the interdependence of research, training, and action in producing social change. Lewin called it "action research." He applied this formula to the study of the person in naturalistic, real life, group settings. He also coined the term "group dynamics." For him it was not the content of what was observed in social groups but the interactions that revealed the essence of group functioning. This emphasis was a new foundation of focusing on the interaction between participants of the group.

Lewin was described by his student (and supervisee), Ron Lippitt (1940), as being deeply sensitive to social problems and was committed to use whatever resources as a social scientist to alleviate them. He was also described as someone that attracted many to work with him because of his congenial personality and he believed in democratic and egalitarian process. He considered and treated his students as equal colleagues. Some prominent cognitive-behavioral psychologists were mentored by Lewin including Leon Festinger (1919–1989), who became known for his cognitive dissonance theory (1956), and environmental psychologist, Roger Barker, Bluma Zeigarnik, and Morton Deutsch, the founder of modern conflict resolution theory and practice (Wikipedia, n.d.d.).

His influence was not so much as in running therapeutic groups as it was on supervising future group leaders in group format. Lewin organized a workshop in New Britain, CT, in 1946 to teach small group skills and community change to community leaders. This workshop led to the creation of National Training Labs (NTL) and to the development of T-groups (Training groups). NTL's seminal contribution is to experiential learning in interaction groups (ntl.institute, n.d.).

Another founding training and supervision model was started by Jewish German-born neurologist and psychoanalyst Siegmund Heinrich Foulkes (1898–1976) who emigrated to England in 1933. He was a refugee with his wife and three children. His training supervisor was Herman Nunberg and was in training analysis with Helene Deutsch, a feminist Freudian analyst. Nunberg was an early advocate (1918) of required "training analysis" for psychoanalysts in training. Nunberg also spoke up strongly in favor of lay analysis, suggesting that behind opposition to it stood nontheoretical motives "such as medical prestige and motives of an economic nature" (Wikipedia, n.d.e). This is significant in that Foulkes was influenced by mentors who were moving toward more egalitarian relationships between the leader and the group, that is, that the group leader was not revered as the main change agent in group therapy for the individual, but that the other members of the group were, and the group-as-a-whole were equal healing agents. As well, the then referred to as lay analysts such as social workers and psychologists, Foulkes believed were of equal regard as neuropsychiatrists. He brought these ideas into his training and supervision of future group therapists in England and was a main influencer in the Group Relations Model.

Two founders of American institutions coming from Europe would train future group therapists during the 1930–1940 decade. They competed to be firsts in establishing group psychotherapy and its supervision and came from differing theoretical points of view, one being loyal to Freudian analysis and the other emphasized social environment. They were Samual Slavson (1890–1981) and Jacob Moreno (1889–1974).

Jacob Moreno, born in Romania, the son of Sephardic Jewish parents moved to Vienna in 1895. In 1917 he received his MD from the University of Vienna. He met Freud on at least one occasion during his education but outright rejected Freud's intrapsychic theories, preferring instead to explore life in the social world through group therapy. His theory and practice were diametrically opposed to Freud's in its foundations.

Moreno first began his group work, 1913–1914, with such diverse populations as prostitutes in Vienna, children and prisoners. He emigrated to the US in 1925 where he developed his practice into theory. Sometimes credited with coining "group psychotherapy," Moreno first used the term and defined it in his *The Application of the Group Method to the Classification of Prisoners* at a meeting held at Toronto in May 1931, and again in several other publications. He founded his training institutes which implemented supervision in 1941 (Giacomucci, 2021, Chapter 2) to promulgate his group methods. His training and supervision sessions replicated his experiential psychodrama methods where participants enacted or reenacted various roles in their life experiences, thus bringing their social situations directly into focus, in group. His foundational contribution to group therapy is the experiential aspect of role play, which would resonate later in Gestalt therapies. Unlike Marsh and Schilder of this era, Moreno lived many years beyond WWII. In later eras Moreno would continue to have influence on traditions of group therapy and many of his group therapeutic elements were precursors of the 1960s and 1970s encounter groups when cultural views attributed human behavior to social context. He traveled extensively in the US and Europe teaching and supervising ("directing" was the supervisor's role) group therapists in his experiential psychodrama methods.

Samuel R. Slavson was Moreno's competitor for being the originator of group therapy and its training as a professional occupation in America. He founded the American Group Psychotherapy Association (AGPA) in 1943. Slavson had arrived in New York at age 13, 1903. Coming from Ukraine, his family escaped from Russian pogroms. He had a natural proclivity for organizing groups in his school and camp. He attended evening school at Cooper Union for a BS in Engineering but was sidetracked by his interest in social justice and child psychology. A natural leader, from 1918 to 1934 he was the departmental director of New York's Walter School, educational consultant to the Pioneer Youth of America, director of research at the Malting House in England, and consultant to agencies treating children in New York.

To qualify himself in the psychoanalytic psychiatric world, during the 1920s Slavson participated in his own personal Freudian analysis (Spotnitz, 1961), but it is unknown with whom or where, another "quiet" supervision. In 1934, he joined his brother, John Slawson, who at that time was executive director at the Jewish Board of Guardians (JBG) in New York, to be the director of group therapy of children where he remained and developed his theories of group and supervision for many years to come.

Slavson may have been group therapy's first training supervisor by virtue of documenting and systematizing its process. He worked in the trend of psychiatry joining hands with social work. He oversaw caseworkers' group leadership, among them Mary Froelich, later to become JBG president, and Betty Gabriel (1902–1995) whom he gave credit for first experimenting with groups of children and adolescents. Gabriel also published an article on her group work (Gabriel, 1939).

In his 1943 book *Introduction to Group*, his "supervisory discussion" of groups was in keeping with his social philosophy and psychoanalytic psychiatry. He advised that children should learn to be autonomous, independent beings in a group with very little intervention from the leader. He applauded the therapist when they stayed out of the interaction. Slavson wrote: "We notice that the group therapist encourages Ann [a child in group therapy] to make a decision (for herself) and accepts Ann's suggestion. This is in line with the general policy of group therapy to build up independence and the status of the children vis-à-vis the adult and wean them away from the domination of adults" (1943, p. 63).

His supervisory analysis of the group process included the roles each child takes on in the group, for example, "equilibrizer, neutralizer, instigator," Slavson's idea of curative factors in the group were "When attachments grow out of the casual contacts during the [group period] they serve as beginnings in developing relationships with others. The relations that originate in the … therapy work room lead to better adjustment on the part of the patient to people within and outside the institution" (p. 315).

For Slavson, the authority of the therapist was to be diminished in group therapy as children learned to be more autonomous. Interestingly, or perhaps paradoxically, the group leader's psychotherapeutic role, although less didactic, structuring, directive and authoritarian than in Pratt's groups, was however operating under psychodynamic principles of the leader being the center of patient projections and transferences, evidence of Slavson's adherence to Freudian therapy. Slavson's 1943 original writings on supervision were based on psychoanalytic Freudian psychology and aimed at understanding and accommodating the individual in the group therapeutic setting. Slavson discussed the responses needed from the therapist, as well as the therapist's countertransference (Levin & Kantor, 1964). There was very little written at the time and for some time to come in the way of supervision of group therapy beyond Slavson's original writings (Levin & Kanter, 1964).

In Slavson's supervision of groups the social worker as caseworker jointly contributed to diagnosing and treatment planning as a way for the social worker to learn how to run the groups. Between the 1920's and 1936 Slavson's method of supervision of the caseworker had three phases. Initially the caseworker followed the supervising psychiatrist's instructions. When the worker had more of a relationship with the patients, they took on more control of the case. In the third phase the caseworker became the primary therapist. In this third phase was when training (supervision plus didactics) took on greater importance. The caseworker integrated psychiatric knowledge and learned diagnostic skills from supervision. Through systematic training in personality development of children, and in psychodynamics and in psychotherapy, caseworkers came to understand better the interaction of the individual personality with social situations. Supervision and casework seminars became important in improving casework techniques (cf. Slavson, 1940, 1992). These were quite organized and structured supervision models for the time. It's still a basic model of supervision used in most internship sites today, both for individual and group therapy supervision.

In conclusion, most of the precursor innovators of group therapy were motivated by German and Viennese intellectual culture which was scientifically driven and competitive: "To be an academic in Vienna at that time and make any headway you had to make a lot of noise. By that I mean publish or spout new ideas. No matter what you were, you always had to blow your own horn. You had to be highly individualistic, intellectually and socially aggressive, and as independent as possible" (Parker, 1980, Chapter 1, p. 21). This same ethic was carried over to America with the added ingredients of freedom and individualism (Van Schoor, 2000). In America there were different and more varied opportunities for employment for the burgeoning psychiatry profession that would include group therapy.

Before WWII, the establishment of Institutes was the vehicle for supervision. Psychoanalytic institutes lead the way, the first examples being in Europe with the Vienna, Budapest, and Palestine Psychoanalytic Societies, and then in America, with the APA. Pioneers of group therapy in America began their training institutes according to their own brands of group therapy such as the Moreno Psychodrama and Slavson's AGPA. Authorized by the medical profession, founders developed their own model of group therapy, then supervised and trained in a manner that reflected their model.

Joseph Meiers, in his *Historical Survey 1930–1945* (1945), summarized and defined the major controversies of group therapy of the day. Early on a salient question was whether the focus should be the individual in the group as Freudian analysts espoused, or the group-as-a-whole as suggested by Burrow, Bion and Foulkes. "Group work" as envisioned by social work always entailed a social awareness, even if in addition to an intrapsychic awareness or psychopathology of the individual participants (Giacomucci, 2021, Chapter 2). Still other voices such as social psychologist Kurt Lewin emphasized the importance of a focus on intergroup relations and associated phenomena of group stereotyping and racism.

An additional dimension that evolved in group therapy theory and practice was the dominance and directiveness of the leader vs. the interplay between members as the therapeutic vehicle, and a more egalitarian relationship with the therapist (Giacomucci, 2021, Chapter 2). The idea of "mutual aid" based on the group healing itself through its own resources has roots in social group work practice (Giacomucci, 2021, Chapter 2), and was the main theory of Abraham Low's group work. Also emerging was the tension between action-oriented groups as in Moreno's psychodrama and activity group work with children from social group work, vs. emphasis on contemplative focus on the internal life of the individual from psychoanalytic tradition. Along with this was whether the therapy took place in a designated place, such as a therapist's office, or in a natural setting, for example, a playroom, playground, theater, family home, the battlefield, church, clinic community room, or on a walk in the park. Eventually the medicalization of group therapy and dominance of psychiatry would make the primary location of group therapy and its supervision in designated hospital settings, especially those with an academic connection. Meiers (1945) called for the requisite need for supervised training to advance the new methods of group psychotherapy, arguably the first mention in the literature that advocated training via supervision and apprenticeship specifically of group therapy. He foresaw in 1945 that training institutes, which followed a medical model, would become a necessary ingredient to the professionalization of group therapy.

Many group therapists worked developing theory and practice between the wars but had not published their work until afterwards. When the war came, "most of them came forward with new projects and plans to meet the emergency" (Meiers, 1945, p. 271). At the time of the war, only 20 professionals had defined themselves as group therapists; compared to the 3,000 by 1980. By 1980 also came an "amazing array of group theories and group therapies" (Ormont, 2001).

Group Therapy's Expansion: The Influence of WWII (1940–1960): The Beginnings of Professional Supervision

Events leading up to WWII included violent antisemitism resulting in more emigration to America of European intellectuals and analysts. At the same time in the US there was civil unrest and turmoil due to ideological differences (Maddow, 2023). The US entering WWII with the atom bomb threatened human civilization. The concurrence of all these events set the stage for the resurgent growth of group psychotherapy not only as a treatment for mental illness, but also for society.

Renewed government and military spending was a major impetus. "In the belief that shell shock could be prevented by selection and training, the armed forces had let military psychiatry slip into decline during the interwar period and by 1939 there were only half a dozen regular officers with varying degrees of psychiatric experience, some in administrative roles" (Jones, 2004, p. 495). The treatment success of group therapy in the eyes of the military had been measured by whether the person could return to the battlefield, meaning there had been little use to fund group therapy after the WWI. To remedy the situation, the US and English governments infused money and government support into psychiatric treatments, including group therapy. Medical institutions, scientific methods, the ongoing professionalization of social work and psychology, and group therapy thus benefited in both England and America as a result of WWII.

Several medical hospitals became the center of care for war veterans in England and the US. The US War Department put out bulletins saying that group therapy had advantages over individual therapy "in dealing with suspicious, hostile and guilty feelings … It is suggested that groups be homogenous, patients be seen individually first and then in groups … from 7 to 25 individuals meeting 3 to 6 times weekly for about one hour" (War Department Technical Bulletin 103, in Meiers, 1945; Jones, 2004).

England's main hospital site for group therapy for war veterans was Hollymoor at Northfield (Jones, 2004). Foulkes became a founder, with Bion and Rickman, of the Northfield Experiments. Lewin was a primary supervising consultant to them and, as a result, Jones (2004) noted that "wards were structured 'not as an organization run by doctors in the interests of their own technical efficiency' but as a community 'related to real tasks' to provide opportunities to identify and analyze the inter-personal barriers which stand in the way of participation in a full community life" (Jones, 2004). At Northfield, the dynamic process underlying the social interaction of the ward was termed "Lewinfiltration," a reference to the experiments in the social psychology of groups by Kurt Lewin (Jones, 2004). Bion, having experience on the front lines of WWI, and Rickman, having been through analysis with Freud's group, teamed up. Their theory was that the group would evolve on its own with little intervention from the leader. The leader's role was only to interpret group-as-a-whole dynamics. They focused on the "here and now" between group members without exploring their past. Burrow had written about the here and now 15 years earlier, calling it the "immediate group in the immediate moment." Apparently Bion and Rickman's experiment did not take well with the hierarchical military organization and was ended after six weeks. Because the groups included up to 100 veterans who were to take responsibility for themselves in the running of the groups with little direction from the leaders, there had been a breakdown in authority (Jones, 2004). However, Bion's legacy in terms of his theories about underlying group-as-a-whole processes that evolve when a group is basically left to its own devices, remains a vital part of contemporary views of group work, large group and the Group Relations school of thought.

The next Northfield experiment was undertaken by Foulkes. They involved all levels of authority in the community in their groups. Instead of just focusing on the group-as-a-whole they also focused on the individual and their accountability in the group. These were innovative experiments in group therapy at Northfield so there was really no "supervisor" to show the path, except perhaps those consultations with Lewin, of which there is very little written. However, with Lewin's consultations and the Northfield experiments began the first "therapeutic communities" (since Marsh's), in which group process was held at all levels of administration, therapists, and patients themselves, in addition to community meetings where all met together (Jones, 2004). This would become the prevailing therapeutic group model that included methods of supervision in psychiatric settings in the Community Mental Health Movement of the 1970s and 1980s.

In reflecting on supervision of group in 1945, historian Meiers concluded: "One thing is certain: efficient Group Psychotherapy is *not* a matter of a few medical (or not medical) geniuses or men of peculiar skill and gifts. It *can* be learned; and so, it *must*" (p. 277). He called for setting up of standards and schooling of group psychotherapists. He lamented that in 1945 books in psychiatry rarely mentioned group psychotherapy. However, many of the original pioneers of group therapy did go on later to practice, supervise, and establish training institutes.

Lou Ormont wrote of his own supervisory experience during that postwar period and stated: "Those of us who learned group therapy in the early fifties turned to the pioneers—the therapists who stood alone in the 1930s, shaping the form and format of group treatment. To master our skills we closeted ourselves in their offices for supervision" (1980, p. 176). His wording "closeted" is curious in light of what Alonso would say later in the 1980s related to lack of recognition of supervisors and supervision. One can only guess at the underlying motives to "closet" supervision at the time: The lack of recognition not only that group therapy was not yet recognized as a distinct profession, but also that supervision was not recognized as a craft that required learning. In supervision there was a lack of standardization, close relationships that evolved with questionable boundaries, and a pressure to prove oneself as an originator. As well, the supervisory relationship has historically been considered sacrosanct and confidential, similar to the therapeutic relationship in order for the supervisee to be open and trusting about sharing potential weaknesses. Though experienced as a necessary component to learning group psychotherapy, supervision was far from being defined or recognized as a systematized practice and continued as handed down from Freud's days.

After the war, group therapy was not only seen as a method for treating mental illness, but also to improve society. Slavson, despite his analytic allegiance, still at the forefront of group therapy development wrote after the war:

> The survival of man, especially in the era of expanding technology, automation and atomic developments can no longer be assured by individualism and uncontrolled competition. Cooperation for the benefit of the community and mankind as a whole is no longer an ideal to be hoped for, but an essential practice if mankind is to survive. The group as a concept and as an operational instrument has come to the fore out of the historic and evolutionary imperatives and has been applied with increasing frequency and skill in many of our social functions. It was, therefore, inevitable that it should also become a tool in efforts at correcting as well as educating and reeducating the human personality. Group Psychotherapy has been the outcome of these dynamic forces. Group Psychotherapy has implications far beyond the clinical frontier for just as the individual cannot develop and survive without the group, society's health and survival as well depends upon adequately functioning and healthy groups. Group Psychotherapy has demonstrated that the hostile, aggressive and destructive forces inherent in man's psyche can be employed in the interest of mental health and the welfare of society. It is only when society learns to accept, direct and sublimate man's basic hostility that it can be turned from its disruptive and destructive course toward the enhancement of human happiness and security.
>
> (Slavson, 1951)

Prewar and postwar pioneers continued their work in the latter part of the 1940s and throughout the 1950s. After WWII, Kurt Lewin joined Jacob Fine at Harvard Medical School to assist in the psychological rehabilitation of former occupants of displaced persons camps. He helped found the Tavistock journal *Human Relations* with his article "Frontiers in group dynamics." His instrumental work in the creation of the NTL and their T-groups continue to be a primary resource for training leaders in the experiential study of human interaction in groups.

Foulkes founded the Group Analytic Society, 1952, and the Institute of Group Analysis, 1971, both serving as primary resources for training and supervision of group treatments. He had a long career and in the early 1960s wrote on group supervision of groups (Foulkes, 1975).

Moreno found a home at Harvard in the 1950s where he set up supervisory trainings and brought them around the world. At that time one-third of hospitals were using psychodrama as treatment. In the 1950s he traveled around the country and world to teach psychodrama.

Slavson had founded the AGPA in 1943, in the midst of WWII, and would go on to make substantial contributions to the professionalization of supervision of group psychotherapy. Noteworthy, in America, AGPA was the first organization that required, in a systematized manner, training of group therapists via supervision. In organizing AGPA, Slavson set some membership criteria—some psychotherapy experience, and if not an MD, to be supervised by an MD. The psychotherapy profession was still dominated by psychoanalytic MDs even though social workers and psychologists had begun to do group therapy. To have enough people to make an association, he allowed many to join that were not group therapists. These usually had an interest in becoming group therapists, so began the path to doing so with supervision by a qualified psychiatrist.

Psychologists, social workers, and caseworkers were considered lay analysts, therefore needed supervision by psychiatrists when doing group therapy. Slavson himself became a first supervisor (despite the fact that his degree was in civil engineering and not medicine); qualifying himself by being in analysis himself with a Freudian protégée (unnamed in historical documents). Slavson saw that the oversight by psychiatrists would lend professional status to group psychotherapy and its supervision. On the other hand, having been self-taught, and having taught many case workers to do group therapy, he promoted the training of lay group therapists. Social workers had accepted psychiatric supervision in large part to give both social work and group work professional status. The debate over admitting "lay group therapists" as opposed to only credentialed, experienced group therapists began at the very inception of AGPA. Much later, whether these trained "lay" group therapists could become supervisors themselves would be questioned. Nevertheless, AGPA rules for supervision began to give the practice some structure and standards.

Slavson consulted frequently with numerous other mental health facilities during his tenure beyond this era of expansion, 1945–1960. From 1956 to 1968, he continued his work and shaped new theories on the treatment of delinquent adolescents and institutionalized psychotics. Until his death in 1981, he wrote prolifically, often lectured, supervised, and was frequently honored by his peers and colleagues.

Alongside Slavson was Hyman Spotnitz (1908–2008), a supervising and consulting psychiatrist for the JBG in New York from 1945 to 1954 (Meyers, 2011). He was of the same analytic threads as Slavson. He had undergone a six-year analysis with Lillian Delgar Powers who had been analyzed by Freud. He was further supervised by Sandor Rado, Herman Nunberg, Sandor Lorand, Sara Bonnett and Rudolf Lowenstein. Born in Boston, he attended Harvard, and then earned his MD in Berlin from Friedrich Wilhelm's University in 1934. He went to the College of Physician and Surgeons, Columbia University, for a neurology degree, awarded in 1939. His specialty was group therapy for severely disturbed children and their families.

Spotnitz was among those few supervisors that wrote about training of group therapists. At the time the focus was on the character traits and capacity for psychological minded-ness that would make a good group therapist and supervisee. Their view was that half the success was in selecting the right trainees. This practice started early with Slavson when he oversaw caseworkers and then selected the best to continue training and supervision. One of the characteristics that Spotnitz (1961) considered important was emotional respon-siveness: "Emotional responsiveness is to some extent inborn, but it is fostered by a lively childhood and by contacts with many people during one's formative years" (p. 231). He described his own upbringing outside Boston in an overcrowded neighborhood, with vio-lent street gangs, and an infamous murder on his street. Being the eldest of five children and having parents who worked at their downstairs candy store almost all the time, he was left to arbitrate fights and upsets among his siblings. "The role of parental helper in a large family is excellent conditioning for a group therapist" (p. 232). It seemed he must have been conditioned to tolerate wide ranges of extreme emotions which became the foundation of his theory. He first worked with severely emotionally disturbed children and adolescents, and with schizophrenics at the JBG with Slavson for whom he wrote a laudatory memorial. As colleagues they surely consulted and peer supervised. The two were among the first to employ group psychotherapy and to supervise caseworkers by going over case transcripts in detail with them. Both were psychoanalytically oriented and revered group treatment.

A major contribution of Spotnitz to group therapy and its supervision was the emphasis on the therapists using their feelings that were inspired ("induced") by the group in order to understand the group's resistances. For this to happen well, the supervisee must already be well trained in awareness of their own interpersonal proclivities (countertransference). For example, the therapist might start to notice their feeling of anxiety in response to the group. In order to use this information, the group leader assesses what usually brings up anxiety for them while also recognizing the emotional tenor of the group. The therapist may then recognize that the group is communicating on a very superficial level to resist addressing angry feelings.

This was in line with Paula Heimann's suggestion in 1950 that all the feelings of the group therapist were important information about what was going on with the patient, and here it's being applied to the group. In addition, Spotnitz also taught therapists to not directly con-front group members' resistances but join them by way of reflecting. To continue the above example, instead of telling the group they are avoiding angry feelings and need to start talk-ing about them, the group therapist might reflect that "the group tonight is talking to each other in a very comfortable way which might be keeping the peace." As in this example Spotnitz moved toward understanding the group-as-a-whole as a frame of reference for the therapist to respond to. This was in contrast to Slavson who mostly advocated addressing and treating the individual in group. Spotnitz was a prolific supervisor, training analyst, lecturer and group therapist and founded Modern Analysis, as well as publishing over 100 articles.

The Beginnings of Formal Supervision and Training Programs

The chief settings for the advancement of systematized supervision of group psychotherapy were hospitals where training programs were set up. Here were the practicums in group therapy and often the first opportunity to practice as a leader of group therapy, whether social worker, psychologist, or psychiatrist. In the hospital practicums, given that psychiatrists had the credentialed status, and psychoanalysis was the treatment method, it makes sense that the first training programs in group psychotherapy would be for psychiatry residents, followed by psychologists and social workers. Geller (1958) provides a prototypical example of such a program he devised with psychiatrists at Rockland State Hospital. At the time psychiatrists were conducting the groups in the hospital, even though they had little group therapy training, but some psychoanalytic/psychodynamic training. Geller was able to gain administrative support to offer a supervision program. He called it a "seminar" approach. He and the psychiatric staff met weekly for two hours on a 13-week rotation basis. The seminars were conducted along the lines of a psychodynamic model: First some didactic material provided by the supervisor, followed by a 30-minute presentation by a therapist of a therapy group. After that it was a "permissive" environment where all the participants were encouraged to explore. The three general foci were "The interaction of the patients within the given group, … what went on between the therapist and the patients, and interactions within the therapy seminar itself … There was about equal emphasis placed on the presentation material, and upon interaction within the seminar" (p. 314). Often what was explored was the meaning of the group dynamics, as well as technical details of how to organize the groups. The groups also dealt with anxieties and resistances and personality styles of the therapists, as well as those of their patients. This model continues to be a primary way of supervising today.

Just a few years after Searles (1955) introduced the idea of parallel process, which he called "reflective process" and English analysts called "mirroring," Geller used the method in these supervision groups. Not only was parallel process discussed but also how the therapist's usual ways of relating to people was carried over to their leadership style of the groups.

> There was found a close correlation between the therapist's usual attitudes and ways of relating to people, and his attitude toward the patients in his group. The didactic, overly intellectual person carried this feature over into the group. The very friendly, strongly emotionally identifying person reacted this way with his patients. In time he took over the patient's problems and anxieties to the point of making it unnecessary for them to work on these things in the therapy. The very narcissistic and opinionated therapist tended to intimidate patients, etc. Here a good opportunity was available to re-emphasize with the therapist the importance of personality understanding and development within themselves if they wanted to become proficient in psychotherapy.
>
> (p. 317)

Geller's post-seminar research found that the important aspects of group supervision of group therapy (as reported by the supervisees) were catharsis, intragroup communication, and developing understanding of defensive processes. Concerns and benefits from the group supervisory format are very similar to concerns heard today about this nondirective, experiential approach. Most participants, once they established some safety and trust, thought the nondirective spontaneous participation approach was valuable experiential learning, while some persisted that they wished for more didactic and guidance from the leader. Significant responses by the supervisees to the follow-up question about the advantages of this type of seminar included that it increased interest in doing group psychotherapy, that it increased the respectability of this modality within the hospital, and that it improved cohesiveness of staff members. And finally, the essence of supervision as typically done today was expressed: "Learning by doing and experiencing has more impact and is more a part of one's life than learning any other way" (Hahn et al., 2022, p. 704).

Influence of Supervision of Individual Psychotherapy

Geller's 1958 work notwithstanding, most psychotherapy training programs in the 1950s and 1960s concerned the supervision of individual therapy, which influenced the supervision of group psychotherapy, particularly the work of Searles (1955), and Eckstein and Wallerstein (1958) in their identification and explorations of the concept of parallel process. Searles viewed the "reflective process" as a transitory unconscious identification of the therapist with the patient, which causes a block in the treatment and entails the therapist's responding to the supervisor in the same manner as the patient responded to the therapist. That is, the dyadic therapeutic interaction that the patient is experiencing with the therapist is stored unconsciously by the therapist, who then replicates it with the supervisor.

Epstein and Wallerstein also incorporated the use of parallel process in supervision in the comprehensive individual supervision program they developed over 10 years starting in 1948 at the Menninger Institute. As for supervision of group psychotherapy, they acknowledged that it adds complications and needed further study. At the Menninger School of Psychiatry (Ekstein & Wallerstein, 1958), psychiatrists began supervising postgraduate psychologists and composed a workshop for psychiatrists to learn how to supervise. They proposed a developmental model of supervision: the training phase, beginning phase, learning process, and the end phase. They explored the multiple relationships among the supervisor, therapist, patient and administrator (of the hospital or clinic setting), including the identification of a conflict of interest that often continues today in institutions, namely the clash that can arise between the administrators' objectives and the clinical supervisory and treatment objectives.

Of significance since it indicated a change in culture of psychiatry, Eckstein and Wallerstein advocated humility in the supervisory role. "The teachers of psychotherapy should preferably be people who are identified with a philosophy in which the true helper has humility rather than power motives toward the helping process. Such humility is a part of genuine self-acceptance, the basic ingredient without which the best of techniques will not bear fruit" (p. 31).

On the other side of the Atlantic, "Group Analytic" supervision was emerging (Smith & Gallop, 2024) following the notions in individual psychoanalytic supervision, including an expanded view of countertransference. At first countertransference was considered unconscious enactments and reactions by the therapist to the patient that needed to be uncovered by the supervisor. Paula Heimann (1950) refined the definition to include *all* the reactions of the therapist in response to a patient, "all the feelings which the analyst experiences towards the patient" (p. 81). This is significant in that the therapist is not obligated to hide, neutralize or disregard countertransference, but to use it to understand the patient more, and in that countertransference could be both conscious and unconscious.

Another important contribution from England at this time was Foulkes who had started the teaching, therapy and supervision of groups with the use of setting of boundaries between therapy and supervision: "The supervisory seminar was not a therapeutic group: it could not be under the circumstances. We deliberately confined our discussion to the interaction between the doctor and his group of patients ... On occasion we also took into account the reactions within the seminar itself" (Foulkes, 1964, p. 251).

In the US, psychologists were beginning to supervise psychologists and not rely on MDs. Bernard Riess (1960), a psychologist, noted that the "master–disciple" model of psychotherapy supervision was still in the "guild" stage where "one certificated master lends his [sic] skills and techniques to a group of apprentices" (p. 111). Riess goes on to say, "For most psychotherapists the supervisor is still the magic initiator whose word is apt to be the encoding of law" (p. 112). By 1960, the role of the supervisor for individual therapy was fairly well defined as including not only didactics about theory, but also the in-vivo reflection of the process between patient and therapist, the countertransference resistances of the therapist, and the transference resistances toward the supervisor. However, there were contrasting views on whether the supervisor was to be the expert, or a collaborator.

As well, by 1960 the supervision of group therapists was well established in many training facilities, but with little distinction between how supervision of group therapy vs. supervision of individual therapy was done, perhaps none. What was being debated was how far to explore the supervisee's history and personality versus leaving that domain to personal therapy, the beginnings of defining boundaries. Relatedly was the question about how necessary individual analysis was to the trainee as part of training (in or out of group), and whether it should be required or optional. What stood was the need for the therapist under supervision to be able to recognize and moderate their countertransference (all their feelings toward the patient) so that it left more room for the therapist to understand and explore the issues of the client/patient (Riess, 1960). It was formulated that the issues (countertransference) of the therapist that interfered with treatment could be addressed in supervision without going into the supervisee's personal history. Contrasting views on countertransference were also apparent into the 1960s despite Heimann's contributions; on the one hand countertransference was bad and needed to be resolved, and on the other hand it was considered an enlightening tool in understanding the therapeutic relationship.

A significant change in perspective in the 1960s was whether the social worker, or psychologist needed to be in continued supervision by a psychiatrist, and at what point they should be able to practice independently. There clearly was a move in the direction of a less authoritarian, psychiatry dominated, structure in the supervisory relationship, and toward each of the professions supervising their own discipline.

In the 1960s, objective methods to evaluate the progress of a supervisee were just beginning. This was the beginning of formulating competencies of the therapist as evaluated by the supervisor. Reiss offered a method that entailed three main pillars: (1) "Technical Skill" comprising diagnostic skill, treatment planning, handling of the patient in beginning and middle phases of treatment, (2) "Personality of the Therapist" including ways of relating to the patient, supervisor, and administration, and (3) "Direction of Growth and Promise" including openness to learning from patients, understanding areas of competence, and willingness to seek future consultation, growth of individual style, awareness of countertransference, and continued scientific interest. In summary Riess stated: "The supervisor helps the trainee a) to develop skills, b) to recognize the areas and ways in which the therapist's character problems enter into the therapeutic relationship, and c) to overcome resistances of learning" (p. 114). These three pillars of evaluation remain today the foundation of assessing supervisees. He went on to emphasize the need for supervisors to receive training specifically in supervision.

Riess acknowledged that analytic training up to that point had ignored social responsibilities of psychotherapists which he refers to as the "analytic deep freeze" (social awareness frozen because analysts historically believe that intrapsychic struggles are universal and biologically inherent, and not subject to political or social forces). He purported that supervisors need to be aware of their own social judgments, biases and values, while at the same time impart the necessity of that awareness to supervisees, who in turn make it part of their therapeutic treatment of clients/patients to help them become aware also. Individual supervision was catching up to group therapy's interest in sociocultural forces as determinants of personality, interpersonal relating and group dynamics.

Derner (1960), a psychologist, moved away from the analytic intrapsychic to interpersonal psychotherapy in the vein of Harry Stack Sullivan, Clara Thompson, Rollo May, and Karen Horney. Derner advocated for the scientific method of observing behavior. Regarding supervision, he stated supervision "becomes a model of successful interpersonal interactions" (p. 140). Derner refined the definition of supervision by distinguishing it from consultation, administrative control, or personal therapy. He stated: "One person is by virtue of his extensive experience senior to the supervisee who is less well trained and experienced. The focus is on suggestions on technical handling of the patient and his problems" (p. 133). Transference and countertransference are to be identified with suggestions of how to deal with them. He viewed the two main problems that supervisees have are (1) the need to be the omnipotent savior, able to cure everyone, and (2) the alternative of feeling like they are not doing anything helpful and should not even receive pay for their efforts.

The papers by Riess and Derner, as psychologists, are significant to group therapy supervision in that up to this point, psychoanalytic psychiatrists were the prevailing and reigning supervisors of individual and group psychotherapy in universities and hospital settings in the US. Analyzing the individual in group continued to predominate in group theory and practice, and they articulated a turn toward importance of the interpersonal group process. Challenging supervisors to emerge from the "analytic deep freeze" of psychoanalytic thought and to take into account social judgments, values and biases, and observations of interpersonal interactions, including parallel process, was a significant move toward legitimizing group behavior and dynamics in psychotherapy.

The Community Mental Health Movement (1960–1970): Whither Supervision?

The fourth-era Community Mental Health Movement (1960–1970) which included The Encounter movement came with American cultural liberation, antiracist movements, the second wave of feminism, and another significant war, the Vietnam War. There was an expansion of community services and community group psychotherapy. The abusive treatment of mentally ill in institutions came to light. At first a social concern, over the years deinstitutionalization became a monetary issue. In addition, there was the discovery and proliferation of psychotropic medications, so that the severely mentally ill were thought to be able to function outside the institution, perhaps with some outpatient psychotherapy.
The government once again provided financial support for mental health services. The Mental Health Act of 1963 provided federal funds for inpatient, outpatient, partial hospitalization, 24-hour ERs, and consultation and education. Community mental health clinics were created by physicians, and they continued to hold authority over psychology and social work in psychotherapy and supervision. This caused the more innovative group therapies to go outside of the medically legitimized psychotherapy institutions and into the general public domain (Kaslow et al., 1977).

An era of tug of war in the role of the supervisor was brought on between professional psychoanalytic psychiatry and new egalitarian, socially influenced clinicians. Social workers and psychologists wanted professional independence. Supervision was being questioned and redefined in the direction of the supervisor becoming a humbler guide who would not delve into personal unconscious motives of the trainee, particularly in a judgmental manner. The supervisee's professional individuation was encouraged. It was about providing a space where the supervisee could feel accepted where they are in their growth process, and experience trust from the supervisor in their ability to grow and develop in their own unique way. It should be noted that up until the 1960s, almost all group therapists and supervisors, particularly psychiatrists, were men. Women were seeking more professional recognition.

The Encounter movement brought an explosion of small and large group experiences for the general public, mental health professionals, educators, as well as the mentally ill. Mental illness was considered a social adjustment problem versus an intrapsychic, biologically driven problem (Kaslow et al., 1977). Group methods pursued divergent tracks but had mutual influence. There was the "group psychotherapy" track—geared toward mental health populations, and the "human relations" track—geared toward training the general population and frequently mental health professionals (Shaffer & Galinsky, 1974). "Models" of group therapy became experimental and often were defined by the genius of the leader, a repeat of the early 1900s. However, there were foundations—Lewin's Training groups (T-groups) and Carl Rogers Encounter groups, both grounded in research. T-groups emphasized the here and now process of the group-as-a-whole and encouraged group cohesiveness, and were meant for professionals, the general population, as well as psychiatric groups. Carl Rogers inspired authentic expression in Encounter groups and also wrote and researched prolifically his humanistic therapy.

Moreno also participated in the Encounter movement. He believed in restoration of community-as-a-whole, was very spiritual, believing that God was in everyone. In early 1970s, several movements incorporated Moreno's techniques—human potential movement, the Encounter movement, T-groups and sensitivity training, and therapeutic communities. However, Moreno denounced these movements as not really being trained in *his* model. He claimed they lacked training and supervision. In 1973 he cofounded the International Association of Group Psychotherapy (IAGP) with Foulkes but died a year later. His wife, Zerka Moreno, took up the teaching and practicing of psychodrama and that's when a certification process started which would professionalize supervision in the psychodrama modality.

Encounter groups were a time of experimentation, self-actualization, and getting in touch with feelings and authentic self. These groups proliferated under a broad range of labels— gestalt, psychodrama, EST, encounter marathons, consciousness raising, nude encounters, primal scream groups, and confrontation groups. Utopian societies were conceived of, and some experimented with living in communes. Some groups devolved into cult-like adherence to an ideal model with strict rules, worshiping the leader, much like how Freud described the danger and dark side of human groups. Others did lead to self-individuating, higher awareness of self, and improved ability to communicate. The paradox of self-actualization groups was that people were drawn to the newest, charismatic, powerful leader who could claim to bring them insight and happiness in self and community. The danger brought on by the encounter groups was the idolization of the leader, the teachers, the supervisors. Titles of popular books began to pop up: "If You Meet the Buddha in the Road, Kill Him," and "I'm OK, You're OK."

The preponderance of psychoanalytically trained psychiatrists from 1945 to 1972 who had worked in universities and hospital residency programs (Shuster et al., 1972) held onto the hard-earned legitimacy of a conservative psychoanalytic psychiatry-oriented view of psychotherapy. Spotnitz (1961) observed that there was a counter-reaction to the large-scale use and immediate popularity of group therapy after the war among some professionals who argued that it wasn't really scientifically sound. Spotnitz figured that it would take another decade to "build the structure of group psychotherapy on firmer foundation" (Spotnitz, 1961, p. 44).

In fact, many were so wary of the spread of experimental group therapies that they adhered to traditional psychoanalytic views of individual psychotherapy, eschewing the value of group therapy. At best, in training, they believed therapists should learn individual therapy—which often took many years, before group therapy, and that the social pressure to provide groups was an "unsound" approach. "Despite the social pressures of 'a sick society,' the sine qua non of a psychiatric clinician is his understanding and judgment of the unique individual psyche" (Shuster et al., 1972, p. xiii). These authors went on to say that once the psychiatrist has seen, treated under supervision a wide array of psychiatric patients, inpatient and outpatient, "he can apply his perception to wider fields: to groups, to organizations, to the community, and finally to cultural and trans-cultural issues" (p. 2).

Many earlier pioneers of group psychotherapy went on to supervise in hospital training centers and academic settings and incorporated a less authoritarian stance toward the supervisee and psychosocial considerations in assessment. Several more figures emerged that really began to systematize and professionalize the supervision of group psychotherapy during the 1960s. Among them was Aaron Stein (1913–1983). He was considered a pioneer in group psychotherapy and an inspiring teacher by in colleagues in AGPA. American born in Philadelphia, graduate of Johns Hopkins University in 1933, and with a medical degree from University of Maryland in 1938, he served as an early president of AGPA (*New York Times*, 1983, obituary). He wrote a chapter on training of group therapists in 1963 that had been presented at the fourth Annual Institute of AGPA in 1960. Stein had trained group therapists since 1954 in various settings: The Group Psychotherapy Project of the Girls' Service League, NY, The Hillside Hospital in Glen Oaks, NY, and at Mount Sinai Hospital in New York. He created and supervised group therapy training programs at all three places beginning in the early 1950s. He was "a highly regarded teacher of group psychotherapy at the Mount Sinai School of Medicine in New York, where he founded the Division of Group Psychotherapy" (MacKenzie, 1992, p. 329).

In supervision, Stein (1963) observed that having previous experience of treating individuals and didactic training in group therapy were important in lowering the anxiety of his trainees in group therapy; but they all had trouble using the group as the vehicle of therapy and thinking in terms of group-as-a-whole. At the beginning they wanted to focus only on the individuals in group. Although sitting in on experienced group therapists, observing and taking notes was an important part of preliminary training, Stein found that actually doing group therapy under supervision was the best way for trainees to learn and feel confident. His view was "that only experienced psychotherapists with adequate knowledge of basic psychopathology should undertake group psychotherapy since it is much more difficult than individual psychotherapy method" (Stein, 1963, p. 564). Stein's main contribution to supervision training was to have group therapists in training use the group as a therapeutic vehicle, rather than doing individual therapy in group. Delineating the techniques for this process would come later with Spotnitz and Lou Ormont's work.

Louis Ormont (1918–2008) was also born and raised in Philadelphia and received a Bachelor of Arts degree from Temple University. Subsequently, he was a graduate of the Yale School of Drama and later Columbia University's clinical psychology program (Keene News obit online, n.d.). He was a Buddhist and believed in the mindfulness and living in the moment that Buddhism teaches which informed much of his here and now thinking in the group therapy process (Collins, 2005).

Ormont was supervised and trained in group psychotherapy by supervisors from a wide range of theoretical orientation—Alexander Wolf, Asya Kadis, Fritz Perls, and Hyman Spotnitz, the latter with whom he worked for 45 years. Ormont (2001) described his early experience in supervision of group:

In traditional fashion we presented a group the way we were trained to present an individual patient. Our concerns were with diagnosis, ego strength, family dynamics, and current stresses. We traced the tangled relationships our patients developed with other group members. This one-to-one guidance offered us a rare chance to illuminate what was hazy, confirm us in our methodology, and acquaint us with more effective interventions. The supervisor would leisurely explain each patient's pattern and point out how it echoed and repeated itself. He or she would indicate what we were to expect and might offer ways to meet the difficulties that would arise. If we wanted to explore some troublesome area outside our practice, we could stop the talk about patients and delve into our inner lives.

(p. 176)

Ormont began to see in this one-on-one supervision that the "group as a whole" themes were not being identified and that group therapy was the treatment of the individual in group. He also felt that the supervision veered toward the supervisor's interest, and sometimes a one-sided view of the group. Even the supervisor's personality and the way the supervisor interacted colored the supervision as it was a form of modeling for the supervisee. In the one-on-one supervision it was assumed the supervisor knew best, and the supervisee was "flawed" and didn't realize others might have the similar challenges with their groups (Ormont, 2001).

"The outstanding limitation was that we were not getting our technical information in the medium in which we had to function. The consistent one-to-one discussion of the one-to-many felt unnatural and strained" (p. 177). A major difference he noted between group and individual therapy was that individual is based on report, in group one sees firsthand, in the "here and now," the enactments of aspects of a person's character, in relation to others. There were added transferences to group members in addition to the therapist. Ormont saw this as a revelation in group therapy, "The study of what a group could do, and not merely of what a therapist could do inside a group, became the guiding purpose of the new stage of group therapy—what we now call Modern Group Therapy" (p. 30).

In 1960, Ormont started his all-group private practice, the first psychotherapist to do so (Brook, 2009). He ran his first supervisory group of eight group therapists (Ormont, 2001). Instead of presenting cases, the members presented problems in their group. "Then we would try to make sense of the presenter's communication. What was going on? What were the patients trying to say? We relied on our spontaneity for clues" (p. 177). This led to the unveiling of parallel process: Was the group responding to the therapist the same way the supervision group was responding to the presenter? Another discovery by doing supervision this way was appreciating the difference between subjective and objective countertransference where the former was a repetitive pattern for the supervisee and thus considered a characterological response pattern of that therapist, while the latter was an atypical response for the supervisee, and thus considered "induced" by the patient or group. Ormont also added the idea of "reparative" countertransference where the therapist tries to give his group and patients what he did not get in their family life. Like Spotnitz, Ormont trained and supervised multitudes of group therapists who continue to practice today. Group therapy and group supervision were his only form of professional practice, of which he also wrote prolifically.

In the American vein of group psychotherapy which had been flourishing further west in Chicago was Carl Rogers (1902–1987). With Abraham Maslow, he started the Humanistic psychology movement which became popular in the 1960s, the major tenet of which was expanding one's creative potential (Van Schoor, 2000). Born in a suburb of Chicago, to a civil engineer and homemaker, both devoutly religious, he was the fourth of six children.

As another example of American religion and group therapy merging, Rogers was an altar boy growing up and changed college career choices from agriculture to ministry to child psychology and obtained his PhD from Columbia University in 1932. Pre-WWII, he worked as director at the Society for the Prevention of Cruelty to Children in Rochester, NY. Post-WWII, Rogers went to the University of Chicago where he was invited to set up a counseling center. It was there, from 1947 to 1957, that he formulated his theories of person-centered and humanistic therapy, and scientifically tested them at his university labs.

Always socially concerned, Rogers opposed McCarthyism in the 1950s and carried this social concern to inform his group therapy projects. Rogers basic tenant that human beings were driven to self-actualize if unfettered by environmental pressures or direction from an authority was adopted by the encounter group movement. He devoted the last decade of his life to traveling worldwide to improve social conflict with his theory. He went to Belfast, Northern Ireland, South Africa, Brazil, Japan and Russia. He focused on cross-cultural communication, personal growth, self-empowerment, and learning for social change.

In training and supervision, Roger's focus was on using person-centered empathy, authenticity, and genuineness in relating to supervisees to stimulate trainee/therapist personal growth and self-understanding. The assumption was that their own actualization will transfer to more effective practice. Being genuine and authentic as a group leader and group participant encouraged egalitarianism and psychological growth of the participants. Empathy was the tool to hear not only words of a participant, but also their emotional communication. Of Rogers, Ormont said, "From Carl Rogers (1961) we learned to follow the feelings in a communication" (Ormont, 2001, p. 30), a major tenet of Modern Group Analysis and supervision.

Growth and Controversy (1970–1980): Supervision Recognized

It was during the fifth-era Growth and Controversy (1970–1980) when supervision of group therapy became recognized in America as essential. The era found competing theories of group therapy, along with criticism of the Encounter movement's expansion into popular culture. Different models of group therapy were being mixed together in all different ways, "a bewildering variety of groups appeared on the scene" (Shaffer & Galinsky, 1974, p. xi). Shaffer and Galinsky cautioned that to combine different models and theories was only considered legitimate if the leader was well versed in those models of group therapy and had adapted them to their unique style. They emphasized the importance of supervision in the training process: "We consider it extremely irresponsible for any professional who has not had supervised experience in leading … groups … or, to conduct groups solely on the basis of didactic information from a book" (p. xiii).

In short, controversy and concern revolved around those therapists who were considered entrepreneurial and not having sufficient traditional and scientific training and supervision. In 1975 in the first edition of his highly influential book *Theory and Practice of Group Psychotherapy*, Yalom compared similarities and differences of Encounter groups with psychotherapy groups. In the same text he argued the importance of training group therapists and outlined a training program that emphasized supervision.

Yalom pointed out that knowledge of supervision of individual cases does not translate adequately to supervision of group therapy since conducting group therapy has immensely more pitfalls and variables to handle than does individual therapy. As many supervisors recognized at that point in time, the trainee of group therapy was very anxious before starting their first group. To have a good experience, it was helpful to have support of a supervisor at the outset. Yalom's method was that the supervisor observes, by whatever method available, the actual group, and for the supervisee to take notes immediately after the group of themes of their group, members' contributions, and the therapist's interventions and countertransference toward the group. Additionally, Yalom advised the supervisor to monitor the supervisee's attitude and openness in presenting material, and to attend to the relationship so that the supervisee will feel comfortable sharing as much as possible about their group. Yalom believed that the supervisee was apt to be present to their group in much the same characteristic manner as to the supervisor. And finally, he suggested that since it takes time to assimilate all the data about a group, that in group supervision of group, each supervisee present for a whole session. These were the foundations of the supervisory relationship and process that would persist to present day.

Group analytic supervision in England in the 1970s was also evolving. It typically was conducted according to the personality of the supervisor (Smith & Gallop, 2024), but in turn students were also encouraged to develop their own style as group leaders. At the Institute of Group Analysis (IGA), founded in 1971 by Foulkes, the first cohorts of supervisees were supervised by him. In their journal *Group Analysis*, several papers were published on supervision of group. Topics ranged from calls for more clarity in supervisory roles, to advocating again for supervision in combination with personal therapy, and for using free association to the material being presented by supervision group members and the presenter. Aspects of the group process to focus on were the therapist's interactions with the group, their feelings and countertransference in their leadership role, their personality, and the dynamics of the therapy group *and* of the supervision group (Bott, 1979). To date that was the most sophisticated explanation of the many foci involved in supervision of group therapy .

In 1975, Foulkes laid out his training recommendations, mostly having to do with the qualities of potential candidates for doing group analytic work. Among these traits he valued honesty with self and others, an awareness of current "problems of the time," and an ability to see differences between people and regard them all as equal, regardless of one's own religious or personal biases. He cautioned that the group leader must be able to tolerate not being perfect or omniscient without collapsing. As far as training format he suggested two to three years in a training group. If recommended by a consultant for further training, they should sit in with another group therapist as a participant observer. Then they might be trusted to run a group themselves under supervision. After about a year of running their own group, they can "start reading the relevant literature." Foulkes believed that no theory or technique should become a "straight jacket" and that the therapist should be able to develop their own style. Unlike many after him, he advised experiencing, observing and conducting groups before taking in any theoretical knowledge from the literature. In reality, many group therapists to this day begin running groups before any formal supervision or didactic learning about group. Although Foulkes recommended "supervision" he did not describe what the process of supervision consisted of.

Bott (1979) and Napoletani (1979), two more Europeans, wrote papers on supervision in the late 1970s that organized some of the aims and processes of group analytic supervision—Bott promoted free association to material presented by the supervision group, then fed it back to the presenter who could gain insight, understanding of group dynamics, understanding of their unconscious motives, and reduce resistance to using supervision. Such a method would shift away from intellectualized solutions while increasing awareness. Napoletani took it a step further and identified five foci of supervision for the supervisor to keep in mind: (1) the therapist's interaction with the setting, (2) their countertransference and comfort with leadership, (3) the group dynamics of the therapist's group, (4) dynamics of the supervision group, and (5) the therapist's personality. He suggested switching between these foci when the supervision group stalled.

Back to America, Erich Coche (1977, Chapter 11) worked at Friends Hospital in Philadelphia and experimented with supervisory training modules there with both staff and students that combined didactic work with supervision for two to three years. A main role of the supervisor was to "help the trainee to make the connection between his book knowledge and the group interactions" (p. 237). He also noted that understanding dyadic transferential relationships is different in the group context. He posited, "The most important task of supervision is to help the beginning group therapist use his or her own person as an effective tool in therapy. One needs to learn when to trust one's intuition, how to use the data from within, when to self-disclose and to what extent, when to push, and when to back off" (p. 237).

Coche went on to spell out the actual process of supervision, where the supervisee reports to the supervisor his version of what happened in the group, which often contained distortions that are a result of the supervisee's resistances in the presence of his superior. A good supervisor can detect the resistances and offer a discussion "in order to reopen communications." This could lead to a discussion of personal characteristics of the supervisee, "blurring the distinction between supervision and therapy, with concomitant interpersonal and ethical problems" (p. 238). On the other hand, if this impasse is not dealt with in some way, then the transferences toward the leader and the dynamics of the group might not be addressed. The model that he came to endorse was supervision that addressed equally the didactic literature on group therapy, combined with process material of the self-study of the therapist and interactions in the groups.

While informed by Yalom, Foulkes, Bott and Nepoletani, Coche, Spotnitz and Ormont, during the 1970s there were still few professional standards recognized for the training of supervisors, or for the supervisory role and function of supervisors of group therapy. Formulations of how it was to be conducted remained relatively experimental so that the supervision of group therapy varied greatly depending on the requirements of the institutional administration, the personality of the supervisor and supervisee, and the extent of use of individual supervision methods for group supervision. There was little guidance for supervisors, except their own therapeutic training and their own experiences with supervisors.

Conceptual Integration, Pluralism, and Maturation (1980–1990): Supervision Formulated

While the 1960s and 1970s brought group therapy to the public and became quite innovative and experimental in its expansion, there was controversy and concerns expressed by some of the founders and the more psychoanalytically inclined. Nevertheless, group therapy became a social phenomenon, not only to heal mentally ill, but to cure society. Community mental health models brought group therapy to hospitals and clinics as the treatment of choice (Kaslow et al., 1977), and an increased need for supervision of group therapy.

In the 1980s, many more papers began to appear about supervision of group, and even the training of supervisors, from Europe, America, and Canada. In *Group Analysis* alone, where there had been only four papers on supervision during the 1970s, there appeared 17 in the 1980s (Smith & Gallop, 2024). One of these, a substantial work by Sharpe and Blackwell (1987), was considered foundational for articulating how supervision was conducted at IGA. It was similar to Foulkes's group supervision of group, although with a greater emphasis on group leaders' personality and needs than on the supervisor. As they described the method, each group leader in the supervision group presented cases which were then explored on two levels—the clinical material presented plus the supervisory groups' associations and reactions to the material presented. The aims of the supervision were greater awareness of the therapists' own dynamics that come out in their work, and with those insights, an expansion of possible interventions for the group leader to employ. In essence, the supervisory work flexibly included various foci: (1) the group process in the presented clinical group, (2) the particular and relevant theoretical constructs such as countertransference, (3) the study of the role and participation of an identified patient in the clinical group, (4) a specific issue or problem in the group, (5) the free associations of all the trainees in the supervisory group, and (6) the use of a structured activity such as role playing. Sharpe and Blackwell stressed the importance of flexibility and openness in encouraging the training therapist to find their own style in learning and developing as a group therapist (Sharpe & Blackwell, 1987).

Sharpe and Blackwell's methods were among many different ones that were being practiced. In her 1985 book *The Quiet Profession*, Anne Alonso (1933–2007) in an academic clinic setting in Massachusetts wrote: "While there are many fine articles and books about supervision, I found myself wishing for a single text that would define the supervisory process and describe its application in a generalizable way … supervision has been thought of as an addendum to a clinician's work, rather than as a professional subspecialty worthy of distinction" (p. vii). She ventured reasons why up to that point that supervision had not received professional recognition, even though it occurred in almost every treatment setting by then. First, she suggested tradition—or adherence to convention since "it's worked so far, so no need for change." She countered, "Even our best supervisors could function more creatively with better theoretical and practical road maps" (p. 5). Her second point was that clinicians in general have the personality characteristic of wanting to help in a nonjudgmental manner and are uncomfortable with the power inherent in supervision, and consequently don't ask for help in becoming a better supervisor nor claim any acclaim for supervising. Alonso argued this leads to supervisors remaining in a "static position," unavailable to the learning that could make supervision more rewarding for them. Her third musing of why supervision had not proceeded as a profession is "cultural bias." Alonso pointed out the aspect of supervision of "caretaking and teaching of the young" was, in Western culture, a feminine responsibility and therefore devalued and poorly paid. The remedy she envisioned was of the loosening of gender roles so that both the authoritative masculine, scientific aspect of supervision can be combined with the artful, feminine caretaking function of supervision.

Alonso also pointed to the permeable and poorly defined boundaries between teaching, administration and psychotherapy. Was the supervisor's "allegiance to the student, to the training institution, or to the patient?" Then there was the uneasiness of discussing students' problems and resistances with colleagues and administrators. Another factor, particularly in hospital settings, was "diminished financial resources for training" (p. 139) which she experienced in her own work setting, a situation aggravated by "managed care" that viewed supervision as not as billable as direct patient care, therefore not an efficient cost. And lastly, she ventured, "The absence of supervisors' professional societies and the scarcity of journals dedicated to publishing research on supervision adds to the overall tendency to ignore the supervisors" (p. 7). She suggested that more scientific and theoretical inquiry into supervision needed to be undertaken, and a model of supervisory competence be established.

Alonso described three, then current, models of supervision—all components of any supervision, except for emphasis. The first model she identified was the "cognitive psycho-educational" model, which was primarily didactic. The model sees the supervisory role as hierarchical, without focus on the supervisee's personal needs or reactions, growth or countertransference. It is focused strictly on what the patient needs. She said supervisors can be interchangeable in this model because it does not consider aspects of the supervisee's or supervisor's character or needs, but rather is focused on the therapist's requisite techniques with regard to the patient.

The second model she called "emotional," as it focuses on the supervisee's emotional growth as a therapist and delves into characterological transferences, countertransferences, and defenses and resistances as they pertain to the therapeutic treatment of patients. What Alonso called the emotional approach was mostly embraced by psychoanalytic circles. Supervision was seen to play a role in the emotional, professional growth of the supervisee. Here the focus is first on the supervisee and secondarily on the patient. However, instead of the analytic intention of regression in the transference, supervision should support progression, according to Alonso. She stated: "Supervision … is distinguished from psychotherapy in its process and in its goals. It is assumed that a transference relationship will develop between therapist and supervisor and that this transferential field will become a primary vehicle for influencing the student's clinical growth. For the purposes of supervision, the training situation is regressive enough [presumably because of the inherent hierarchical relationship]. The emphasis is on the progressive rather than regressive movement: there is a concerted effort to shore up and strengthen the supervisee's healthiest defenses, either by reducing the ambiguity or by helping the trainee to tolerate the inevitable confusion of clinical work" (p. 17).

The third model was an in-between model where parallel process is considered primary focus, which incorporates both the cognitive and emotional aspects of the supervisee. Additionally, it incorporates the supervisor's self so that there is a synchronous learning between supervisor and supervisee. In Alonso's opinion, some regression in the supervisory relationship is "a rite of passage" as long as the supervisee returns to baseline with some support. If there is no regression, she stated that there is probably too much distance between the supervisor and supervisee. The relationship between supervisor and supervisee is highly personal so that neither one is interchangeable, meaning that the relationship is made up of the unique personalities of the supervisor and supervisee. Alonso referred to Searles's (1955) philosophy when she stated: "The supervisor and the student are engaged in a similar process of helping each other to mutually develop through the synergy of their relationship" (p. 18).

Alonso (1984) called for the development of supervision as a profession above and beyond psychotherapy with its own training and standards. She proposed seminars for new supervisors where experienced supervisors attend to the "process and theory of supervision" which also benefits experienced supervisors by "revitalizing" their practice of supervision. She suggested there should be an association of supervisors. "Supervisors need a louder and clearer voice; they need to speak to one another, to train new supervisors in their profession, and to stand apart as specialists who present a major subspeciality in the clinical field" (p. 4).

Lonergan in her 1985 book *Group Intervention* described starting and maintaining groups with the support of supervision in psychiatric hospital settings. Most of the treatment in psychiatric hospitals at the time was done in groups, from therapy groups to activity groups, occupational therapy groups, to family groups, community meetings, addiction groups, medicine management groups, and pre- and post-group processing groups among staff (author's personal experience). Lonergan's supervisory focus was on the tension between the culture of hospital administration and the culture of psychotherapy. The former, she argued was often characterized by administrative pressures on clinical staff to run more cost-effective programs by working long hours with difficult to manage patients. Meanwhile the treatment teams carry on their shoulders the need to be empathic toward patients within a culture from above that shows little compassion. In fact, at times "supervision" was required by administration to be used in an evaluative fashion, evaluating job performance and productivity, so that supervisors were stuck between having to be supportive and evaluative at the same time. It was in this kind of environment that Lonergan wrote, "Given the morale problem that is so prevalent in medical and psychiatric hospital settings, supervision needs to be a source of support." On an optimistic note: "Since all parts of the system are connected, a new ingredient, such as a new, well-supervised group, can have (positive) repercussions throughout the entire hospital structure" (p. 58) in an isomorphic manner.

What made for a "well-supervised group" in the hospital setting in the 1980s? Lonergan suggested the importance of allowing for the supervisee to become aware of their role within the whole hospital system and explore the systemic pressures leading to possible burnout. Further, the supervisor needed to encourage processing, validate the trainees' perceptions and feelings, reality test them, and ultimately instill hope and ideas about how to move forward in their role. A good way to instill this hope was to explore the ways the supervisee's skills and creativity in leading a group could be developed. The supervisor should attend to the group leader's needs, anxieties and questions about how to handle particular situations in the group. For trainees in the very beginning stages of the work, offer concrete examples of group scenarios with exactly what the therapist could say to handle them. Another task of the supervisor, as Lonergan posited, was to ascertain the learning needs of the supervisee regarding their knowledge base, learning style, and areas of potential creativity.

Supervisees came with different knowledge bases about group leadership and about the patient populations they serve. Lonergan suggested that the supervisor assess how the supervisee learns best and tailor the supervision to their individual needs. It was beneficial to encourage the group leader's creativity in choosing what special populations they might like to work with and follow their interests in creating a group. Learning how to conduct an effective group for a particular population can be rewarding and inspiring. In summary, for the ingredients for a "well-supervised group" that Lonergan detailed were meeting the supervisee's individual needs with respect to their anxieties about leading groups, their learning styles and attending to the professional growth of the supervisee. Both the supervisor and supervisee were to be aware of their roles within the larger organization, which required the supervisor to have some knowledge of group-as-a-whole dynamics and a systems perspective. All in all, Lonergan emphasized the many ways the supervisor in a hospital setting needed to be supportive of the supervisee for a group program to work.

The Advent of Managed Health Care: A Cloud on Group Psychotherapy's Horizon (1990–2015): Supervision Starts to Become Professional

Despite the challenges imposed on psychotherapists with the advent of managed care and the rise of evidence-based practice, perhaps for the first time, in this era supervision was recognized as the "single most influential element within training of group therapists, regardless of the theoretical model of group therapy employed" (Leszcz & Murphy, 1994, p. 99). In the face of cost-effective, regulated psychotherapy, group therapy researchers were challenged to provide evidence that group therapy was effective, equivalent or better than other therapeutic modalities, and efficient (Burlingame & Strauss, 2021). On the other hand, the supervisors of group therapy in this era worked hard toward "how to best prepare the next generation of clinicians to successfully practice the craft of psychotherapy, which continues to be an amalgam of art, science, and interpersonal relatedness" (Klein et al., 2011, p. xi). This created a tension between research and practice of group psychotherapy (cf. Greene,

2012). While empirical science continued to be an important validating aspect of group therapy theory, it had not yet caught up to the nuances of psychotherapeutic intervention, which has been best learned through the supervisory process.

While supervision of group therapy was by this time widespread, it was mostly conducted one on one with the group therapist, due to convenience of scheduling and tradition (Bernard, 1999). Nevertheless, group supervision of group therapy, begun in the 1960s by Ormont, expanded in the 1990s to include delineation of many ways of presenting group material, and many ways to conduct the supervisory group itself. This era saw a flourishing of the use of supervision groups for group psychotherapy with deepening and increasing pluralistic approaches to work. Although in many cases, individual supervision of a group therapy leader still predominated, methods of group supervision of group therapy became a focus. And, as Bernard (1999) stated: "The models for group psychotherapy supervision conducted in a group form are as varied as the ways in which different group therapists conduct their groups, and thus the rationales for conducting supervision in a group setting are quite varied as well" (p. 155).

Several substantial volumes on this topic were published in this time span, among them a special issue on "Group Supervision of Group Psychotherapy" introduced by Bernard and published in 1999 in the *International Journal of Group Psychotherapy (IJGP)*. Here several authors emphasized the tasks of the supervision group in response to the presenter's material. Although most had psychoanalytic roots of using free association, unconscious and conscious transferences, there were many variations and emphases for how the supervisor would direct the group.

In this issue Kleinberg (1999) focused on the supervisory relationships and alliances among members of a group supervision using parallel process to understand their treatment groups. Tylim (1999) held firmly to the "frame" of the supervision group—time, place, and payment are consistent and are the first level of interpretation by the supervisor if not adhered to by group members. He maintained neutrality and a "blank screen" as leader and has the group members decide entirely what to present from their groups, or process among themselves. As leader supervisor he only made interpretations when he discerned an impasse, resistance, or obstacle to the group process. He based the relationships in the group on transferences and countertransferences to each other, which were understood as repetitions of past relationships, primarily in their families of origen. He included that in the group social influences are internalized and brought into the intrapsychic object relations of each individual in the group. Tylim considered a group context to tend to mob regression and that the supervisor needs to be on top of whatever regression might be occurring so that the group does not become destructive. By working with the supervisory group's parallel process, he intended that the group leaders would bring their same dynamics and insights gained in the supervisory group to their own groups. He modeled almost precisely his theory of group therapy with the supervision group.

A Modern Analytic supervision of group was described by Rosenthal (1999). He added to the literature a detailed analysis of individual and group supervisory resistances. Resistance is detected when members fail to fulfill the contract of presenting openly their group material, or when members do not participate in a constructive manner with the group. Following the Modern Analytic method started by Spotnitz and Ormont, resistance is first detected in an accepting manner and considered to be protecting the individual or group in some way. The function of the resistance to the supervisee is explored nonjudgmentally, then what in their group brought it up, and finally whether the supervisee's mode of resistance was an adaption to early familial relationship experiences. Only if treatment destructive resistances that included attacking or being consistently critical of other members, not attending, or not paying for the group supervision, did the supervisor directly intervene. Rosenthal relied heavily on his modeling of group leader behavior (Glatzer, 1971) as an example of exploring resistance in groups.

Another contributor to this issue, Agazarian (1999), the founder of Systems-Centered Therapy (SCT), described a very specific, active approach by the supervisor to lead the group through developmental stages of fight or flight with authority, separation/individuation, and then the mature intimacy phase. She used specific language, such as "role-lock" and "mind-reads" for defensive operations, and another set of specific language for interventions—"structural," "functional," "vectoring," and "contextualizing" interventions. There are seven steps to the supervision process which the supervisor actively leads the presenting supervisee through, while others in the group also participate. The first step is the most important—the stating of the problem. It must be stated in a specific way of the supervisee having a strong feeling toward someone or an event in their group. From there the dynamics of the presenter in relation to members in their group, and the stage of development of the group are explored. Agazarian built her theory on Lewinian systems theory. Stages of development are gone through by joining in similarities—"subgrouping" with other members in the group; then, when the group is ready, offering a "difference," which again others may join in. There is always a tension between staying safe with old patterns and the innate desire to evolve. To become a supervisor takes quite a bit of training to learn the language and methods of intervention, and particularly having a sense of when to use them. Agazarian founded the Systems Center Training Institute in Philadelphia which currently has many group therapists in training and supervision.

Atfield (1999) in this issue expanded on Altfeld and Bernard (1997). The presenter started with a question or concern. The group was then instructed to give only emotional free associative responses. After the round of free associations, there was a cognitive component to make sense of what might have resonated and bring creative insight to the presenter's leadership and their group's process.

The 1999 issue of *IJGP* endorsed the psychoanalytic supervisory format of supervision in the US. In the same analytic vein, in England Meg Sharpe expanded a paper she had authored with Blakewell (1987) in her 1995 book *The Third Eye: Supervision of Analytic Groups*. Of significance here is her how-to chapter about the various formats that can be utilized for the work of group or individual supervision of group.

Sharpe refined and categorized the methods of therapists presenting material in group supervision. She stressed that all supervisees, and groups of supervisees have their own best ways of learning so that having various options of presenting to choose from could be tailored to the supervisee. Her categories included: (1) the "single issue" where a particular behavior in the group is focused on, like a group member not showing up, or acting out in some other disruptive manner; (2) the "spontaneous report" when the therapist reports from memory in the moment of supervision without notes; (3) "focusing on an individual" group member that usually holds some special significance or projective identification with the group leader, and can lead to fruitful exploration of countertransference and the evolution of therapy for the patient; (4) a "theoretical analysis," that explores a particular theoretical construct such as transference or resistance and applies it to the data of the group interactions; (5) The "kaleidoscopic approach" where members of the supervision group take on scripted roles of a supervisee's therapy group; and (6) "Brainstorming" or free associating on the part of the supervision group to offer solutions of how to handle an uncomfortable event, or perceived mistake of the therapist presenting. Still another method, (7) a "written summary" of the group is given in advance to the supervisor and supervision group so there's more thoughtful discussion time (Sharpe, 1995). She suggested that not only is it helpful to have a variety of methods to suggest to supervisees, but the supervisor may also feel more comfortable, or be more adept, with certain methods of presentation than others.

With the cumulative advances of theory and practice in the 70's, 80's and 90's, the first years of the 21st century clearly saw supervision as the cornerstone of training in group therapy. Yalom and Leszcz (2005) advised about the particular importance of "close supervision at the beginning of one's experience leading groups," and Stockton et al. (2014) argued that the "best practice" approach to learning group leadership is "practice leading or co-leading under close supervision." Even later in training, supervision is important according to Brabender's (2010) five-stage schema of development of the group therapy leader. While the first stages include acquisition of knowledge of the didactic kind, in later stages the group leader internalizes all that goes into supervision—particularly relationships, identifications, and disidentifications with various supervisors.

In 2006, as a first teaching of supervisors' method, Bernard and Spitz created a supervision manual to train supervisors of group psychotherapy. Though these authors were primarily psychodynamic in orientation the manual was pan-theoretical and taught the basics of the supervisory process: creation of a format for supervision, the supervisory relationship, ethics, and special situations that arise in groups. Much of the teaching manual continues to be relevant and is a founding precursor to this book.

In sum, the "cloud" of managed care in the 1990s and first part of the 21st century encouraged a scientific foundation of group psychotherapy and it's supervision, and dialectically, a creative, humanistic approach to supervision. The processes and procedures of group supervision of group therapists were elaborated from many different theoretical orientations. Research on supervision of group therapy was yet to come even though research on group therapy expanded.

The Age of Standardization, Empiricism, and Evidence-Based Practice and Diversity, Equity, and Inclusion (2015 to Present): Supervision Competencies

Perhaps the most significant event for group psychotherapy in this current era is its recognition in 2018 by the American Psychological Association as a designated psychology specialty (Counselman, 2020, MacNair-Semands and Whitingham, 2023), a recognition that serves as a powerful impetus for advancing the work of training and supervising of group therapists. Two reciprocally related and landmark concomitants of this recognition of group psychotherapy are the development of competencies for both practicing and supervising group work and the ascendance of research-based evidence to document why groups work and how they work. The first of these achievements is best represented by Barlow's efforts (2012, 2013), using a competency-based model, to articulate the requisite foundational and functional skills needed for becoming a competent group therapy supervisor. The second byproduct of the recognition of group as a specialty is the augmented push to establish scientifically generated findings to document the validity of this treatment modality. As Leiderman reported (2024) a good deal of work has gone into the establishment of an ongoing data base of significant findings, identifying not only outcomes of group therapy models for specific patient populations but also those specific group processes that promote therapeutic outcomes. Further, the increasing prominence of empirical work also refers to the growing trend toward practice-based evidence.

Practicing group therapists and supervisors have not taken to introducing psychometric assessments into their regular practice since they were introduced over 30 years ago. However, research in the area is progressively recognizing the importance of designing research of real time workings of group and supervision through the use of validated process and outcome measures in as a naturalistic settings as possible.

In the latest edition of their well-known book, Yalom and Leszcz (2020) present an overview of group therapy supervision, which incorporates many of the foundational efforts of the past century. They endorsed "close clinical supervision" (p. 641) and reiterated three basic tasks: "normative" (having to do with establishing the format and procedures for the work), "formative" (entailing the session-level integrating and internalizing of theory and practice), and "restorative" (supporting the trainee in coping with what are the unique challenges and pressures of the work). These authors further endorsed the idea that supervisory work take place in a group of trainees; that is, group supervision of group therapy, positing that it offers several opportunities for further development of the group therapist. The members have opportunities to get feedback from different angles to their cases from each other. They grow through the risk-taking of presenting their work candidly to their colleagues. Support from other group members can have an additional element, in addition to support from the supervisor. To further ameliorate the hierarchical nature of supervision that has the potential of inducing shame, Yalom and Leszcz encourage the supervisor to share mistakes they've made, and vulnerabilities experienced as a group therapist, in other words to be transparent.

Racism in America became a center sociological issue that group therapists and their supervisors have addressed in their practices. Awareness and self-reflection of racist biases have encouraged methods of communication that harken back to Lewin's work. Antiracism has inspired group therapists and supervisors to become more socially aware and attuned to environmental pressures on themselves and clients. Values of diversity, equality, and inclusion are being reexamined at all professional levels of group psychotherapy, including organizational structures, supervision and training structures, and group leadership.

In summary, group psychotherapy and its supervision as a professional medical and scientific discipline has come of age in the current decades. Its practice is unique in that it spans many disciplines from counseling to social work, psychology, and psychiatry. It's been a hundred plus years in development, with deepening recognition of supervision including the necessity of training for supervisors. The various aspects of supervision of group therapy, such as the supervisory relationship, the content and format of supervision have undergone experimentation in practice and debate in the literature. As new research develops to inform the creative aspects of supervision of groups, and as professional training programs of supervisors are recognized, we come closer to answering Alonso's call for recognition of supervision as a profession in and of itself. Hardy and Bobes (2017) endorsed that becoming a supervisor requires specific training: "Supervisors take a quantum leap in their development as they transition from being a therapist to being a supervisor" (p. 5), particularly with the added lens of antiracism. Supervision of group therapists is currently recognized for its importance in the development of professional identity, self-care of the therapist and the refinement of group therapy intervention skills.

Future directions: To answer Alonso's call for supervision as a profession beyond psychotherapy, inroads have been made, particularly with respect to individual supervision with texts such as Watkins (2013). Bernard and Spitz's *Training Manual for Supervisors* (2006) was a beginning to provide training specifically for supervisors of group therapists, and this current book is meant to be an update of that. Standards for individual supervision have been devised (Falender & Shafranske, 2017) and continue to be revised. Seminars, continuing education and supervisory institutes continue to be rare, particularly for supervision of group therapy. A special interest group for supervisors of group psychotherapy has been established at the AGPA; there is still no specific association of supervisors. Alonso's 1984 clarion call, "Supervisors need a louder and clearer voice; they need to speak to one another, to train new supervisors in their profession, and to stand apart as specialists who present a major subspeciality in the clinical field" (p. 4), is still in the works and may become a reality in the next couple of decades.

References

Adler, A. [Alexandra] (1965). The work of Paul Schilder. *Bulletin of the New York Academy of Medicine, 41*(8), 841–853.

Agazarian, Y. M. (1999). Systems-centered supervision. *International Journal of Group Psychotherapy, 49*(2), 215–236.

Alonso, A. (1985). *The quiet profession: Supervisors of psychotherapy.* Macmillan.

Altfeld, D. A. (1999). An experiential group model for psychotherapy supervision. *International Journal of Group Psychotherapy, 49*(2), 237–255.

Ambrose, C. T. (2011). Joseph Hersey Pratt, MD: The man who would be Osler. 38th annual meeting of the American Osler Society in Boston, MA, May 7, 2008.

Ambrose, C. T. (2013). Joseph Hersey Pratt (1872–1956): An early proponent of cognitive-behavioral therapy in America. *Journal of Medical Biography, 22*(1), 35–46.

Barlow, S. H. (2012). An application of the competency model to group-specialty practice. *Professional Psychology: Research and Practice, 43*(5), 442–451. https://doi.org/10.1037/a0029090

Barlow, S. H. (2013). *Specialty competencies in group psychology.* Oxford University Press. http://dx.doi.org.visn1kis.idm.oclc.org/10.1093/med:psych/9780195388558.001.0001

Barton, W. E. (1987). *The history and influence of the American Psychiatric Association.* American Psychiatric Press.

Bender, L. (1985). *Paul Schilder mind explorer.* Human Sciences Press.

Bernard, H. S. (1999). Introduction to special issue on group supervision of group psychotherapy. *International Journal of Group Psychotherapy, 49*(2), 153–157.

Bloom, S. L. (1997). By the crowd they have been broken, by the crowd they shall be healed: The social transformation of trauma. In R. G. Tedeschi, C. L. Park, & L. G. Calhoun (Eds.), *Posttraumatic growth: Positive changes in the aftermath of crisis* (pp. 179–213). Lawrence Erlbaum.

Bogardus. (1939). The philosophy of group work. *Sociology and Social Research, 23,* 567.

Bott, P. (1979). A systems model for group psychotherapy supervision. *Group Analysis, 12*(2), 134–136.

Brabender, V. (2010). The developmental path to expertise in group psychotherapy. *Journal of Contemporary Psychotherapy: On the Cutting Edge of Modern Developments in Psychotherapy, 40*(3), 163–173. https://doi.org/10.1007/s10879-010-9142-4

Burlingame, G and Strauss, B. (2021). Efficacy of Small Group Treatments: Foundation for Evidence-Based Practice. In *Bergin and Garfield's Handbook of Psychotherapy and Behavior Change.* Wiley.

Burrow, T. (1924). Social images versus reality. *Journal of Abnormal Psychology and Social Psychology, 19*(3), 230–235. https://doi.org/10.1037/h0064512

Burrow, T. (1992). The basis of group-analysis, or the analysis of the reactions of normal and neurotic individuals. In K. R. MacKenzie (Ed.), *Classics in group psychotherapy* (pp. 31–38). Guilford Press. (Reprinted from "The basis of group-analysis, or the analysis of the reactions of normal and neurotic individuals," *British Journal of Medical Psychology, 8,* 1928, 198–206.)

Coche, E. (1977). *Supervision, consultation, and staff training in the helping professions.* Jossey-Bass.

Collins, Michelle (September 2005). "Book Review: The Technique of Group Treatment: The Collected Papers of Louis R. Ormont". *Group.* 29 (3): 391–393. JSTOR 41719079.

Counselman, E. (2020). Group as specialty. The Group Psychologist, Div. 49 Newsletter, American Psychological Association.

Derner, G. F. & Monroe, R. R. (1960). An interpersonal approach to training in psychotherapy. In N.P. Dellis & H. K. Stone (Eds.), *The training of psychotherapists: A multidisciplinary approach* (pp. 130–150). Louisiana State University Press.

Drury, N. & Tudor, K. (2022). Trigant Burrow and the social world. *International Journal of Applied Psychoanalytic Studies, 19*(2), 187–201. https://doi.org/10.1002/aps.1743

Durkin, H. E., Cooper, N., Deutsch, A. L., Fielding, H. G., Krasner, J. D., Langner, H., McCormick, C., Rosenbaum, M., Ross, E., & Thorne, R. (1971). A brief history of the American Group Psychotherapy Association 1943–1968. *International Journal of Group Psychotherapy, 21*(4), 406–435. https://doi.org/10.1080/00207284.1971.11492125

Ekstein, R. & Wallerstein, R. S. (1958). *The teaching and learning of psychotherapy.* Basic Books.

Emmanuel Movement. (n.d.). *Emmanuel Church in the City of Boston; emmanuelboston.org/mission/history/emmanuel-movement*

Ettin, M. F. (1989). "Come on, Jack, tell us about yourself": The growth spurt of group psychotherapy. *International Journal of Group Psychotherapy, 39*(1), 35–57.

Falender, C. A. & Shafranske, E. (2017). *Supervision essentials for the practice of competency-based supervision.* American Psychological Association.

Foulkes, S. H. (1964). *Therapeutic group analysis.* George Allen & Unwin.

Foulkes, S. H. (1975). *Group-analytic psychotherapy: Method and principles.* Gordon and Breach.

Foulkes, S. H. (1985). *Paul Schilder mind explorer.* Human Sciences Press.

Frawley-O'Dea, M. G. & Sarnat, J. E. (2001). *The supervisory relationship: A contemporary psychodynamic approach.* Guilford Press.

Freud, S. (1965). *Group psychology and the analysis of the ego.* Bantam Books, Inc.

Gabriel, B. (1939). An experiment in group treatment. *American Journal of Orthopsychiatry, 9*(1), 146–169.

Galdston, I. (1985). *Paul Schilder mind explorer.* Human Sciences Press.

Gay, P. (2006). *A life for our time.* W.W. Norton.

Geller, J. J. (1958). Supervision in a hospital psychotherapy program. *International Journal of Group Psychotherapy, 8*, 313–322.

Giacomucci, S. (2021). *Social work, sociometry, and psychodrama.* Springer.

Glatzer, H. T. (1971). Analytic supervision in group psychotherapy. *International Journal of Group Psychotherapy, 21*(4), 436–443. https://doi.org/10.1080/00207284.1971.11492126

Greene, L. (2012). Group therapist as social scientist, with special reference to the psychodynamically oriented psychotherapist. *American Psychologist, 67*(6) 477–489.

Hahn, A., Paquin, J.D., Glean, E., McQuillan, K., & Hamilton, D. (2022). Developing into a group therapist: An empirical investigation of expert group therapists' training experiences. *American Psychologist, 77*(5), 691–709. https://doi.org/10.1037/amp0000956

Hale, Jr., N. G. (Ed.) (1971). *James Jackson Putnam and psychoanalysis: Letters between Putman and Sigmund Freud, Ernest Jones, William James, Sandor Ferenczi, and Morton Prince, 1877–1917.* Harvard University Press.

Hardy, K. V. & Bobes, T. (Eds.) (2017). *Culturally sensitive supervision and training: Diverse perspectives and practical applications.* Routledge.

Heimann, P. (1950) On counter-transference. *International Journal of Psychoanalysis, 31*, 81–84.

Jones, E. (2004). War and the practice of psychotherapy: The UK experience 1939–1960. *Medical History, 48*(4), 493–510. https://doi.org/10.1017/S0025727300007985

Kaklauskas, F. J. & Greene, L. R. (Eds.). (2020). *Core principles of group psychotherapy: An integrated theory, research, and practice training manual.* Routledge.

Kaslow, F. W. (Ed.). (1977). *Supervision, consultation, and staff training in the helping professions.* Jossey-Bass.

Klein, R. H., Bernard, H. S., & Schermer, V. L. (2011). *On becoming a psychotherapist: The personal and professional journey.* Oxford University Press.

Kleinberg, J. L. (1999). The supervisory alliance and the training of psychodynamic group psychotherapists. *International Journal of Group Psychotherapy, 49*(2), 159–181.

Le Bon, G. (1903). *The crowd: A study of the popular mind.* T. Fisher Unwin.

Leiderman, L. (2024). An interview with Gary Burlingame, PhD, CGP, AGPA-DF on the new Evidence-Based Group Therapy website. *Group Circle*, Summer, p. 3.

Leszcz, M. & Murphy, L. (1994). Supervision of group psychotherapy. In S. E. Greben & R. Ruskin (Eds.), *Clinical perspectives on psychotherapy supervision* (pp. 99–120). American Psychiatric Association.

Levin, S. & Kanter, S.S. (1964). Some general considerations in the supervision of beginning group psychotherapists. *International Journal of Group Psychotherapy, 14*(3), 318–331. https://doi.org/10.1080/00207284.1964.11642757

Lex, B. (1979). The neurobiology of ritual trance. In E. G. d'Aquili, D. C. Laughin, Jr., & J. Mcmanus (Eds.), *The spectrum of ritual: A biogenetic structural analysis.* Columbia University Press. Scribd.com/document/797927846/Lex-1979-Ritual-Trance

Lippitt, R. (1940). An experimental study of the effect of democratic and authoritarian group atmospheres. *University of Iowa Studies: Child Welfare, 16*(3), 43–195.

Lonergan, E. C. (1985). *Group intervention: How to begin and maintain groups in medical and psychiatric settings.* Jason Aronson.

Low, A. A. (1984). *Mental health through will training.* Willett Pub.

Low, A. A. (1943). *The techniques of self-help in psychiatric after-care.* Illinois OCLA 42198367. Recovery.

MacNair-Semands, R. & Whitingham, M. (2023). *Group psychotherapy assessment and practice. A measurement-based care approach.* Routledge. http://dx.doi.org.visn1kis.idm.oclc.org/10.4324/9781003255482

Maddow, R. (2023). *Prequel: An American fight against fascism.* Crown.

Marsh, L. C. (1931). Group treatment of the psychoses by the psychological equivalent of the revival. *Mental Hygiene, 15*, 328–349.

Marsh, L .C. (1933). An experiment in group treatment of patients at Worcester State Hospital. *Mental Hygiene, 17*, 396–416.

McWilliams, N. (2021). *Psychoanalytic supervision.* Guilford Press.

Meiers, J. I. (1945). Origins and development of group psychotherapy: A historical survey, 1930–1945. *Sociometry, 8*, 261–296.

Meyers, M. (2011). Guide to the Hyman Spotnitz Archive 1920-1990: Center for Modern Psychoanalytic Studies

Napolitani, F. (1979). Co-therapy by alternate conduction and reciprocal supervision. *Group Analysis, 12*(1), 52–55.

New York Times. (1983). Obituary for Aaron Stein.

NTL Institute, (n.d.) *NTL-Kurt Lewin's Legacy, NTL's Legacy: Changing the World Through Transformative Learning.* ntl.org/ntl-legacy

Ormont, L. R. (n.d.). *The Keene Sentinel*, Nov 18, 2008; keenoesentinel.com/news/obituaries/dr-louis-r-ormont/article

Ormont, L. R. (2001). Training group therapists through the study of countertransferences. In L. B. Furgeri (Ed.), *The technique of group treatment: The collected papers of Louis R. Ormont, Ph.D.* (pp. 175–189). Psychosocial Press. (Reprinted from "Training group therapists through the study of countertransferences", *Group*, 4, 1980, 17–26. https://doi.org/10.1007/BF01456624).

Parker, S. (1980). *Paul Shilder mind explorer.* Human Sciences Press.

Perlina, A. (2015). *Shaping the field: Kurt Lewin and experimental psychology in the interwar period.* Unpublished doctoral dissertation, Humboldt-Universität zu Berlin.

Pertegato, E. G. & Pertegato, G. O. (2018). *From psychoanalysis to group analysis.* Routledge.

Pinney, E. (1978a). Paul Schilder and group psychotherapy: The development of psychoanalytic group psychotherapy. *Psychiatric Quarterly, 50*(2), 133–143.

Pinney, E. (1978b). The beginning of group psychotherapy: Joseph Henry Pratt, M.D. and the Reverend Dr. Elwood Worcester. *International Journal of Group Psychotherapy, 28*(1), 109–114.

Pratt, J. H. (1908). Results obtained in the treatment of pulmonary tuberculosis by the class method. *British Medical Journal, 2*, 1070–1071.

Recovery International. (n.d.). About Recovery International, History of Recovery International. international.org/about-recovery-international/

Richmond, M. E. (1930). *Some next steps in social treatment.* Russell Sage.

Riess, B. F. (1960). The selection and supervision of psychotherapists. In N. P. Dellis & H. K. Stone (Eds.), *The training of psychotherapists: A multidisciplinary approach* (pp. 130–150). Louisiana State University Press.

Rogers, C. (1961). *On becoming a person. A therapist's view of psychotherapy.* Houghton Mifflin.

Rosenthal, L. (1999). Group supervision of groups: A modern analytic perspective. *International Journal of Group Psychotherapy, 49*(2), 197–213.

Scheidlinger, S. (2000). The group psychotherapy movement at the millennium: Some historical perspectives. *International Journal of Group Psychotherapy, 50*(3), 315–339.

Schilder, P. F. (1936). The analysis of ideologies as a psychotherapeutic method, especially in group treatment. *American Journal of Psychiatry, 93*(3). https://doi.org/10.1176/ajp.93.3.601

Schuster, D. B., Sandt, J. J., & Thaler, O. F. (1972). *Clinical supervision of the psychiatric resident.* Brunner/Mazel.

Schwartz, J. (1999). *Cassandra's daughter: A history of psychoanalysis.* Routledge.

Searles, H. S. (1955). The informational value of the supervisor's emotional experiences. *Psychiatry, 18,* 135–146.

Shaffer, J. B. & Galinsky, M. D. (1974). *Models of group therapy and sensitivity training.* Prentice-Hall.

Sharpe, M. (1995). *The third eye: Supervision of analytic groups.* Routledge.

Sharpe, M. & Blackwell, D. (1987). Creative supervision through student involvement. *Group Analysis, 20,* 195–208.

Shaskan, D. A. & Roller, W. L. (1985). *Paul Schilder, mind explorer.* Human Sciences Press.

Sicherman, B. (1980). *The quest for mental health in America 1880–1917.* Arno Press. Reprinted from "The quest for mental health in America 1880–1917," 1967, doctoral dissertation, Columbia University.

Slavson, S. R. (1940). Group therapy. *Mental Hygiene, 24,* 36–49.

Slavson, S. R. (1943). *Introduction to group psychotherapy.* Commonwealth Fund, International Universities Press.

Slavson, S. R. (1951). Current trends in group psychotherapy. *International Journal of Group Psychotherapy, 1,* 7–15.

Slavson, S. R. (1992). Are there "group dynamics" in therapy groups? In K. R. MacKenzie (Ed.), *Classics in group psychotherapy* (pp. 166–182). Guilford Press. (Reprinted from "Are there 'group dynamics' in therapy groups?" *International Journal of Group Psychotherapy, 7,* 1957, 131–154.)

Smith, M. & Gallop, M. (2024). *Group analytic supervision.* Routledge.

Spotnitz, H. (1961). *The couch and the circle: A story of group psychotherapy.* Alfred A. Knopf.

Stein, A. (1963). The training of the group psychotherapist. In M. Rosenbaum & M. Berger (Eds.), *Group psychotherapy and group function* (pp.558–576). Basic Books.

Stockton, R., Morran, K., & Chang, S.-H. (2014). An overview of current research and best practices for training beginning group leaders. In J. L. DeLucia-Waack, C. R. Kalodner, & M. T. Riva (Eds.), *Handbook of group counseling and psychotherapy* (2nd ed., pp. 133–145). Sage Publications. https://doi.org/10.4135/9781544308555.n11

Thomas, G. W. (1943). Group psychotherapy: A review of recent literature. *Psychosomatic Medicine, 5,* 166–180.

Tylim, I. (1999). Group supervision and the psychoanalytic process. *International Journal of Group Psychotherapy, 49*(2), 181–198.

Van Schoor, E. P. (2000). A sociohistorical view of group psychotherapy in the United States: The ideology of individualism and self-liberation. *International Journal of Group Psychotherapy, 50*(4), 437–454. https://doi.org/10.1080/00207284.2000.11491023.

Watkins, C. E., Jr. (2013). The beginnings of psychoanalytic supervision: The crucial role of Max Eitingon. *American Journal of Psychanalysis, 73,* 254–270. https://doi.org/10.1057/ajp.2013.15

Wender, L. (1945). Group psychotherapy. *Sociometry, 8,* 3/4, 108–111.

Wikipedia. (n.d.a). *Apprenticeship.* https://en.wikipedia.org/wiki/Apprenticeship

Wikipedia. (n.d.c). *Abraham Low.* https://en.wikipedia.org/wiki/Abraham_Low

Wikipedia. (n.d.d). *Recoveryinternational.org.* https://en.wikipedia.org/wiki/Recovery_International

Wikipedia. (n.d.e) *Nunberg.* https://en.wikipedia.org/wiki/Hermann_Nunberg

Wilson, G. (1956, May). Social group work theory and practice viewed against new trends and developments. National Conference of Social Work, 1956, Box: 8, Folder: 15, Gertrude Wilson Papers, SW 224, Social Welfare History Archives.

Yalom, I. D. & Leszcz, M. (2005). *The theory and practice of group psychotherapy* (30th ed.). Basic Books

Yalom, I. D. & Leszcz, M. (2020). *The theory and practice of group psychotherapy* (6th ed.). Basic Books.

Chapter 2

Group Therapy Supervision
Qualifications and Competencies, Tasks, and Methods

Noelle L. Lefforge

Becoming a supervisor/consultant of group psychotherapy requires several areas of competency. A good supervisor not only has experience as a group therapist but is also a good teacher and is aware of ethics of the profession, including multicultural aspects. In addition, the group therapy supervisor needs to be competent in the work of clinical supervision, being adept at forming mentoring relationships with supervisees by developing close empathic connections while respecting good boundaries. Fortunately, over the past couple of decades, competencies and standards both for the practice of group psychotherapy (Bernard et al., 2008; ASGW, 2021; Barlow, 2013; Group Specialty Council, 2018) and for clinical supervision (APA, 2014; Barlow, 2013) have been significantly developed.

Competency in Group Psychotherapy Practice and Competency in Supervision

The goal of group psychotherapy supervision is to facilitate the development of group psychotherapy competencies of the supervisee. Adopting the competency assessment toolkit for general professional psychology (Kaslow et al., 2009), Barlow (2013) delineated the foundational competencies (professionalism, reflective practice/self-care, scientific knowledge/ methods, relationships, issues of diversity, ethical/legal standards/policy, and interdisciplinary systems) and functional competencies (assessment, intervention, consultation, research/ evaluation, supervision/teaching, management/administration, and advocacy) necessary for the practice of group psychotherapy. Barlow's *Group Competency Benchmarks Document* (available as an appendix in Barlow, 2013) identifies the essential components and behavioral anchors of each these competencies, specifically for group psychotherapy practice, at three levels of specialist development: doctoral readiness, postdoctoral/residency readiness, and ABPP (board certification) readiness. While many aspects of competency development of a group psychotherapy specialist overlap with general practice, Barlow's work provides in-depth descriptions of specialized areas of group work such as group-specific assessment strategies and tools, case formulation at the group level, relational aspects unique to group such as cohesion and member-to-member attachment, and group-specific therapeutic factors, processes, and dynamics. This work served as a major part of the efforts of the Group Specialty Council to establish the formally recognized competencies for group psychology/ psychotherapy (listed and defined in the appendix; Group Specialty Council, 2019; recognized by the APA Commission on the Recognition of Specialties and Subspecialties in Professional Psychology).

DOI: 10.4324/9781003410621-3

Those who supervise group psychotherapy must have a good understanding of what competent group psychotherapy practice is and, in addition, of what makes for competencies in clinical supervision, both general clinical supervision and for group psychotherapy supervision specifically. For psychologists, the American Psychological Association (APA) has established competency benchmarks (Kaslow et al., 2009) and guidelines (APA, 2014) for clinical supervision which expects clinical supervisors to understand and enact their role, the supervisory relationship, and processes and procedures related to supervision. Barlow (2013) took an important step in applying these general supervisory competencies to the supervision of group psychotherapy.

Supervision versus Consultation

The role of an experienced group practitioner providing training and guidance to develop a group psychotherapist's knowledge, attitudes, and skills can occur through supervision or consultation. The distinction is based on differences in responsibility and authority and thus should be clear from the onset of the arrangement. Supervision occurs when the supervisor retains ultimate authority over the care of the patient/s because they hold the ultimate responsibility for that patient's care (i.e., the patient's care is delivered via the supervisor's professional license). While the supervisor has obligations to the developing supervisee, their primary responsibility is the welfare of the patient/s. Therefore, the supervisor's directives supersede the supervisee's plans when there is conflict between them, particularly when the disagreement concerns the welfare of the patient/s. Because the supervisor holds the authority and responsibility for the welfare of the patient, they make the decisions about the course of care, and can be as directly involved as they see fit to serve the welfare of the patient/s. Consultation, on the other hand, is a less formalized arrangement in which the developing clinician maintains ultimate authority and responsibility for the patients. The consultant will provide guidance and advice in the service of the developing clinician, which can be rejected or implemented to the extent that the developing clinician decides. The patient/s are seen under the authority of the developing clinician's license, and the consultant holds no formal obligation to the patient/s or licensing boards regarding the services delivered. While "supervision" is utilized throughout this manual, the concept is intended to equally apply to consultation throughout.

Additional complexity of supervision arrangements should also be understood. *Supervisor-in-training* models are intended to develop supervisory skills in developing professionals. A supervisor-in-training would provide "supervision" to a junior colleague while being supervised by a licensed professional. In this case, the supervisor-in-training's supervisor retains authority and responsibility for the patient. The supervisor typically meets with and provides supervision to the supervisor-in-training, who in turn meets with and provides supervision to the trainee, although the supervisor may be as directly involved with the trainee and patient/s as the supervisor sees fit. This type of arrangement is referred to as *vertical supervision* and usually occurs in university settings.

Group Psychotherapy Supervisor Expertise and Competency

Evidence is mounting to indicate that the ethical delivery of group-specific services requires specialized training, despite widespread training practices that neglect the importance of the supervisor's specialized expertise (Whittingham et al., 2021). While group psychotherapy is as effective, and in some cases more effective than individual therapy for treating many patients in need of psychological treatment (Burlingame et al., 2016), it also poses increased risks for iatrogenic harm, particularly when facilitated without knowledge and skill specific to conducting group therapy (Whittingham et al., 2021). Supervisors must be able to triage their supervisees' growth areas. Specifically, the group psychotherapy supervisor differentiates among deficits that are suboptimal (e.g., will slow down the potential for therapeutic growth) versus those that are likely to cause direct harm (e.g., colluding with processes resulting in scapegoating), and intervene differentially. For example, the group supervisor has broad discretion for utilizing all processes and methods of supervision (see section below) as they see fit to promote optimal functioning of the supervisee. However, when the supervisees' competency deficits are likely to cause harm, the supervisor is responsible for intervening quickly and directly with a targeted plan to address the issue/s. In serious situations, the supervisor may need to become directly involved with the service provision or consider removal of the trainee.

Utilizing a supervisor with specialized expertise is needed to ensure that supervisees practice in alignment with the most up-to-date clinical practice guidelines (e.g., Bernard et al., 2008; Group Specialty Council, 2018) so that the supervisor can uphold their duties regarding the welfare of patients. Specifically, training should include appropriate *orientation and screening* of group members as evidence-based methods for mitigating the risks of iatrogenic harm of group psychotherapy, including reduction of premature termination/dropout. Supervisees should learn how to adequately conduct *pregroup interviews* and identify *group selection* factors (i.e., "Is this person likely to benefit from the group treatment?") and *group composition* factors (i.e., "Who should the group be comprised of to meet its goals?"). It is impossible to know exactly how any one person might interact in a group, but the screening process can go a long way in imparting some group norms to the potential group client, and in assessing the likelihood that there might be mutual benefit between the group and the prospective member. Group therapies are often implemented in settings in which the group facilitator has limited autonomy and authority to determine group selection and composition. For example, in psychiatric hospital settings, administration may expect that all patients on the unit attend the group. This can produce suboptimal, and even risky, group compositions such as a group in which there is a large amount of heterogeneity in terms of ego functioning among the members (particularly when there is a sole outlier; Yalom & Leszcz, 2020). Thus, supervisors need to ensure that the supervisee is tracking group composition for homogeneity/heterogeneity and adapting the group as needed to prevent harm, for example, by increasing structure in response to a problematic composition. Not all problems that can occur in groups can be avoided, which is exactly why supervision and/or consultation is helpful.

Supervisors' own expertise in group psychotherapy is typically developed through training and experience. This expertise can be formally recognized through certification, such as the Certified Group Psychotherapist (CGP; International Board of Certified Group Psychotherapists). Reputable credentials verify the supervisor's expertise and can be helpful to trainees' own pursuit of specialty credentialing because it is easier for them to provide documentation that they received qualified training and supervision. Supervision is one aspect of developing a group psychotherapist that can be supplemented by other types of training, such as didactics/courses, unsupervised clinical practice, and scholarship (Group Specialty Council, 2024).

Clearly, the expectations of group psychotherapy supervisors vary greatly depending on the setting. Academic institutions, particularly accredited ones, are prone to have many formalized standards for supervisors. Some large organizations and agencies (e.g., VAs, hospitals, large healthcare systems) may also have requirements or incentives for group psychotherapy supervisors to hold credentials in the group therapy specialty, but many do not. Group psychotherapy supervisors in independent practice and other less regulated settings will likely have much less formalized arrangements or requirements in place to practice as a group psychotherapy supervisor.

Group Psychotherapy Supervision Tasks

While there is a great deal of similarity between supervision of individual psychotherapy and supervision of group psychotherapy, and much of what is known about supervising group psychotherapy is based on literature in supervision of individual therapy, there are worthy distinctions. Given that group psychotherapy is a specialized modality of intervention, a supervisor of group psychotherapy must be familiar with developing *competencies* in the domain of intervention that are *unique to group psychotherapy*, particularly the complex matrix of interactions that occur in group psychotherapy.

Levels of Analysis

Attending to multiple levels of group interaction is one skill unique to group psychotherapy that needs to be developed within trainees (King & Hunt, 2015; Tasca et al., 2014). A consultant can be extremely helpful in this respect because of the complexity. Group psychotherapists are expected to work on five levels of organizational processes simultaneously. Specifically, they attend to processes within each individual of the group (intrapersonal), between salient dyads in the group (interpersonal), the group-as-a-whole, among various functional and dysfunctional subgroups that emerge in the group, and the group embedded within larger social contexts such as the local community and the host organization. Therefore, a skilled supervisor of group psychotherapy supports and guides the supervisee's ability to attend to, track, and respond effectively to all of these levels at once, and when necessary, prioritize which level is problematic or moving the group. This is often a challenging skill to impart and many novice group psychotherapists, presumably applying the skill set they are most familiar with from individual psychotherapy, are overly concerned with the *intrapersonal level* only; that is, with each individual's experience in the group. In terms of the *interpersonal level* of work, it is common for novice group psychotherapists to become overly invested in their own relationship with each individual in the group. The group psychotherapy supervisor needs to continually intervene to ensure that the group leader is not just delivering individual psychotherapy in a group setting, but rather conducting group psychotherapy including the reinforcing of group therapeutic factors (Yalom & Leszcz, 2020) (i.e., instillation of hope, universality, imparting information, altruism, corrective recapitulation of the primary family group, socializing techniques, imitative behavior, interpersonal learning, group cohesiveness, catharsis, and existential factors) utilizing opportunities offered by *all* of the interpersonal relationships within the group. Optimizing the therapeutic factors of groups requires developing the supervisee's ability to work at the *group-as-a-whole level*. Group psychotherapy supervisors need to have a nuanced understanding of all levels of group work to facilitate depth and complexity as their group therapist builds intervention competencies. The group psychotherapy supervisor will want to have the supervisee practice shifting between discussing what may be occurring for each of the group members, what may be occurring between particular group members, and what themes are emerging in the group-as-a-whole. The group supervisor can encourage the group therapist to have case conceptualizations and treatment plans (intentions for interventions informed by the conceptualization) to address each of these levels. For example, there may be a particular group member who was regularly expected to overperform in their family of origin who becomes a monopolizer in group therapy. At the individual level, the therapist could understand this behavior as an enactment and be interested in helping this patient to relinquish time and space in the group in an effort to develop a broader interpersonal style. At the same time, the group therapist will also want to track the group-as-a-whole's involvement in this systemic enactment. Why is the group so readily willing to hand over the time and space to one individual? What is going on in the group that resentment simmers rather than being directly expressed? The supervisor can work with the group leader to help shift the group norm to a more functional one in which needs and boundaries are openly negotiated and responded to.

Additional group dynamics and processes are worthy of continued attention in the development of group therapists. For example, the emphasis on group cohesion as the primary therapeutic factor of group psychotherapy (according to research on group psychotherapy) (Burlingame et al., 2018) often leads trainees to overpathologize all subgrouping when, in actuality, both *functional and dysfunctional subgroups* occur in groups (Agazarian, 2011). For example, in working with functional subgrouping, a common experience (e.g., parental loss, overt discrimination due to marginalized identity, generational specific stressor) may unite some members while others lack personal experience in that area. In the initial stages of processing the shared experience, the group therapist recognizing dynamics of functional subgrouping can allow a subgroup to connect and relate to one another and tolerate that some members may be "sitting on the sidelines" rather than trying to force a theme common across the entire membership. They will likely find that entry points for other members will emerge as processing unfolds. On the other hand, the group therapist-in-training will need to recognize and intercede in dysfunctional subgrouping. For example, if the group facilitator starts to witness "us" and "them" dynamics, typically evident by overly simplistic labeling and an unwillingness to be curious about the experience of the other, they can help the group by openly describing the phenomenon that is happening. This may seem like an overwhelming and daunting ask to the group therapist at first ("How do I manage problematic human interactions that occur at the foundation of social interaction?"), but the supervisor can help make this more manageable by framing it as always supporting humanizing interactions (as opposed to dehumanizing ones) in group psychotherapy. Group supervisors need to assist their supervisees in differentiating subgroups and responding by supporting functional subgrouping and disrupting dysfunctional subgrouping.

Lastly, *interorganizational level* awareness and skill is often needed in supervision of group. Very often the group is influenced by the organizational structures that surround the group, including the group therapist-in-training, the group therapy supervisor, and their relationship/s with each other and the systems in which they are embedded. Groups that occur within hospital settings are often influenced by the structures, hierarchies, and rules of the hospital system. For example, suppose a therapist working in a hospital walked into their regularly scheduled group to find 20 patients when the previous day there were only 10. There were not even enough chairs in the room for everyone at the time. To cope with the situation, the supervisor departed from the typical model of coleading the group with the trainee and decided to split the group and instructed the trainee to lead one of those sections in another space. Given the scarcity of rooms in the hospital, imagine that the only space that is available for the trainee's section is a small utility room. Certainly, it would not be surprising if patients in this group experienced and potentially expressed negative feelings toward the hospital administration during this group session. For example, a protective dynamic toward the trainee could be enacted if the group perceived the trainee to be relegated to a lower status (and thus the patients relegated to the lower status) as evidenced by the less-than-ideal setting. The culture of psychotherapy in general and group psychotherapy in particular may clash with the culture of the embedding host organization, including differences in how resources are to be allocated and money spent, and supervision needs to attend to helping the trainee contain such potentially disruptive and conflictual dynamics. Many aspects of the larger societal context influence the dynamics of group psychotherapy, and supervisors can help supervisees learn to navigate their influence.

Another contextual dynamic to be reckoned with in supervision is the evaluative component of the trainee's performance and development. Imagine a university-based group being co-led by a junior faculty member and student-supervisee. They are struggling with the group, noticing that all the members are careful and reserved and that extensive moments of seemingly empty silence occur. Group members share little of themselves and are reticent to interact with one another. The supervisor and supervisee come to understand that the group fears "doing it wrong" which is a paralyzing undercurrent. They realize that they are both living with this fear themselves, the supervisee afraid of doing group "wrong" in the supervisor's presence, as well as the junior faculty member supervisor fearing doing it "wrong" in front of their supervisee/s, senior faculty, and administrative leadership (who, though not physically present, may be readily present in their mind). Openly discussing this dynamic in supervision—exploring such questions as "what kind of grade will we get?"—is needed to free the leaders from paralyzing anxiety about evaluations and permitting them to work without being perfect.

Intervening and Observing

Supervisees, particularly novices, often feel *overwhelmed* as they begin to comprehend what is required of a skilled group psychotherapist. However, occasionally the group supervisor may encounter the *overly confident* trainee who underestimates the distinctiveness and therapeutic opportunities of groups, for example, by overequating it with something like teaching a class. It is the responsibility of the group psychotherapy supervisor to meet the trainee where they are in terms of their level of competency and their view of self in leader role and respond effectively. The *anxious trainee* needs to feel supported and have attention paid to their areas of efficacy while being encouraged to take risks and act with increasing independence, while the overly confident trainee needs to be challenged and encouraged to view the nuances and complexities of their group.

A key intervention competency in group psychotherapy is the need to know when the therapist should intervene versus when they should let the *process unfold*. Many supervisees have been trained in active orientations that place a great deal of responsibility on the therapist to generate and direct therapeutic content. The group psychotherapy supervisor may need to encourage these supervisees time and again to trust the group process and the therapeutic relevance of each group member to another. Group psychotherapy supervisors need to be aware of where on the *intervening to observing stance* will be most effective for the group psychotherapy trainee to take, which depends on both *persistent contextual factors* (e.g., the orientation, duration, and purpose of the particular group psychotherapy) as well as *transient contextual factors* (e.g., the stage and foci of the group at a particular moment). The point is to help develop the therapist's capacity for active intervention and its timing and be aware of countertransference barriers or resistances within the group therapist (e.g., lack of confidence, shame). On the other hand, the therapist's capacity to inhibit active responses and recognize when the group is working well without the facilitator's increased involvement. Moreover, the group supervisor's role is to hone the supervisees' ability to know what type of stance (active to observing continuum) is best under what group circumstances. Sometimes this involves the supervisee's building tolerance to sit with ambiguity which might include some anxiety while still emotionally and cognitively processing all that is happening in the group.

This supervisory skill is particularly important to counteract the potential for *iatrogenic* group dynamics and processes (e.g., Roback, 2000). Specifically, group supervisors track the groups they supervise for the harm that can come from scapegoating, monopolizing, group think, attacking, silence and a host of other anti(therapeutic)-group processes (Greene et al., 2019). Supervisors facilitate intervention competencies in their trainees to also recognize these processes early and intervene effectively. Sometimes, if the group leader is unable to stand back and observe these dynamics, they might actually end up getting pulled in and colluding. Meanwhile, a group leader who is particularly sensitive to these dynamics may too quickly intervene to stop the harm in its tracks thereby unwittingly attacking, blaming or shaming a member or the group-as-a-whole for going down that road. As with generally all components of group psychotherapy, this too is an area of nuance. For example, silence can be both a problematic group process, but also a needed and healthy one, possibly to slow down the pulse or cool down the temperature. Again, the group psychotherapy supervisor's role is to support the therapist's knowledge and skill in making useful discriminations. This is yet another challenge for the group psychotherapist to navigate; the supervisor both provides broad algorithms for appropriate and sound decision-making by the trainee, while also cautioning against applying overly simplistic rules to what are actually nuanced and complex processes. This is best done by examining the supervisee's actual interventions and the group's process to provide many example applications. Many trainees, particularly at early stages of training, long for "answers" and demand step-by-step instructions for conducting their work. The group psychotherapy supervisor can validate this desire, but not acquiesce to it, instead focusing on developing a strong foundation for the supervisee's ability to broaden their monitoring of the group dynamics at hand and responding differentially to the unique context of each moment, with developing observational skills, deepening and broadening conceptual skills, sharpened sense of timing, and enhanced clinical judgment. Sometimes reassurance with certain principles of group therapy and examples of possible interventions are reassuring, and at other times giving examples of what the therapist might exactly do or say can be helpful. There are too many variations in the here-and-now process of a group to give tried and true algorithms for every case. This is the special arena of a supervisor, versus a teacher of group dynamics, to visit the supervisee's actual work and discuss various interventions based on the complex interplay of the general principles of group therapy, the supervisee's personality and stage of development, and the group's stage of development, while keeping in mind the individual participants' therapeutic progress.

Group Stages

Understanding and knowing how to effectively work with the group's *stage of development* is another intervention competency that is attended to by the group psychotherapy supervisor (cf. Brabender & Fallon, 2009). The supervisor assists the trainee with understanding the various stages of group process, where the group currently is situated and the journey it has traversed. There are several models of group developmental stages established in the literature that the group supervisor can adopt and utilize for training. While all group psychotherapists should be well-versed in their understanding of each stage, what challenges and needs the group is currently coping with, and how they are best met by the facilitator, the group psychotherapy supervisor has the added challenge of recognizing ways that their supervisee may be challenged to meet the needs of the group at each developmental stage. Supervision from a stage-based perspective is advantageous when the group psychotherapy is less structured, and/or when the group psychotherapy is more process focused. Group stages are likely to unfold regardless of the extent of group structure so that an awareness of each stage is warranted even if the therapy group being supervised is a highly structured, skill-focused, manualized treatment. For example, many DBT skills groups are arranged to convey a particular skill set in a more efficient manner than individual psychotherapy. However, participants in these skills groups will be more readily able to learn and practice the skills if the current group dynamics are attended to. Specifically, the group leader will want to build some sense of group cohesion and sense of safety so that participants will ask questions when they have them, even though it requires some degree of vulnerability in the presence of others to do so. Similarly, group leaders who ignore conflict in such a group may miss participants who have gone into fight-flight-freeze mode and therefore are incapable at the time of learning the didactic material being presented (Vogel & Schwab, 2016).

At the *forming stage*, occurring at the beginning of treatment (and reemerging when the group needs to restabilize or reconsolidate, as when a new member joins the group), themes of dependency and inclusion become salient (Tuckman, 1965). The supervisor should anticipate that the trainee is likely beginning the group with their own anxiety, which is likely to be higher with the less experience the trainee has in group psychotherapy (and psychotherapy generally). At this stage, the group members are often reliant on the group leader/s. Some supervisees will experience this as pressure from the group to perform and become more anxious, while others will experience some (defensive) comfort in taking on a role that is more analogous to individual psychotherapy. The group supervisor will do well to encourage the group supervisee to recognize and manage their own internal reactions, while facilitating foundations for cohesion which include interaction among the members. However, the supervisor will also want to ensure that the trainee does not become overly attached to the forming stage, and thus act in ways that prevent the group from moving into the next stages.

The *storming stage*, with its themes of counter-dependency and flight as reactions to the dependency issues in the first stage, is important for the therapist to handle competently, as conflict among people and authority is inevitable (and very often has therapeutic potential). However, this stage is often the most daunting for the developing group psychotherapist and thus the group supervisor plays a particularly important role. It is important that the group supervisor counteracts attempts of the trainee to avoid this developmental stage which can occur when the group leader is overly acquiescent to the group's demands, unnecessarily increases the structure to circumvent challenges, becomes too flexible with enforcing elements of the group contract to avoid conflict, and so on. The supervisee often needs reassurance that storming is an inherent (and often needed) group dynamic. Instinctive reactions to shut down or circumvent conflict in the group may lead to less desirable outcomes such as intensifying the revolt or burying it into underlying, insidious processes. Even in highly structured groups, unaddressed conflict will interrupt the group's ability to complete the working task. For example, a group member who feels attacked during group is unlikely to bring genuine examples to work through in the group setting. Similarly, a member who is used to high conflict relationships in which conflict almost always leads to abuse will likely be triggered by unaddressed conflict. Their survival instinct may kick in and circumvent their ability to engage with the content in a learning mode. Group psychotherapy supervisors have the opportunity to help their supervisees learn to approach rather than avoid the conflict in the group and then respond with curiosity and openness rather than defensiveness. To do this, the group leader often benefits by having an outlet for their own unfiltered reactions, for which supervision can be an optimal container. It is typical for storming to induce feelings that range from helplessness ("I don't know what to do!") to resentment and anger ("Why is my group doing this *to* me?!"). Group supervisors who are able to welcome and normalize these reactions during supervision can help their group therapists respond effectively in the room with their groups. It is essential that the group supervisor navigate the therapist's tendency to personalize the storming phase ("I must be doing this wrong") and instead view it as a normal group process that may actually be indicative of progress ("The group trusts one another enough to be forthcoming about their differences").

The focus of the *norming stage* is trust and structure. Trust is built on consistency and predictability which can be facilitated by providing a reasonable degree of structure. Thus, maintaining the "frame" of the group (i.e., the parameters on time, space, task definition as well as the content of the group agreement) is crucial and the supervisor will need to ensure that their supervisee appreciates the therapist's role in holding that frame. In particular, the supervisor adapts their focus depending on the supervisee's response to the role of the facilitator in holding the frame. For example, some group therapists are inclined to be overly rigid and harshly respond to normative group attempts to push on the boundaries set by the frame. These supervisees can become defensive when the group challenges the frame, rather than seeing the inherent necessity and value of group negotiations. The supervisor may find it helpful to bring up that exploration of the boundaries is inherent in group dynamics and explore with the therapist the countertransferences that can be elicited by the group testing the boundaries, while offering support as the therapist practices balancing the need for both flexibility and limit setting.

On the other end of the continuum, the supervisor may work with a supervisee who tends to be overly permissive. The supervisor may need to assist the well-intentioned helping professional to internalize that limit setting is compassionate and ultimately facilitates therapeutic dynamics and mitigates potentially harmful dynamics. Supervisees who only have experience conducting individual therapy may be unfamiliar with situations requiring authoritative positioning. Again, the supervisor may have to work with the trainee to identify and work through countertransference that can emerge when the groups' problematic dynamics need direct interruption and redirection.

Overall, the group supervisor assists the supervisee to differentiate which rules/agreements/norms are negotiable (and to what degree) and which are not ("treatment destructive"). Along these lines, they will need to decide how active a role the facilitator needs to take in holding the parameters compared to allowing the group to determine and maintain them. Here again, the supervisor must avoid any pull to oversimplify decision-making, and instead develop the supervisee's ability to hold in mind many layers of contextual complexity.

The *performing stage*, sometimes referred to as the *working stage*, is marked by maturity and productive group processes. During this stage of group development, the supervisor may need to help their supervisee allow the group to work and resist the urge to overfunction on behalf of the group. The group leader needs to remain attentive, engaged, and present while also permitting the group to do its own work. Supervision can be a good outlet to process the experience that often arises for group facilitators at this stage who are tempted to join the group as a member rather than a leader.

The final stage of group development, the *adjourning stage*, focuses on the termination process. In parallel processes, this important stage merits emphasis. In a society that is largely avoidant of goodbyes, many group patients/clients' unprocessed losses are activated as the group comes to an end. The group supervisee is just as susceptible as their clients/patients to avoid the true ending as it approaches. The group supervisor must manage their own avoidance of endings, to support the group supervisee through this stage of group. This process may be magnified if the group's ending coincides with an ending for the trainee and their supervisor. This stage offers great opportunity for the group supervisor to directly work with their supervisee to acknowledge both the loss that all endings pose, as well as the hope of a new beginning. The role of self-awareness on behalf of the supervisor is imperative; the supervisor must be aware of the timeline of both the group and the work with the supervisee and allow ample time and space for processing. It is common for supervisees to have intense reactions to endings. The supervisor who can be responsive to the full range of these reactions which often include sadness, relief, fear, possessiveness, disconnection, and so on, will likely help the supervisee to be present and responsive to their group as it comes to an end.

Group Psychotherapy Supervision Methods

Clinical supervision utilizes a variety of methods. While the standard methods are derived from individual psychotherapy supervision, each contains nuanced considerations for utilization in supervision of group psychotherapy. The *multiple methods* lend themselves to different developmental area/s (knowledge, skill, self-awareness) and provide many ways of learning. They can take into account different learning styles and the developmental level of supervisees, to consider which method to utilize when. When selecting methods of supervision, supervisors will also want to consider aspects of the supervisees' work and the targets for development. For example, the supervision may shift depending on whether the focus of the group work is here-and-now versus there-and-then; structured versus unstructured; cognitive versus affective.

Didactics

Didactics involve the supervisor taking on a teaching role, presenting information in an explanatory form. This method focuses on promoting the group leader's acquisition of foundational and functional knowledge, hopefully at their developmental level. The supervisor delivers the information clearly, utilizing case material to illustrate the content and offering opportunities for engagement with the material. Scaffolding (i.e., gradually increasing complexity and providing temporary support to aid in understanding and applying learning that is faded out) of didactic material is helpful (Taber, 2018).

Modeling

Modeling involves the supervisor performing desired behaviors while being observed and interacting with the supervisee(s). This is an experiential method with the ultimate goal of the group leader(s) internalizing therapeutic methods fitting to their interpersonal style and theoretical orientation. The trainee usually has many supervisors throughout their career to learn and emulate from, and eventually consolidates their own therapeutic knowledge base and style. Additional modeling examples can come from the many videos of group therapists conducting group. These can be reviewed in supervision by the supervisor and supervision group.

Role-Playing

In *role-playing*, the supervisee performs desired behaviors outside of an actual session, often observed by or interacting with the supervisor and/or group supervision colleagues. There are many methods of role-play. Psychodrama and Gestalt therapists, while having specific techniques, have also made role-play a mainstream therapeutic method which is extremely useful in supervision. One method is for the supervisor to model an intervention. It's beneficial to follow the modeling with role-play, using a "watch then do" approach. Repetition is often needed for effective modeling, and the skills modeled should be within the supervisee's range of attainment. This method primarily promotes skill development (Bearman et al., 2013). To decrease anxiety, the supervisor models the behavior first and removes the evaluative component. Role-playing is best used to anticipate likely scenarios, though group leaders often prefer to role-play the most difficult situations. In group supervision, multiple supervisees can be utilized to role-play group processes.

Audio-Video Review

Utilizing audio-video recording review involves the supervisee and supervisor watching recordings of sessions by the supervisee, marking moments to discuss and providing feedback. Audio-video review offers the opportunity for process coding, in which real-time performance can be evaluated for micro-outcomes, such as a client's engaged versus disengaged response to the clinician's verbalization. Evaluating which clinician behaviors promote desired in-session responses and which deter are considered an important tool for improving overall clinical outcome and thus process coding in clinical training is being promoted (Westra & Di Bartolomeo, 2024). This method addresses knowledge, skill, and self-awareness. It is crucial to ensure that the supervisees' successes are observed and discussed as valid feedback, as they may mistakenly believe that only critical feedback counts. The quality of the audio and video is important, so positioning cameras and microphones optimally is necessary. Multiple cameras with automation technology (e.g., OWL, e-meet) can be considered for group settings. Supervisees can be encouraged to watch recordings outside of supervision and mark specific times and requests for the supervisor to review. This type of recording and supervision is often required in university training settings because it offers the most immediate objective data of what happens in the group session.

Progress Note Review

In progress notes review, the supervisor and supervisees review progress notes (the official documentation in the healthcare record that is typically drafted by the supervisee and reviewed/edited/finalized by the supervisor) of a previous group session as the data for the supervision. Sometimes the supervisor and/or supervision group reads documentation provided by the supervisee and provides feedback through an iterative process to finalize the progress note. This method focuses on knowledge and skill development. It increases the supervisor's familiarity with the case if they are not directly observing or coleading.

Feedback helps the supervisee consolidate materials to what is most important, align with documentation standards, and complete progress notes efficiently.

Process Notes

Process notes are different from progress notes in that they focus more on the therapist's subjective experiences rather than overt observations of what happened in the group, including the therapist's reflections, hypotheses about what happened, affective and countertransferential reactions, and plans for the next session. Unlike videotapes which record what actually took place overtly, process notes might be more advantageous in capturing the group leader's resistances, anxieties and defensive reactions. Optimally the supervisee relates as closely as possible the events and process of the group as it occurred, including internal experiences, with the expectation of an optimal nonjudgmental but honest and informative supervisory experience. An astute supervisor can sensitively detect and in a timely manner address the supervisee's anxieties about presenting their work. Often parallel processes between the group leader's behavior in supervision and in the conducting of their groups can be gleaned. This is where the therapeutic skills of a supervisor can benefit the group leader—hopefully without pathologizing the supervisee which is not helpful. This method targets self-awareness. Supervisors and supervisees should be aware of regulations related to process notes, as they are distinct from progress notes and may have protections from compelled released, but not always. There should be an agreement on whether the process notes will be reviewed by the supervisor. Both supervisees and supervisors may keep process notes of clinical services and/or supervision.

Case Conference

The case conference method involves group sharing of case material, often with a specified structure in a group setting. This method helps the supervisee develop a coherent and meaningful narrative, a story of what happened, an integration of "facts" (who said what, and who did what) with dynamic understanding and interpretation of the observations. The emphasis here is on developing an integrated case formulation of the group session. This method addresses knowledge, skill, and self-awareness. Supervisors should be aware that group dynamics are likely active in the case conference itself and utilize the audience to promote growth while interfering with any problematic group dynamics. The degree of evaluation should be agreed upon beforehand, and utilizing a rubric for evaluation can be considered.

Live Observation

Live observation involves the supervisor watching a session as it occurs, either as a live observer in the room, or hidden via use of a one-way mirror or live audio-visual stream. It is important to consider the supervisor's observation on the group and whether the group is aware when the supervisor is observing. Technologies like bug-in-the-ear can be used for the supervisor to provide input or coaching while observing, and debriefing can be included. Direct observation has been found to increase supervisee satisfaction and promote their performance, but is widely underutilized (Amerikaner & Rose, 2012).

Cofacilitation

Finally, cofacilitation focuses on skill and self-awareness development. This method involves the supervisor and supervisee coleading sessions, allowing the supervisee to gain practical experience and receive immediate feedback. Cofacilitation in group psychotherapy offers a dynamic supervisory structure that enhances collaborative learning and professional development, yet it also introduces complexities in authority perception and execution. While coleaders model therapeutic interventions and provide real-time feedback, the division of authority can lead to challenges such as deference, passive resistance, or idealization of one facilitator over the other. Group members may struggle with conflicting leadership styles, interpreting disparities in authority as inconsistency or favoritism, which can disrupt cohesion and therapeutic progress. Clear role delineation and mutual respect between coleaders is needed to mitigate these challenges and foster a balanced supervisory environment (Freedman & Diederich, 2018). Integrative models emphasize the need for structured communication and alignment in leadership approach to optimize cofacilitation outcomes.

Supervisors are encouraged to be creative and consider adapting or combining the methods mentioned here, which is not intended to be a comprehensive list. However, it should be noted that any of these methods can likely be utilized to develop any area, particularly if implemented with the specific intention of doing so. Supervision is an area ripe for innovation and constantly evolving. Adjusting methods of supervision to align with both the target of training and individual characteristics of the trainee is likely to enhance the process.

Conclusion

This chapter outlined the qualifications, competencies, tasks, and methods required for effective supervision in group psychotherapy. It emphasizes the importance of supervisors being experienced group therapists, as well as ethically aware and culturally responsive professionals, who can impart their knowledge and skill to others. Supervisors develop their supervisees' competencies in intervention unique to group psychotherapy, understand and work with various stages of group development, and use various supervision methods such as didactics, modeling, and role-playing. This chapter highlights the complexity and multi-layered nature of group psychotherapy supervision, emphasizing the need for supervisors to be adaptable and innovative in their approach. Following this chapter that spells out many of the salient parameters of supervision, Chapter 3 will illustrate, up close and personal, the many ways it is practiced.

References

Agazarian, Y. M. (2011). Functional subgrouping in systems-centered groups and the theory from which it emerged. In S. P. Gantt & Y. Agazarian (Eds.), *Systems-centered therapy: Clinical practice with individuals, families and groups* (pp. 97–111). Karnac Books.

Amerikaner, M. & Rose, T. (2012). Direct observation of psychology supervisees' clinical work: A snapshot of current practice. *The Clinical Supervisor, 31*(1), 61–80. https://doi.org/10.1080/07325223.2012.671721

APA. (2014). *APA guidelines for clinical supervision in health service psychology.* www.apa.org/about/policy/guidelines-supervision.pdf

ASGW. (2021). *ASGW guiding principles for group work.* https://asgw.org/wp-content/uploads/2021/07/ASGW-Guiding-Principles-May-2021.pdf

Barlow, S. H. (2013). *Specialty competencies in group psychology.* Oxford University Press. https://doi.org/10.1093/med:psych/9780195388558.001.0001

Bearman, S. K., Weisz, J. R., Chorpita, B. F., Hoagwood, K., Ward, A., Ugueto, A. M., Bernstein, A., & Research Network on Youth Mental Health (2013). More practice, less preach? The role of supervision processes and therapist characteristics in EBP implementation. *Administration and Policy in Mental Health, 40*(6), 518–529. https://doi.org/10.1007/s10488-013-0485-5

Bernard, H., Burlingame, G., Flores, P., Greene, L., Joyce, A., Kobos, J. C., ... Feirman, D. (2008). Clinical practice guidelines for group psychotherapy. *International Journal of Group Psychotherapy, 58*(4), 455–542. https://doi.org/10.1521/ijgp.2008.58.4.455

Brabender, V., & Fallon, A. (2009). Introduction to stage development in psychotherapy groups. In V. Brabender & A. Fallon (Eds.), *Group development in practice: Guidance for clinicians and researchers on stages and dynamics of change* (pp. 3–8). American Psychological Association. https://doi.org/10.1037/11858-001

Burlingame, G. M., McClendon, D. T., & Yang, C. (2018). Cohesion in group therapy: A meta-analysis. *Psychotherapy, 55*(4), 384–398. https://doi.org/10.1037/pst0000173

Burlingame, G. M., Seebeck, J. D., Janis, R. A., Whitcomb, K. E., Barkowski, S., Rosendahl, J., & Strauss, B. (2016). Outcome differences between individual and group formats when identical and nonidentical treatments, patients, and doses are compared: A 25-year meta-analytic perspective. *Psychotherapy, 53*(4), 446–461. https://doi.org/10.1037/pst0000090

Freedman, W. & Diederich, L. T. (2018). Group co-facilitation: Creating a collaborative partnership. In M. D. Ribeiro, J. M. Gross, & M. M. Turner (Eds.), *The college counselor's guide to group psychotherapy* (pp. 159–172). Routledge.

Greene, L. R. & Kaklauskas, F. J. (2019). Anti-therapeutic, defensive, regressive, and challenging group processes and dynamics. In F J. Kaklauskas & L. R. Greene (Eds.), *Core principles of group psychotherapy: An integrated theory, research, and practice training manual* (pp. 49–55). Routledge.

Group Specialty Council. (2018). *Draft Clinical Practice Guidelines.* www.apadivisions.org/division-49/leadership/committees/draft-practice-guidelines.pdf

Group Specialty Council. (2019). *Postdoctoral residency competencies for group psychology and group psychotherapy specialty.* www.apadivisions.org/division-49/leadership/committees/postdoctoral-residency-group.pdf

Group Specialty Council. (2024). *Education and training taxonomy for group psychology and group psychotherapy.* www.cospp.org/cos-approved-specialty-e-t-taxonomies

Kaslow, N. J., Grus, C. L., Campbell, L. F., Fouad, N. A., Hatcher, R. L., & Rodolfa, E. R. (2009). Competency assessment toolkit for professional psychology. *Training and Education in Professional Psychology, 3*(4, Suppl), S27–S45. https://doi.org/10.1037/a0015833

King, A. & Hunt, T. (2015). Use of the group to enhance learning opportunities. In K. O'Sullivan, A. King, & T. Nove (Eds.), *Groupwork in Australia* (pp. 268–299). Institute of Group Leaders.

Roback, H. B. (2000). Adverse outcomes in group psychotherapy: Risk factors, prevention, and research directions. *Journal of Psychotherapy Practice and Research, 9*(3), 113–122.

Taber, K. S. (2018). Scaffolding learning: Principles for effective teaching and the design of classroom resources. In M. Abend (Ed.), *Effective teaching and learning: Perspectives, strategies and implementation* (pp. 1–43). Nova Science.

Tasca, G. A., Francis, K., & Balfour, L. (2014). Group psychotherapy levels of interventions: A clinical process commentary. *Psychotherapy, 51*(1), 25–29. https://doi-org.du.idm.oclc.org/10.1037/a0032520

Tuckman, B. W. (1965). Developmental sequence in small groups. *Psychological Bulletin, 63*(6), 384–399. https://doi.org/10.1037/h0022100

Vogel, S. & Schwabe, L. (2016). Learning and memory under stress: Implications for the classroom. *Science of Learning, 1.* https://doi.org/10.1038/npjscilearn.2016.11

Westra, H. A. & Di Bartolomeo, A. A. (2024). Developing expertise in psychotherapy: The case for process coding as clinical training. *American Psychologist, 79*(2), 163–174. https://doi-org.du.idm.oclc.org/10.1037/amp0001139

Whittingham, M., Lefforge, N. L., & Marmarosh, C. (2021). Group psychotherapy as a specialty: An inconvenient truth. *Psychotherapy, 72*(2), 60–66. https://doi.org/10.1176/appi.psychotherapy.20200037

Yalom, I. D. & Leszcz, M. (2020). *The theory and practice of group psychotherapy* (6th ed.). Basic Books.

Appendix: Competencies for Group Psychology/Psychotherapy

Integration of Science and Practice

- Demonstrates the use of evidence-based knowledge and interventions for planning and facilitating groups.
- Conducts effective group organization practices such as screening, orientation, and group process commentary.
- Applies the scientific principles from current research findings to group members' problems, issues and concerns.

Ethical and Legal Standards/Policy

- Recognizes ethical dilemmas and concerns related to group psychotherapy and uses an ethical decision-making model when ethical dilemmas arise in groups.

Consultation and Evaluation

- Demonstrates an ability to work constructively with interdisciplinary mental health professional teams.
- Engages in evaluative practices as applied to groups such as cohesion, group progress, and the like.

Supervision and Teaching

- Applies a supervision model when working with mental health professionals in training such as in practicum and internship.
- Presents information relative to group psychology and group psychotherapy in venues such as case presentations, grand rounds and the like.

Assessment

- Demonstrates an ability to evaluate the group's and group members' needs and progress.
- Uses appropriate assessment measures and instruments for screening and progress.

Professional Values, Attitudes, and Behaviors

- Demonstrates an awareness of personal values, attitudes and behaviors that have the potential to affect the therapeutic process
- Conceptualizes and implements a self-reflective process related to group facilitation.

Intervention

- Facilitates the emergence of group therapeutic factors such as universality, hope, catharsis and cohesion.
- Effectively intervenes to prevent and/or address problematic group member behaviors such as monopolizing, story-telling, and help-rejecting.
- Effectively and safely manages members' expression of difficult emotions such as anger, fear, guilt and shame.

Individual and Cultural Diversity

- Facilitates the therapeutic experience for groups composed of diverse individuals.
- Conceptualizes the role of power dynamics in groups.
- Demonstrates an ability to intervene effectively when issues such as marginalization and microaggressions occur in groups.

Chapter 3

Contemporary Approaches to Group Psychotherapy Supervision

Editor: Michelle A. Collins-Greene

Authors: Molyn Leszcz, Nina W. Brown, Ellen Wright, Scott Giacomucci, Les R. Greene, Susan P. Gantt, Leah M. Niehaus, Francis Kaklauskas, Michelle A. Collins-Greene, and Tony L. Sheppard

Introduction

This chapter captures the work of contemporary supervisors of group psychotherapy, all of whom have practiced many years and have trained and supervised innumerable group leaders. They demonstrate the diversity of settings and theoretical orientations that are prominent in the current era. Their essays speak for themselves and provide wonderful illustrations and models for supervisors-in-training and consultation to emulate. They also talk about who influenced, mentored, and supervised them.

An Interpersonal Approach

Molyn Leszcz

Structure, Frame, and Format of Group Psychotherapy Supervision

I work in the University of Toronto's Department of Psychiatry and have throughout my career. It has been my base for clinical work in group psychotherapy, research, and importantly the training and supervision in group psychotherapy that I provide.

There have been a number of group supervision foci over the years. These have included training and supervision of group therapists in protocol-driven, funded group psychotherapy trials, including for cancer populations, genetic predisposition to cancer, and for patients with schizophrenia. I have also developed group therapy training programs in China and provided supervision over 10 years with the attendant cross-cultural challenges. The bulk of my supervision, however, and what has been ongoing over 40 years now, has been supervision of three to four cotherapy teams yearly who lead interpersonal group therapy as part of the training program at the University of Toronto. I will focus my comments on this cohort because it has been the largest and most continuous part of my supervision work.

The usual model is of two residents agreeing to work in cotherapy over a year-long period. I supervise the cotherapy team from the conceptualization of the group including assessment, preparation, and orientation of new members to the group, and then provide weekly supervision of the cotherapy team over the duration of the year. Typically, it takes three months to assemble the group and then the cotherapy team leads the group for approximately 28–32 weekly sessions to its conclusion. The groups are comprised of 8–10 people, closed for the duration of the group, and, since Covid, meeting via Zoom. The groups are heterogeneous and consist of patients referred with a range of diagnoses, including depression, anxiety, substance use, trauma, and personality difficulties.

DOI: 10.4324/9781003410621-4

A good deal of time is spent in the pregroup period, recognizing the important contributions to clinical outcome that come from good selection and pregroup training. By front-end loading the work, we are generally able to achieve cohesive and durable groups with few dropouts and with good clinical effectiveness. Each cotherapy team establishes with each patient an etiological formulation that helps align goals, tasks, and quality of the therapeutic relationship, building a therapeutic alliance which then feeds into the development of group cohesion. We refer to these foci as "compass statements," establishing direction and clarity about patient goals and expectations of how group members will work in the group to advance their goals. Clarity of focus is particularly important in the time-limited group model.

Once the group launches, the cotherapists provide a detailed summary of the group session noting key themes, key interactions, progress toward completion of the compass statements, challenges, risks, and counter-transference challenges. Generally, this is a two- to four-page summary the residents create after each group. Prior to Covid, when groups were led face-to-face, I would regularly observe from behind the one-way mirror.

Group Contract

The group contract is shaped by the setting in which I am working. I am transparent about the multiplicity of goals that I have in the academic training program with responsibility both for clinical care of the patient, education and training of residents, and their evaluation. I aim always to align these three dimensions, emphasizing the fact that if we provide good clinical care and a good training experience, evaluation becomes a secondary concern. In our system, I serve as the most responsible physician for these patients and the patients all have met me at some point in their trajectory as part of the selection and assessment process for group therapy.

In the same way that we establish a therapeutic alliance and a clear therapeutic contract of patients, I aim to establish an educational alliance with my supervisees regarding goals, tasks, and the quality of our relationship. We meet weekly for 45 minutes and as noted review the process notes from the preceding group session.

The group experience is demanding and rewarding, as reported to me by many residents. It is often one of the longest single clinical commitments they make during their training which normally involves a series of three to six month rotations.

In addition to providing excellent clinical care, the purpose of training is to promote the resident's ability to grow and develop into an individual who thinks about groups as a group therapist rather than just a therapist who does groups. An overarching training goal is removing obstacles to the trainees' growth and development as therapists, so that they can use themselves fully as therapeutic agents. This involves deep understanding of our patients and recognition of the role of empathy, both with regard to *receptive empathy*—our understanding of our patients—and *expressive empathy*—how that understanding is communicated. This involves attention to counter-transference and recognizing how certain patients may elicit interpersonal impacts, maladaptive transaction loops and articulation within the social microcosm of their core interpersonal difficulties.

The formulation model we employ is informed by the Plan Formulation Model (Weiss, 1993). This identifies patients' goals; obstacles to those goals that emerge from early life experiences that may concretize into pathogenic beliefs and negative expectations about self and other; and the way in which these pathogenic beliefs gain expression in interpersonal terms within the social microcosm of the group. It demands deep engagement on the part of the group therapists. Working closely together as cotherapists can create professional intimacy that can be highly valued, but it can be challenging at times. Throughout, I maintain clarity about educational boundaries. I have made very good use over the years of Anne Alonso's maxim that the psychotherapy supervisor in effect must "listen with the clinician's ear and speak with the teacher's mouth" (Alonso, 1985). I find it helpful to be judiciously transparent in sharing common challenges that I have encountered in my own professional work as a way of normalizing and reducing the risk of shame and humiliation in my trainees.

I aim to provide ongoing feedback about resident performance and their growth and development. This serves two purposes. One is creating a collaborative approach to feedback and evaluation for the trainee and the second is facilitating greater clinical effectiveness through the use of that feedback.

Stage of Learning

The residency training is a five year program and residents who seek to do group therapy generally are senior residents, certainly in the second half of their training. Because it is an elective it is of appeal to those who are interested in psychotherapy.

Supervision seeks to promote the link between theory and practice and how to operationalize concepts into clinically relevant terms. Often supervisees will comment that they understand what to do in principle but have difficulty putting that into practice. Group therapy often involves higher levels of therapist self-disclosure and exposure than other forms of psychiatric care and hence levels of anxiety initially are quite high. I emphasize the importance of seeing themselves on a developmental path. A paper by Zaslav (1988) is a welcome read for many because Zaslav describes progressing through the stages of group shock, reappraisal, feeling one step behind, using the here-and-now and polishing one's skills. I try to normalize the learning challenges and the apprehension about group psychotherapy. I also assign a range of readings to bolster their confidence. Most residents are familiar with the textbook that I have coauthored, with Irvin Yalom, *The Theory and Practice of Group Psychotherapy* (Yalom & Leszcz, 2020).

Role of Group Supervision of Group Psychotherapy

Supervision, together with didactic learning, experiential learning, observation, personal therapy, and attendance at conferences all contribute to the growth and development of our trainees. In my view, supervision is the linchpin of these elements. I am influenced in understanding my role as a supervisor of group therapy by the literature on training that addresses the normative, formative, and restorative tasks of group psychotherapy (Leszcz, 2011). The *normative* task of supervision is to help establish the frame and clarity of the task and the administrative processes of the group; the *formative* tasks relate to training group therapists how to practice and link theory to practice. This is the bulk of the supervisory task but the first task, normative, sets the stage for success and the third task, *restorative*, becomes more important at times of great challenge when residents become discouraged, demoralized, and lose confidence. In addition, supervision brings into discussion the evidence base of effective group psychotherapy leadership with regard to how to develop group cohesion, how to maintain and establish a therapeutic alliance, the role of empathy, and how to use counter-transference constructively.

Many trainees find working in the here-and-now to be a challenge in group psychotherapy. They feel exposed, apprehensive, and unable to readily articulate what the group and individual patients need in the moment. This is part of what supervision provides—helping residents to anticipate being "one step behind" initially and then narrowing the gap between understanding and therapeutic action. At the *micro level*, supervision helps articulate the interpersonal model, the role of interpersonal learning, the social microcosm, how to work in the here-and-now, and how to promote an adaptive spiral from in group to outside of the group. The interpersonal model demands therapists being much more active than they are in other forms of psychodynamic psychotherapy or other kinds of structured groups. The interpersonal model demands a greater use of self which is a challenge for trainees in their professional development. Another key component of supervision is exploring group dynamics, group development, and group process. I share with residents that processing skills are our superpower. It is the way in which we can make sense of things that other people see more narrowly. We can appreciate the overdetermination of what is in front of us, which helps keep us humble and avoid premature or pathological certainty.

At the *macro level*, supervision plays a key role in the development of the therapist as a professional. Allied with this is transmitting the core values of our profession to our trainees: respect for our patients, humanity, empathy, interpersonal flexibility, integrity, respect for boundaries, and therapeutic humility. These issues have all become much more important with the growing appreciation and awareness of the impact of racism, discrimination, and oppression on our patients. Supervision hence must also promote cultural awareness, cultural opportunity, cultural humility, and cultural openness so that we create training environments that in turn create therapeutic environments in which there is a clear sense of safety, inclusion and a welcoming of diversity.

Training Influences On My Development as a Group Therapist and Supervisor

I have benefited enormously from both supervision and mentorship throughout my development. I did fellowship training at Stanford University with Dr. Irvin Yalom, which was my true introduction into group psychotherapy. I am grateful that our relationship has continued for these many years into friendship and collaboration. Dr. Yalom taught me the importance of caring for patients, the vitality of doing meaningful work throughout one's life, the value of working in the here-and-now, the importance of therapeutic presence, and that the relationship is the healing force. I also learned from Dr. Irv Yalom the importance of therapeutic humility. I recall vividly watching him lead a group. I was observing behind the one-way mirror, and the group was a complete failure. There was no engagement, no interaction, and every moment felt like it was pulling teeth. Dr. Yalom joined us later for a discussion of the group. He declared there will be group sessions like this throughout your career. There will be times when you think the quality of your life would be better "if you were a shoe salesman rather than a group therapist." That has provided me with great comfort over the years as I have encountered similar difficulties in groups. Coupled with Dr. Yalom, is the important influence of Dr. Danny Silver, a psychiatrist and psychoanalyst. He was not a group therapist, but I learned from him the value of therapeutic persistence and commitment and his belief that everyone we see is potentially treatable if we can engage them.

The third important influence has been working in cotherapy. Over the years I have worked with at least 60 different coleaders, each for a year of weekly group psychotherapy. During this time, I have also had my work observed by trainees and benefited enormously from the questions they asked in our postgroup rehash. Scrutiny and feedback are essential in our professional growth and development and are hallmark aspects of deliberate practice.

I have also benefited enormously from participation in groups myself, most recently a two year experience in group therapy focused on racism and discrimination. I am grateful to Dr. Will Ashley for facilitating this group. It has helped me to become more empathic and better attuned to the experience of marginalization and discrimination. I have learned that if I do not inquire about these issues with my patients, these issues may not come up spontaneously in treatment. Participation in the American Group Psychotherapy Association (AGPA), which has been a professional home for me for many years has also promoted my growth and development through my participation and demonstrations of my work and the feedback and scrutiny that that has elicited. We only get better at what we do through feedback and deliberate practice.

Finally, I would underscore the importance of being in a community of practice. AGPA has provided that for many years as did the Canadian Group Psychotherapy Association while it was operational. We do difficult work. It is hard to do it in isolation. Social connection, learning from colleagues, and being supported by others in our profession, allows us to continue to do this important and difficult work.

References

Alonso, A. (1985). *The quiet profession: Supervisors of psychotherapy*. Macmillan.

Leszcz, M. (2011). Psychotherapy supervision and the development of the psychotherapist. In R. H. Klein, H. S. Bernard, & V. L Schermer (Eds.), *On becoming a psychotherapist: The personal and professional journey* (pp. 114–138). Oxford University Press.

Weiss, J. (1993). *How psychotherapy works*. Guilford Press.

Yalom, I. D. & Leszcz, M. (2020). *The theory and practice of group psychotherapy,* (6th ed.). Basic Books.

Zaslav, M. (1988). A model of group therapist development. *International Journal of Group Psychotherapy, 38*, 511–519.

A Psychoeducational Approach

Nina W. Brown

The Structure, Frame, and Format of Group Consultation

Psychoeducational groups have three major components: educational, affective and group factors that are balanced for group sessions and treatment. These groups are short term, have a narrow focus and are atheoretical which means they can use components from any theory, foster skill development, enhance self-awareness and assist with collaborative learning. (Brown, 2024, cf. Brown, 2013, 2018)

The supervision I usually provide is for doctoral counseling and psychology students. The supervision occurs in a class setting, "Advanced Group Counseling and Psychotherapy," on a weekly basis for three hours. The course is required for counseling students and an elective for psychology students. The major requirement is for student group leaders to facilitate an interpersonal process group for undergraduate students enrolled in a required course on interpersonal relations. All group sessions are scheduled during the day and during the time scheduled for the undergraduate course. There are 8–12 groups of these sessions consisting of approximately 10 undergraduate students during a semester.

The student supervisees are expected to follow the syllabus, attend class sessions, and to actively participate. They are also expected to submit weekly journals and leader critiques.

This allows me to intervene when needed, to assess growth in learning, identify lack of knowledge and encourage growth in leader responsibilities. Class supervision sessions use role play and demonstration groups, allowing them to discuss personal concerns, group concerns or dilemmas, and discuss case studies, readings and group situations. Although lectures are deemphasized, there are times when the lack of knowledge makes lectures the best way to provide the needed information. Supervision sessions are conducted as would be group sessions so that the role of the leader (instructor) serves as a model for group leadership and demonstrates how to provide process commentary, interventions, boundary maintenance, and address out of group concerns with encouragement to bring out of group interactions back to the group.

The supervision class time is used to provide a balance of cognitive and affective information, show modeling of some group leadership strategies, and to guide students to inner self-development to moderate potential counter-transference that could negatively affect the groups they facilitate. Lectures are kept to a minimum, planned for topics emerging from the sessions and where lack of knowledge is identified. Examples of educational topics include confidentiality, ethics, cultural competence, and self-care.

The Group Contract

The doctoral students (supervisees/trainees) are oriented to the requirements for the group they will facilitate, and the requirement for a weekly written report that addresses a specific topic. They meet once a week with me to provide supervision and to extend their knowledge. The topics for the written report have to do with the group dynamics and their leadership. They can include effective and counter-productive member behaviors, personal resistance and feelings aroused, feelings directly and openly expressed by others, the degree of the session's present centeredness, the theme for the session, identification of the group-as-a-whole resistance, and how the group managed conflict.

Students also agree to submit a written critique of their leadership addressing all of the following: the strategies they used to manage their personal anxiety, metaphors emerging in the session, the ease or difficulty they had in maintaining an emotional presence, identification of their actions to foster member to member interactions. They also are asked to make process commentary and include the strengths and needs for improvement of their leadership, and the strengths and weaknesses of their interventions. This model and format have been used for over ten years, and the feedback from the undergraduate group members and their course instructor is positive citing reduction of stress, improved communications, and increased self-understanding as just some of the outcomes for group participation.

Stage of Learning of Participants

I served on the American Psychological Association's Commission on Accreditation and was able to review syllabi from many psychology programs in the US. The doctoral degree at that time was the culminating degree for practice, but that has since changed so that the master's level is considered a degree sufficient for practice. While counseling students are required to take a course in group counseling and psychotherapy, many students from psychology programs have only received a lesson or so on group topics as part of another course in their programs. Hence, there is usually a variety of knowledge about leading groups which means that the supervisor will have to supply considerable information about groups and my courses are prepared for that lack. Readings and lectures are presented on various group leader topics such as group dynamics, making group process commentary, group-as-a-whole concepts and other major group leader topics.

Students usually arrive to the course with a varying degree of having led group therapy already. Many have participated in practica and internships where they led groups or are currently enrolled in these. In addition, many are employed as clinicians in agencies, schools, or even in private practice which means that they bring a richness of experiences to the course and enhance discussions of the didactic material.

Another variable that contributes to the use of psychoeducation for supervision for group leaders is their experiences as members of a therapeutic group. Because some have not had any experience, although counseling students are required to take a personal growth group course as part of their program, it is not unusual to find that many students have not had such an opportunity. I usually begin a course with asking about their experience as members of a group to get an idea of whether there will be resistances to work on, or if they had a good experience which adds to the understanding of the power and promise of group counseling/therapy/psychotherapy.

Role of the Group Supervisor of Group Psychotherapy

I consider the role of the group supervisor to take care to prevent shaming, to build confidence, to show the constructive use of inner experiencing as a reflection of the group's feelings, resistance, experiencing and the like. The supervisor structures the sessions to capitalize on the students' experiences as group leaders, promote their inner self-development, and explore personal reactions, thoughts and ideas that emerge or are triggered by group interactions. It is an opportunity to explore various theoretical perspectives as related to topics relative to group psychotherapy, and to fill in learning gaps.

Training Influences On My Development as a Group Therapy Supervisor

My training began with the course I took at William and Mary for the doctoral degree. After working at Old Dominion University, we initiated an accredited counseling program which requires a course in group counseling and psychotherapy. It turned out that I was the only faculty member in the program who had taken a course in group counseling and psychotherapy. I quickly realized that I needed to know much more about groups and group leadership. Yvonne Agazarian directed weekends on teaching group at Temple University and I attended those for several years. It was during those weekends that I met someone who told me about the Mid-Atlantic Group Society and began to send me newsletters about the organization and their offerings. I began attending their weekend conferences where I was able to learn from experienced clinicians. I attended every workshop I could find sponsored by the American Psychological Association and the American Counseling Association relative to group therapy and finally attended an AGPA's conference and realized how much I could learn from these effective and knowledgeable professionals.

In addition to attending the conferences at AGPA, I also participated in their Institutes, National Designate Instructor Training and other workshops and webinars. This describes my formal training, but there are many other informal training experiences that have contributed to my instruction and supervision for group counseling and psychotherapy. A rich source for much of the information I received were the readings and the research I had to do for the books I wrote and published (N = 41+ at this point). Examples of books' topics include *Psychoeducational Groups* (2018), *Facilitating Challenging Groups* (2014), *Creative*

Activities for Group Therapy (2023), and *Teaching Facilitation of Group Therapy* (2024). Learning and training for group counseling and psychotherapy continue to be priorities for my continued growth.

References

Brown, N. W. (2013). *Psychoeducational groups* (3rd ed.). Routledge. (Translated into Turkish.)
Brown, N. W. (2018). *Psychoeducational groups* (4th ed.). Taylor & Francis.
Brown, N. W. (2024). *Teaching facilitation of group therapy: Processes and applications*. Routledge.

A Modern Analytic Approach

Ellen Wright

Structure, Frame, and Format of the Group Psychotherapy Supervision

I typically organize my group supervision of group psychotherapy by asking one member to present an issue or concern and any relevant information they think will aid listeners in understanding the group process. The supervisory group is asked to be aware of the potential for parallel process (i.e., the recreation of the treatment dynamics in the interaction between group members) and to study which party the listeners ally or identify with—the leader, the group member, or the group-as-a-whole. These suggestions help group members study feelings induced by the presentation and can aid in identifying resistances present in the group be they, individual, group, status quo, or treatment destructive resistances. Members are invited to be curious about the types of counter-transference (objective, subjective, social, concordant or complementary) that may be elicited by the presentation.

Case presentations are examined with attention to understanding deviations from the group agreement which shed light on the historical patterns of the group members. Methods that highlight and resolve individual and group resistances are explored, specifically interventions whose goals are to increase immediacy, that is, group process between members into the here-and-now. Supervisees are asked to be aware of risk and vulnerability involved in presenting and to be alert to the appearance of a self-critical narrative in the presenter. Research (Haen & Thomas, 2018) has highlighted how experiences of shame and self-criticism drain precious emotional energy away from more constructive responses such as introspection and exploration of relevant dynamics. This dynamic is also present when members present in group supervision. In order to minimize the impact of shame and self-attack, the group leader will selectively discuss relevant parallel scenarios from her practice that help normalize transference enactments and therapist errors and demonstrate the working through process.

Modern Analytic supervision also highlights defenses and resistances related to aggression and to intimacy. Hyman Spotnitz, the founder of Modern Psychoanalysis, introduced the concept of the "narcissistic defense," the idea that maladaptive processing of aggression, the turning of aggression toward the self, underlies many psychological and somatic disorders. Spotnitz's theory and technique revolutionized the treatment of preoedipal disorders, many of which are related to the self-destructive internalization of aggression. Techniques that address the narcissistic defense are particularly amenable to use in group therapy, where maladaptive defenses against aggression can be observed and explored.

Supervisees are helped to identify these defenses, to apply methods for managing the level of anger in the group, and employ new methods for expressing negative affect. Key to the process of becoming more comfortable working with aggression is the exploration of supervisees' familial attitudes and prohibitions against the feeling and/or expression of negative emotions. Techniques for working with negative transference and aggressive interactions between group members are discussed and modeled by the leader in her handling of negative emotions that can occur during the supervisory process. Interventions that focus on the modulation of anger in the group and the constructive expression of anger are discussed within the context of the case presented.

Louis Ormont, a pioneer in Modern Group, expanded the application of Modern Group to include resolving "resistances to intimacy" (Ormont, 1984). Ormont's taxonomy of resistances to intimacy can be used to help group leaders identify and resolve the fears underlying dysfunctional approaches to relationships as they manifest in the members' outside lives and as they are demonstrated in the group process. The discussion of these resistances is then linked to interventions that help the group leader bring the group interaction into the here-and-now of the group where new modes of relating can be practiced and internalized.

The Group Contract/Agreement

I introduce the concept of the group agreement by reviewing the training group/supervisory agreement. This document integrates issues of social equity and systemic oppression into the conventional group contract. It expands on the accepted components of the group agreement (i.e., confidentiality, putting feelings into words, not action) and asks group members to be aware of how differences, both visible and invisible, impact members' participation in a group. Additionally, I ask supervisees to be aware of how privilege and identity may impact the group dynamics they are presenting as well as their colleagues' ability and comfort in speaking candidly about their cases and their own internal process.

I also introduce my group leader agreement which details the leaders' commitment to study and manage the ways in which her positionality and bias impact how she intervenes in the discussion of the cases presented as well as in the group process in the here-and-now supervisory group. This agreement also invites open discussion of injuries that may occur because of these biases. The inclusion of these components of the treatment frame enables group members to practice observing and speaking to charged issues of race and privilege, and to observe, and internalize how the group leader handles these emotionally charged exchanges. Repeated experiences of working with difficult transference and counter-transference issues helps supervisees build the stamina and resilience needed to remain engaged and responsive to difficult group interactions that will occur in the groups they lead.

Stage of Learning of Participants

My interest in the application of Modern Analytic theory to a variety of settings (medical, educational, musical and athletic performance) equipped me to work successfully with clinicians with a variety of training experiences (interpersonal, somatic, art therapy, trauma-informed) in my supervision groups. Often seeking to study psychoanalytic theory as their second training experience, these supervisees benefit from being helped to value their prior training even as they see themselves as beginners in Modern Group. This valuing of prior training efforts enables them to access feelings of competence that counterbalance the inevitable feelings of vulnerability and self-consciousness that accompany learning a new approach to group therapy.

My inclusion of other theories in addition to the Modern Group approach underscores the importance of modeling how group interventions can take multiple forms. This messaging enables supervisees to develop and express their own therapeutic voice, rather than replicating the approach of the supervisor in ways that can feel artificial and inauthentic. Participation in a group composed entirely of mental health providers introduces additional resistances and defenses. I speak directly about the unique pressures that mental health providers can experience when presenting to other clinicians. These can include fear of exposure of personal vulnerabilities, feelings of inadequacy in comparison to other group members and to the leader, shame and self-criticism of their clinical work, and "reputational anxiety" —the fear that disclosure of areas of bias and inadequacy will influence how one is seen as a therapist and adversely affect the willingness of others to refer clients to them. When issues of social inequity and implicit bias are uncovered, supervisees with privilege fear being seen as "bad" and can become silent or even be paralyzed by white guilt and shame. I model bringing my own biases and privilege into the group process and demonstrate how to work therapeutically with these difficult social dynamics when they enter the group process.

The Role of Group Supervisor of Group Psychotherapy

Supervision is an opportunity for participants to learn essential theory and skills while becoming more aware of aspects of their personal history that both limit and enhance their effectiveness as a group leader. It also provides the opportunity to develop and strengthen one's professional ego. Included in one's professional ego is a delineation of one's sense of identity as a therapist, clarification and internalization of emerging skills and competencies, and application of the theory and technique that one chooses to utilize in group work. A healthy professional ego also includes access to the "Valuing Self" (Wright, 2022). Group supervision builds the Valuing Self, a "reservoir of memories and experiences of ourselves, including how we are viewed by others in our lives, that provides a positive, robust connection to the therapist's sense of self" (Wright, 2022). When group leaders are challenged by negative transference and the conflictual feelings they create, accessing the Valuing Self can restore the group therapist's emotional equilibrium and competence.

To build and sustain a successful practice of group psychotherapy requires the practitioner to carefully and consistently monitor their internal reactions and to build and sustain a successful and gratifying Modern Group practice relies on our willingness to share our knowledge, our vulnerabilities, and our emotional resources with others with a similar life goal. This community of colleagues, be they mentors, supervisors, analysts or training group members, provide a chorus of voices that help us reflect on ourselves and our work. Our colleagues provide for us what a therapy group provides for its members, the opportunity to hear how others see us, as well as a setting where we can observe and learn how to do things differently. Group supervision helps us develop the pillars of our professional ego—the repository of our skills, intuition, our sense of purpose and agency. In our supervisory groups we learn to disengage our critical inner voice and accept, even welcome, our imperfection. Mistakes are inevitable, and they can provide some of the richest opportunities for growth for us as well as our patients. As we work to address rupture and then repair, we provide emotional experiences that most of our patients never had in their formative years. Supervision groups help us learn to serve as models for recognizing ruptures, mending rifts, and staying open to deeper emotional connections internally and with each other.

Training Influences On My Development as a Group Therapist and Group Therapy Supervisor

I am a Modern Analyst in private practice. I work with individuals, couples and groups and I train and supervise other therapists. I was introduced to Modern Analysis as I was entering the first year of my training in clinical psychology. Modern Analysis provided me with a theory and technique that valued both my intellect and my emotions. As I came to understand and integrate key elements of Modern Analysis, respecting and joining defenses, and emotional communication to name two, I learned how to help even the most resistant of clients engage in treatment and explore a more constructive life path.

Confronted by the limitations of academic clinical training, my work with Modern Analytic supervisors helped me learn to tolerate and then utilize some of the most difficult induced feelings from very disturbed patients, feelings of helplessness and despair. These supervisors modeled the type of relationship I use now in my work as a supervisor—a relationship where ideas and suggestions are gently and generously, sometimes humorously, offered in an environment of curiosity rather than critique. I credit these supervisors, and my training analyst, with providing me with the intellectual stimulation and emotional nourishment that enabled me to successfully complete my doctorate and become a certified Modern Analyst. More important than these credentials, these supervisory experiences demonstrated to me that modern analytic treatment could help clients create more successful and rewarding lives.

The power of Modern Group was most evident when I was a coleader of an inpatient group with my internship supervisor. I observed how his use of interpretation injured group members, creating disconnection rather than group cohesion. Utilizing Modern Analytic techniques of bridging, and joining and mirroring of resistances (Ormont, 2001), I enabled a disparate group of inpatients to become agents of change for each other and to experience the rewards of emotional connection.

On internship I observed and participated in a variety of group treatments (inpatient, IOP, and outpatient) settings and observed the need for expanded education and supervision in group therapy. Seeking to address gaps in my own experience with groups, I joined a therapy group with Lou Ormont where I addressed my own self-limiting dynamics and internalized the skill and intuitive powers of an icon in the field of group treatment. This group experience, and the many that followed, inform how I work with the supervision and training groups I conduct on a weekly and biweekly basis in my private practice, in my role as faculty member and supervisor at The Center for Group Studies in New York, and as training analyst at the Institute of Contemporary Psychoanalysis in Los Angeles.

Recent focus on intersectionality and the role of the identity of the therapist on group process and treatment outcomes, led me to study more closely the ways in which my history, training, and identities influence my supervisory practices. One specific focus is how my privileged and marginalized identities (e.g., white, female, cis gender and Jewish) influence how I use my relational power and social power as a group therapist and group supervisor. The application of this additional social lens has enabled me to model and help supervisees learn to intervene with humility and to be accountable for their actions when they result in injury. During supervisory sessions we work to identify and understand the impact of implicit bias in our work as therapists. This approach helps supervisees become more aware and receptive to processing of enactments of societal oppression as they manifest in their groups and in enactments that may occur in our supervisory settings (Stevens and Abernethy, 2018).

References

Haen, C. & Thomas, N. K. (2018). Holding history: Undoing racial unconsciousness in groups. *International Journal of Group Psychotherapy, 68*(4), 498–520. https://doi.org/10.1080/00207 284.2018.1475238

Ormont, L. (1984). The leader's role in resolving resistances to intimacy in the group setting. *International Journal of Group Psychotherapy, 38*(1), 29–45.

Ormont, L. (2001). Training group therapists through the study of countertransferences. In L. Furgeri (Ed.), *The technique of group treatment* (pp. 175–190). Psychosocial Press. (Original work published 1980.)

Stevens, F. & Abernethy, A. (2018). Neuroscience and racism: The power of groups for overcoming implicit bias. *International Journal of Group Psychotherapy, 68*(4), 561–584, https://doi.org/10.1080/ 00207284.2017.1315583

Wright, E. L. (2022). *Use of self and care of self: New directions for working with countertransference*. 50th anniversary of the Philadelphia School of Psychoanalysis, Philadelphia, PA.

Psychodramatic and Sociometric Approaches

Scott Giacomucci

The Structure, Frame, and Format of Group Therapy Consultation

My provision of supervision groups takes place in various settings including ongoing online and in-person supervision groups for group therapists seeking to integrate sociometry and psychodrama methods into their practice. Participants' practice settings vary from private practice, residential programs, intensive outpatients, and multiday workshop offerings. My ongoing online workshops include participants from around the country while my in-person supervision groups are usually contracted by addiction or mental health treatment programs to fulfill supervision requirements for credentialing in experiential therapy. I also offer several multiday workshops for psychodramatists that are designed to provide each participant with supervised practice segments where practitioners receive on-the-spot feedback and evaluation regarding their psychodrama directing competencies.

In my ongoing online groups, the structure involves a brief check-in from each participant about their facilitation experiences since last session, followed by case presentations, experiential demonstrations, and/or discussions of theory, ethics, methodology, and best practices. Some sessions are oriented around specific questions or cases from participants which are encouraged to be sent to me in advance. In supervision groups when there are not many concrete questions, I start with short check-ins and identify any shared concerns or experiences from the check-ins, from which I spontaneously design a sociometric, sociodramatic, or psychodramatic process to address the group's central concerns in action during the session.

In my in-person supervision sessions with the team of an agency, I warm the group up to a specific reoccurring issue emerging in client–staff interactions. Using role play, we will reenact the situation, then utilize doubling (which is when a participant stands next to a role and attempts to articulate what the role is experiencing beneath the surface—for example, "I am feeling helpless and angry" or "Being woken up by staff in treatment gives me flashbacks of my abusive father"). This is done for each of the roles in the scene to deepen our awareness of the potential underlying motivations influencing the outcome of the interaction. After which, we will replay the difficult encounter while experimenting with new ways of intervening with the client while role reversing various staff members into the client role so they can feel and experience the impact of different interventions. This structure provides an expansion of insight and empathy, followed by the experiential learning from practicing new responses and/or witnessing others demonstrate how they might respond to the client in the same situation. This will often result in 5–10 different demonstrated interventions to the same tough client encounter.

My psychodrama directing practice workshops are structured to include one to two hour segments of time designated for each participant to facilitate a psychodrama with the entire group or in a one to one setting which is followed by feedback, teaching, and processing. Occasionally, psychodramas are paused midway through to consider the plethora of psychodrama interventions that could be employed in any given moment. These directing workshops offer on-the-spot supervision and allow me as the supervisor to witness the supervisee's facilitation in real time rather than relying on their verbal account of their facilitation with clients after a session.

The Group Contract

My supervision groups include simple group norms and expectations related to participation, choice, confidentiality, respect, and physical touch. The group goals focus on enhancing facilitation skills in psychodrama, integrating trauma-informed principles into practice, addressing counter-transference issues, working through internal barriers in facilitation, engaging in peer support, and building community.

Stage of Learning of Participants

Participants' experience level varies considerably. One of my online groups is for advanced psychodrama trainees and practitioners (with 300+ training hours) while the other group is for newer trainees in psychodrama. My onsite workshops for treatment teams usually include participants who are experienced group therapists but new to psychodrama. My multiday workshops with supervised practicums tend to incorporate more diversity experience levels in that they may include participants who are already board-certified in psychodrama along with folks completing their first psychodrama directing practice.

Role of the Group Supervisor of Group Psychotherapy

I approach the role of psychodrama group supervisor, through the lens of role theory and the subroles of supervisor (educator, manager, and supporter) and psychodramatist (sociometrist, analyst, therapist, and producer). This means attending to the sociodynamics of the group and facilitating sociometric warm-ups, analyzing the group process while connecting theory to here-and-now experience, leveraging my relationship with participants and use of self, as well as attending to the production elements related to psychodrama. I believe strongly in the idea that "more is caught than taught" (Shulman, 2020) in supervision and that I must demonstrate group leadership and psychodrama competencies in action through my facilitation of the supervision group. In this way, the psychodrama *content* of the supervision is integrated with the psychodramatic supervision *process* and teaching structures.

As a psychodrama supervisor, I am frequently employing sociometric tools within the supervision group to assess group needs, desires, and preferences while identifying and channeling shared warm-ups into an appropriate sociometric, sociodramatic, or psychodramatic process in the group. For example, in the check-in of a recent online session, multiple participants had mentioned feeling burnout, wanting to learn more warm-up tools, and how to utilize psychodrama online. In realizing the central concerns in the group, I facilitated a series of breakout rooms, each with a new prompt that led to the concretization of a new role related to burnout. Prompts were "a strength that can help you address burnout," "something that fuels your burnout," and "something you are willing to commit to doing to address your burnout this week." Each participant utilized small objects in their own space (such as a pen, a piece of candy, a paperclip, a coin, an action figure, etc.) to represent each of these roles for themselves and created a simple miniature psychodrama scene which were then presented to the group individually. Participants volunteered to show and describe their miniature scene and were offered doubling statements from other participants to deepen their experience, insight, and empathy. Doubling in online sessions is the same process as in-person sessions but requires more coordination from the director because the group member doubling can't physically stand next to the person they are doubling online. In the case of an online session like the one described above, I simply invited doubling for the person who shared their scene and give them the opportunity to repeat or change the doubling statements from each of their peers. This structure addressed multiple group needs in a 30–40-minute experiential piece in that it helped address burnout, demonstrated a simple warm-up process as well as multiple psychodrama interventions in an online group.

Here's another recent example of utilizing doubling; this example is from my weekly online supervision group at my outpatient center. A supervisee had a client who expressed gratitude to the therapist for their work together through the recent death of a parent. We were celebrating the supervisee's work with their client and invited doubling for the supervisee. Doubling statements from myself and others included: "I'm proud of the work that I do as a counselor," "my work as a counselor gives me meaning and purpose," and "I'm grateful that I've spent the time to do my own grief work so I could show up for my client in their grief work." The supervisee repeated the statements that felt true, and we all seemed to gradually move into a new level of emotional intimacy together as a group. Then we invited the supervisee to take on the role of their client for a few minutes and we offered doubling statements for the client, which the supervisee repeated or changed based on what he thought would fit for his client. Some of these doubling statements included: "I'm grateful for my therapist," "I don't know how I would have navigated this death without the support of my therapist," and "my therapist's empathy and support helped me feel hopeful in my darkest moments." After which, the therapist derolled from the role of his client and we transitioned into some sharing about how we each connected to the doubling statements. These doubling statements helped us as a group further connect to a deeper sense of purpose and meaning related to the impact that we each have in the lives of our clients. Although it was centered around one supervisee and his specific client, the sharing process expands the focus to each supervisee to consider how they relate based on their own experiences. Doubling is one of the simplest psychodramatic interventions that can be integrated into any session.

Furthermore, as a supervisor, I see my role responsibilities also including the management and teaching of best practices, ethics, and connecting theory and research to practice. In this regard, my supervision session frequently includes discussions of trauma-informed principles, mitigating risks of retraumatization in psychodrama, and either identifying theoretical concepts in action or utilizing psychodramatic theories (such as action theory, spontaneity theory, role theory, sociometric theory, Moreno's theories of catharses, child development, human nature, etc.) to help guide supervisees' group facilitation (Giacomucci, 2023). Psychodrama philosophy elevates spontaneity as the most important quality in therapy, learning, systemic change, and supervision. In the psychodramatic context, spontaneity is specifically defined as the energy we access through a warming-up process that allows us to have a new response to old reoccurring situations or an adequate response to a novel situation. Therefore, the primary purpose of supervision from a psychodrama theoretical lens is to help supervisees and their clients access spontaneity, address barriers to both supervisees' and their clients' spontaneity, and help participants develop adequate and new responses in their work so that they can help their clients develop new and adequate responses in their lives (Giacomucci, 2021). Supervision is essentially spontaneity training.

Psychodrama philosophy also challenges traditional power dynamics between leader and participants in that the therapist is seen as part of the group and clients are seen as therapeutic agents of the group. Similarly, in supervision, I engage the group as a supervisor-learner, encourage supervisees to offer supervisory comments to each other, and conceptualize the group-as-a-whole as both the primary *supervisee* and the *supervisor*. This conceptualization leads to an emphasis on mutual aid, peer support, collaboration, empowerment, and engagement between participants. This approach helps with the embodiment of trauma-informed principles while promoting safety and group cohesion within the supervision group. The resulting group climate is characterized by encouragement, affirmation, and peer support between supervisees.

Training Influences On My Development as a Group Therapy Supervisor

I began my career at age 18 working in inpatient addiction treatment which is almost entirely composed of therapy groups and support groups. Nearly 15 years working in this setting provided me with countless group facilitation opportunities with small groups (5–10), medium groups (10–20), and larger groups (up to 115). After completing my master's in social work training at Bryn Mawr College, which was strongly psychodynamic in nature, I began to specialize in trauma therapy and facilitate trauma-focused groups in inpatient, partial hospitalization, and outpatient settings. At this time, I also dove into psychodrama training which was focused on trauma-specific psychodrama approaches. My integration of sociometry and psychodramatic methods into my groups was highly regarded by clients, which led to more demand. After experiencing and working with various clients/trainees who experienced harm in psychodrama and other trauma therapies, I began to critically reflect on psychodrama practice, supervision, and training and incorporate SAMHSA's trauma-informed principles into all domains of my work. My doctoral studies at the University of Pennsylvania included learning related to social work teaching, supervision, and leadership which helped me to synthesize my roles as psychodramatist and clinical social worker while grounding my work more firmly in research. After being awarded board certification in sociometry, psychodrama, and group psychotherapy, I initiated the 3–4-year process of mentorship to become a psychodrama trainer/supervisor. In this rigorous process, I received intensive supervision and mentorship related to stepping into supervisor and trainer roles in my work. Aside from all of the supervisory role models (good and bad) that I have learned a great deal from, I've also been gifted countless ideas on how to improve my effectiveness from supervisees, students, and clients. Frequent and ongoing check-ins, feedback forms, sociometric explorations, outcome evaluations, and research studies have proven invaluable in my professional development. I feel that my supervision groups, training groups, classrooms, and therapy groups have been my best supervisors.

References

Giacomucci, S. (2021). *Social work, sociometry, and psychodrama: Experiential approaches for group therapists, community leaders, and social workers*. Springer Nature.

Giacomucci, S. (2023). *Trauma-informed principles in group therapy, psychodrama, and organizations: Action methods for leadership*. Routledge.

Shulman, L. (2020). *Interactional supervision* (4th ed.). NASW Press.

A Supportive Approach for Working with Lower Functioning Veterans

Les R. Greene

The Structure, Frame, and Format of Group Therapy Consultation

Both the psychotherapy groups and the supervision of those groups occur within the outpatient mental health clinic of a VA medical center. The psychotherapy groups are "slow open" groups composed of lower functioning veterans—male, older, low socioeconomic status, various races and ethnicities—many of whom have participated in these weekly sessions for years. In fact, patients tend to remain in the groups unless they move from the area or die; there are virtually no drop outs. For almost all, the groups represent both a stable and stabilizing space providing affirmation of self despite some idiosyncrasies that are typically less tolerated in the larger society. They provide a sense of connection, including a unifying and salient shared social identity as a "wounded warrior" for people who live relatively impoverished psychosocial lives.

The supervisees are third-year Yale psychiatry residents, working as cotherapists in these groups on a yearly rotation. Some years the supervision group is composed of three pairs of residents, in other years two pairs.

Adding to the complexity of the supervisory group is the supervisory team, composed of myself and two attending psychiatrists, an arrangement designed to best fit the multiple roles the residents assume in this work, namely psychotherapist, psychopharmacologist, and physician. The team follows a loose division of labor, with me assuming primary authority for supervision of group psychotherapy per se and the two attending physicians supervising such issues as medications and medical concerns to the extent they arise within the sessions. Of course, we aim at being flexible with this role differentiation as a way of modeling for the residents how to link or integrate these different kinds of work.

In the initial sessions of the supervisory group in July, we offer a brief introduction to the work of these therapy groups with an emphasis on (1) observing and thinking about the individual patients, particularly in terms of their ego functions such as capacity for adaptive coping and reality orientation and the quality and nature of their relationships, (2) needing to monitor and shape group climate and cultures such as levels of cohesion and engagement (Kaklauskas & Greene, 2020) and (3) appreciating the distinguishing features of and rationale for supportive psychotherapy (cf. Winston, 2014). We also offer an orientation to the work of the supervisory group, particularly the rationale for supervising in a group with its inherent opportunities to learn from peers and to experience and explore group processes in the here-and-now. Other than asking that they provide room for each of the therapy groups to be discussed within the session, the how, why and what of the material to be presented is left to them.

The Group Contract

The residents are oriented to the reality that their work roles—both as cotherapists in the clinical groups and as participants in the supervisory group—are authorized jointly by Yale and the VA, two large and intersecting systems which have implications for what and how they learn. More particularly, they are reminded that, as part of the training requirements of the Yale psychiatry residency program, they are periodically evaluated regarding their developing competencies by all faculty involved in their training. They are invited to explore this evaluation process in the supervision group. In addition, clinical requirements set forth by the VA, such as record keeping and treatment coordination, are reviewed. Because the group psychotherapy and its supervision are embedded within the highly complex VA system, a number of structural and systemic issues are identified that also can be explored within the supervisory group, issues such as confidentiality and its limits, the role relationships of each resident to other clinical staff who may be treating the same patients, and the possibility of dual relationships where residents might serve not only as group therapist to the patients in their groups, but also in other roles such as psychopharmacologist or individual psychotherapist. All of these boundary issues are grist for the mill and the residents are explicitly invited to explore them as legitimate part of the work within the supervisory group. Finally, the role relationships of the cotherapists and of the residents' relationships to their cohort in the VA are further areas that can be explored within the supervisory group.

Stage of Learning of Participants

The residents share an intellectual prowess—they are smart, motivated to excel in their professional and academic pursuits, and already quite accomplished. And while they all share considerable clinical experience, having come through two years of hands-on work in a variety of medical settings, their foundational knowledge of psychotherapy in general and of group psychotherapy in particular is usually quite limited, knowing only the basics such as some superficial distinctions between CBT and what Yale refers to as "insight oriented" therapy. And their actual psychotherapy experience at this point is also quite limited, perhaps serving as a junior cotherapist in a manual-driven, technique-oriented CBT group. Most pertinently and challenging for the work of supervision is the considerable variation in their possessing a psychological mindedness, as it is manifested in enthusiasm and aptitude for thinking about such matters as how the mind works, what processes bring about psychological change, and, most importantly, openness to their own inner worlds. Relatedly, it is important for the supervisors to appreciate the fact that not all the residents are deeply interested in practicing psychotherapy or becoming a psychotherapist. The PGY3 year provides an ideal opportunity for the residents to sort out what professional trajectories they wish to pursue; psychotherapy, research, administration, community outreach are among the many roles and identities that can be developed. Our aim is to provide the residents with a meaningful experience into the world of group psychotherapy precisely to help them sort out whether this is to be part of their professional identity; for a few, group work has become a core part of who they are professionally (cf. Rosenstein & Yopp, 2022)

The Role of Group Supervisor of Group Psychotherapy

My primary effort in their early work on learning psychotherapy is to promote a genuine curiosity about the material, whether it be hypothesizing what a "problematic" patient in the group is actually wanting, developing an understanding of why a female cotherapist is feeling devalued or patronized in the group, or why the group-as-a-whole is feeling deadened and boring and what to do about it. It is less about learning specific technique and more about developing an analytic attitude and some conceptual tools to help guide psychological exploration at the individual, interpersonal, group and contextual levels. We attempt to evolve a culture in the supervisory group away from mere reporting of who said what and toward a more meaning-making illumination of the processes within the therapy groups, within the individual patients, within the selves of the residents, and within the supervisory group.

Of course, our invitation to the residents to explore requires an appreciation of potential countervailing forces not to know and to avoid feelings or thoughts that may be unpleasant. The risk-taking inherent in psychological exploration requires instilling a sense of safety and modeling exploratory behavior. We monitor the group climate in the supervisory group—the spirit of shared exploration and engagement and, conversely, resistances to learning. We have come to appreciate how resident training up to this point can foster certain forms of resistance that are in opposition to the values and aims of supervision. To wit, we can identify these obstacles to thinking about supportive group therapy in our particular setting as tendencies to (1) be symptom-focused as opposed to exploring the inner worlds of the patients and the group, (2) be individual-focused as opposed to witnessing interpersonal and group-as-a-whole processes, (3) be content-focused (as in merely reporting who said what) as opposed to understanding why patients were saying what they were saying, (4) assuming a strictly objective focus as opposed to appreciating the value of subjective experience in self and others, and (5) taking a medical model approach with an overreliance on symptom description and medication management as opposed to a more integrative biopsychosocial orientation. A related resistance that we have witnessed is a subtle devaluing of the enterprise, an unspoken belief that working with lower functioning veterans in long-term supportive therapy is merely a rather unsophisticated kind of "cheerleading," without appreciation of how the work not only provides ongoing stabilization, thus reducing the need for more intensive treatments, but also some actual enhancements of psychosocial functioning. Effectiveness of the supervisory effort is assessed, to a significant degree, in how these prepotent tendencies to distance oneself from the work are modified over the course of the training year so that, as we have frequently witnessed, the supervisory group shifts from a highly regimented, turn taking objective reporting of content to a more spontaneous, interactive, and reflective space.

While there no formal didactics within the supervisory group experience, conceptual tools are introduced organically when they can be usefully applied to and expand upon the material being presented. In particular, three domains are emphasized, the first being the full range of ego functions such as those that facilitate a stable and enduring sense of self, a cognitively and affectively rich internal world, a meaningful and realistic set of connections to others, and the capacities to adaptively endure stress and frustration. At the level of the group entity, we invite exploration of the group processes, both those that promote the experience of the group as a safe, cohesive and coherent psychological space and those that are experienced as disruptive and disturbing. Finally, we draw attention to specific therapist techniques to facilitate optimal functional capacity for each veteran and promote a safe and inviting group space. Here we distinguish more dynamic interventions such as interpretative or confrontive ones that address material not fully conscious but that are not suited for this kind of supportive group work from interventions that encourage, affirm, support and model adaptive ways of being in the group and in the world. This is not to say that we don't encourage the supervisees to think dynamically and deeply about what is going on at the individual, interpersonal, group and contextual levels, but not to intervene in this way. Succinctly stated, our mantra is to "think dynamically but intervene supportively." So, for example, at the periods of transition, where the new cotherapist pair enter the group in July and terminate from the group the following June, the veterans often resort to denial and counter-dependency to cope with the anxiety of the unfamiliar and the sense of impending loss by asserting that their role vis-à-vis the residents is to "train" them how to be therapists, a reversed role relationship that serves to empower them and limit feelings of vulnerability. This dynamic is explored in the supervisory group to help the residents experience and understand the process and, importantly, not internalize or take these dynamics personally. Another frequent kind of work in the supervisory group is explore veterans' cultural values and enactments, as manifested in what are often stereotyped views of women, authority, doctors, and various sociopolitical groups, views that can clash with the residents' views of their own personal and professional identities. Here too the supervision invites the trainees to explore their feelings about these differing worldviews without judgment or defensiveness, manage potential counter-transference reactivity, and help them appreciate what these values serve for the veterans.

Training Influences On My Development as a Group Therapy Supervisor

Naïve would certainly not be an underestimate of my understanding of such ideas as group process, group dynamics, and group therapy before beginning my graduate studies at Yale in the late 1960s. Not that I hadn't had experiences in groups and leadership positions earlier in my life—editor of my high school newspaper, president of my youth group, cub scouts, little league baseball, to name a few. But my initiation into the serious study of group life occurred in the fall of 1967 when a fellow graduate student asked if I wanted to join a T-group led by one of the Yale psychology faculty. "Tea group" I thought, how nice. Tea and biscuits in a stately office situated in the revered Institute of Human Relations. Clearly an invitation to join the club. But like many an initiation, there was shock and awe. I soon discovered that the invitation was not an exercise in esteem enhancement and comradery among fellow Yalies, but rather an offer to join a Tavistock self-study group. No tea and no biscuits here, only deep and mind-blowing interpretations about our frustrated dependency longings onto the idealized but unavailable mother-leader.

As I soon subsequently learned, Yale in that era was one of a very few strongholds of scholarly and practical efforts into the study of group dynamics. First as a member and then as a consultant, I participated in a number of group relations conferences, run collaboratively by the Departments of Psychology and Psychiatry and the School of Nursing. I took advantage of the many opportunities to continue my deep dive into group life throughout my graduate work. I joined the "Group on Groups," a loosely organized assemblage of Yale faculty and graduate students interested in discussing group topics. I embarked on research into group process, my very first publication exploring where group members sat in relation to the leader as a function of their needs for fusion versus differentiation. Finishing graduate and postdoctoral work at Yale, I joined the faculty of UC Davis Department of Psychiatry where I cotaught courses on group dynamics and group therapy. And when I was invited back to New Haven in 1981 to assume positions at the VA and Yale, I continued what was destined to become a career-long interest in the study of group life. Among my work activities, a role that I have now spent over four decades pursuing, is my supervising and training Yale PGY3 psychiatry residents in group therapy, as described above.

References

Kaklauskas, F. & Greene, L. R. (Eds.) (2020). *Core principles of group psychotherapy: An integrated theory, research, and practice training manual*. Routledge.

Rosenstein, D. L. & Yopp, J. M. (2022). *The group: Seven widowed fathers reimagine life*. Oxford University Press.

Winston, A. (2014). Supportive psychotherapy. In R. E. Hales, S. C. Yudofsky, & L. W. Roberts (Eds.), *The American Psychiatric Publishing textbook of psychiatry* (6th ed., pp. 1161–1186). American Psychiatric Publishing.

A Systems-Centered Approach

Susan P. Gantt

Structure, Frame, and Format of Systems-Centered Group Therapy Consultation

All Systems-Centered Therapy (SCT) consultation begins with "My problem is I ... ." This phrase provides a structure for closing the boundary to comprehensive explanations and instead opening the boundary for exploring and apprehensive discovery. This structure provides an alternative fork to our human tendency to explain our problems at the expense of exploring what we do not yet know. The goal of SCT consultation is to enable consultees to discover the conflict or issue or problem in themselves that they are externalizing onto the client, for example, their personal projections (Agazarian, 1999). SCT sees the dynamics of groups and individuals as isomorphic, that is, similar in structure and function. Hence, SCT hypothesizes that an isomorphic version of the supervisee's problem with their group will surface in the supervisory system, especially when the boundary is closed to explaining and "talking about" and the supervisee is vectored to discovering their problem.

For example, when the consultee discovers: "My problem is I ... am anxious," the SCT consultant then introduces SCT's protocol for undoing anxiety.[1] Once the anxiety is lowered, the consultee is asked to see how their identified problem (e.g., "I am anxious") relates to the phase of their group's development (e.g., anxiety signals the flight subphase), that is, isomorphy (similarity of structure and function) for systems in a nested hierarchy. SCT consultants hypothesize that all living human systems have the goals of *survival* by maintaining the status quo, *development* which requires opening to similarities in the apparently different, and *transformation*. In consultation consultees are likely to replicate the survivor roles which are activated in their group's phase of development. Once the problem and phase context are clear, consultees learn to identify the type of intervention most likely to support system development in their work with the group. SCT interventions are either *structural* (modifying boundary permeability by weakening noise in the communication), *functional* (enabling discrimination and integration of differences with functional subgrouping), *vectoring* toward a goal where the supervisee chooses what fork to explore first, and *contextualizing* by developing an awareness of the phase of development as the context both for the group-system and the work of consultation.

All of these interventions support "the major goal of the SCT supervisory approach: to work in such a way that the supervisees' insights into their own restraining forces will be isomorphic with the work that is being done in their groups" (Agazarian, 1999, p. 228). At the end of the consultation, the consultee rates their satisfaction with the consultation on a scale of 1–10 where 10 is high. When the score is below 10, the consultee is asked what restraining forces they would need to weaken next time around to have their full satisfaction. This structure orients members toward the norm of taking active membership in the consultation in the service of their learning. After each consultation, both the individual and the group share surprises, learnings, satisfactions, dissatisfactions and discoveries. This gives all members a chance for joining in resonance and integrating new learnings.

SCT consultation puts into practice Agazarian's theory of living human systems, which defines a hierarchy of isomorphic systems that are energy-organizing, goal-directing, and system-correcting. The basic hierarchy in any SCT group is defined as a nested triad: system-as-a-whole, member-system/subgroup-system and person-system. The consultation process itself builds system-as-a-whole norms in which the restraining forces can be weakened toward discovering and identifying the central consultation issues.

The Role of Group Consultant

I supervise group leaders both in group and individual consultation using SCT's consultation framework. I also include time for consultation in all of my SCT training groups. For example, one SCT group meets twice a year for three days in person. Between group meetings, we meet on video calls to explore theory or do consultation. I lead two other SCT training groups that include one hour for consultation in the six-hour training days where members learn both by getting consultation and taking the role of giving SCT consultation.

SCT introduces the phrase "role, goal and context" as a pathway for contextualizing, which lowers our human pull to personalizing. In SCT consultation groups, I first ask: "Who would like to *get* a consultation today? And who would like to practice *giving* one? Who would like to observe?" These questions orient the group to our system context (a consultation group), and its learning goals (getting and giving consultation) and to the roles of consultant (giving consultation), consultee (getting consultation) or observer (learning to see the whole consultation system and its isomorphy with the client context). In a recent group, three members wanted consultations, three others then volunteered to be consultants and two claimed the role of observer. Having the three roles available supports learning from different roles with different goals. Each consultee in turn picks one of the available consultants. The learning is usually quite rich in all three roles. In my group leader role, I set the time boundaries and consult to the consultant either when they ask for consultation or when I notice the structure is being dropped.

As all SCT work starts with centering[2] into the present, the member taking the role of consultant asks the consultee whether they want to center on their own or have the consultant lead them both in centering. Naming this fork-in-the-road gives the consultee an active choice, again building the consulting system norms to support active membership. SCT's centering introduces a structure in which all members sit centered by sensing one's body, and the energy from the earth and the universe as a way to shift out of everyday roles and into an exploratory role in contact with one's bodily experience and knowing. Connection to our energy fuels our membership roles whatever our context or role, that is, as consultant, consultee, or observer. In more advanced consultation groups, I offer the option of taking the "consultant to the consultant" role with me available to consult. Once the system of consultant and consultee are centered, the consultant orients the consultee to the structure of "My problem is I … ."

Consultant to Consultee. Start with the words "My problem is I …" and say the words slowly so that you can use each word as a steppingstone for dropping from your head and thinking into your center where you can sense. Prepare to be surprised about what you discover about your problem. I will say "My problem is I …" with you, you start and I will follow.

Tracking closely, the consultant restarts the process whenever the consultee pauses for more than a few seconds or looks up, both of which signal the pull to "explaining" at the expense of exploratory discovery, for example, the consultant interrupts the human pull to explain one's problem (a "flight" restraining force) or blame the client or group (a "fight" restraining force) and restarts the journey of "My problem is I …" to discover so that the consultee can discover what they do not yet know. This is a fundamental fork-in-the-road in SCT, the fork between "explaining" which takes us to what we think or know already and exploring which takes us to the "edge of the unknown" which is the place of all potential discovery. This fundamental fork is first introduced in the flight phase of all SCT work.

The Role of Group Leader as Consultant

SCT group consultants build the group-system context in which the consultee is supported to "address the different levels of transference manifestations by modifying the specific constellation of defense [restraining forces] … in the context of the subphase of development that elicits them" (Agazarian, 1999, p. 229). Drawing from Lewin (1951), SCT redefines each phase of system development as a force field of driving and restraining forces. In all SCT work, the consultant works to weaken the simpler restraining forces in the flight subphase first, enabling reality-testing before working with fight phase restraining forces and in turn the more complex work with survivor roles in the phase of roles and role locks. This work prepares the consultation group to recognize and explore their authority issue as it impedes taking their own authority as group leaders. It is only after the work of exploring the authority issue as it arises in the consultation context that the consultation group transitions to the challenges of how to weaken their restraining forces related to separation and individuation and then the ongoing work of norm-setting in role, goal and context (cf. Gantt et.al., 2021).

The Group Contract

Rather than a contract, SCT consultation groups establish group norms, for example, doing our human best to attend all sessions, to start and stop on time, undoing "yes, but" communications and finding out which side of the "yes, but" fork the consultee wants to explore first. This fork opens the door to explore conflicts which SCT operationally defines as two subgroups. All SCT groups use functional subgrouping whenever there is a difference, exploring both sides of the conflict one at a time until the differences can be integrated. SCT sees the process of discriminating and integrating differences as the essential work of development for all living human systems. Using the SCT structure of "My problem is I …" is a commitment to opening to the unknown where all discovery happens (which often surfaces a conflict or a restraining force for opening to the unknown) and discovering instead of explaining (which blocks us from the unknown). Working with these norms puts SCT into practice and is based on the theoretical foundations that underlie SCT, that is, that all living human systems survive, develop and transform through the process of discriminating and integrating similarities and differences—both differences in the apparently similar and similarities in the apparently different (Agazarian, 1997).

Stages of Learning of Participants

Participants have varying levels of experience, training and knowledge of group therapy, and some are new to SCT. In consultation, more experienced members typically volunteer to be a consultant while less experienced members often start by taking the role of consultee. The advantage of group consultation is that members learn from each other whether in the role of observer, consultant or consultee.[3] Consultation is an essential context for this learning. SCT is based on theory and every intervention tests the validity of the theory and the reliability of the practice. SCT trainees are encouraged to see their groups and group members from the lens of a theory of living human systems, for example, the whole-system of the group as the context for the member-system and subgroup-system roles, which in turn is the context for the person-system.

Contextualizing is the antidote to personalizing both for group leaders and members. I often remind members in consultation that who they can be in working with their groups has more to do with the group and its phase of development than just with the group thera-pist's skill and resources. Learning to see ourselves as leaders and our group members as voices for subgroups in the context of the group-system-as-a-whole and its phase of devel-opment is a vital step in the ongoing learning to be SCT group leaders.

Training Influences On My Development as a Group Therapy Supervisor

My first group experience was as an undergraduate in the early 1970s when I attended a 24-hour T-group led by Charlie Holland, the clinical psychologist at my college. He was influenced by National Training Laboratory (NTL), which had been spawned by Kurt Lewin's work in small group effectiveness and community building. Working with Charlie led me to attend some group trainings with the Mid-Atlantic Training, an affiliate of NTL. Some years later I participated in a psychodynamic training group for many years with David Hawkins (a former president of AGPA). David recommended Yvonne Agazarian's institute at AGPA which I attended in 1991. Soon after this, I actively sought out SCT with Yvonne, continuing my training, learning and collaborating with her until her death in 2017. Yvonne was a highly skilled group therapist yet just as important, if not more, are her contributions in her theorizing where she integrated the work of psychoanalysis and systems thinking along with the work of Lewin (1951), Shannon and Weaver (1964), and Bennis and Shepard (1956). AGPA was an invaluable context for Yvonne over many years as she developed a theory of living human systems with operational definitions of each theoretical construct that put the theory into practice in SCT and training (Agazarian, 1997).

References

Agazarian, Y. M. (1997). *Systems-centered therapy for groups.* Guilford. Reprinted in paperback (2004: Karnac Books).

Agazarian, Y. M. (1999). Systems-centered supervision. *International Journal of Group Psychotherapy, 49*(2), 215–236. https://doi.org/10.1080/00207284.1999.11491582

Bennis, W. G. & Shepard, H. A. (1956). A theory of group development. *Human Relations, 9*(4), 415–437. https://doi.org/10.1177/001872675600900403

Gantt, S. P., Carter, F., Gibbons, D., & Hartford, R. (2021, October). *Systems-centered training & therapy: Seeing the system, not just people. Commemorating the work of Yvonne Agazarian.* Systems-Centered Training & Research Institute. https://youtu.be/KWm762r7sAM

Lewin, K. (1951). *Field theory in social science.* Harper & Row.

Shannon, C. E. & Weaver, W. (1964). *The mathematical theory of communication.* University of Illinois Press.

Systems-Centered Training and Research Institute. (2011). *SCT foundation manual.*

An Integrative Approach for Working with Adolescents

Leah M. Niehaus

The Structure, Frame, and Format of Group Therapy Consultation

I run a supervision group of five prelicensed clinicians and one licensed clinician; some lead groups, while others do individual therapy. We meet weekly for supervision and also have a once monthly supervision solely dedicated to the supervision of leading group therapy with adolescents, and have an additional group therapy supervision once monthly for two hours where we focus solely on group work. Group therapy questions and concerns are welcome at any supervision gathering.

Members are all employees in my group practice and work together daily. We offer open-ended process groups for elementary kids, adolescents, and young adults. In order to lead adolescent groups effectively, it is important that the clinician is up for a challenge and enjoys the developmental stage of adolescence. They must be able to relate and build rapport easily with teens and have appropriate boundaries while knowing how to professionally self-disclose. They must be adept at risk assessment, management of a diverse group of young people, capable of handling ruptures or crises in group, curious, and have a sense of humor. It is rewarding to run adolescent groups, but it is also demanding and challenging!

There is a rhythm and consistency to the structure and frame of clinical supervision in my practice. We often do a check-in as we settle into supervision; often there is a learning/teaching/didactic instruction component, and they do case presentations/group therapy presentations. Each clinician touches on challenging cases each week, but we also rotate each person doing a formal lengthy case presentation on occasion where we review symptoms, differential diagnosis, treatment planning concerns, and transference/counter-transference. We also rotate each clinician teaching the group a particular skill (like a DBT concept), an expressive arts activity, or leading a discussion around a topic (like cultural humility). They can select what they would like to teach or demonstrate to the supervision group. In addition, I like to incorporate inspired clinical supervision techniques—and often weave in creative exercises, "sculpting" a challenging clinical issue, considering a clinical vignette, utilizing journaling, exploring activities to awaken clinical intuition, watching a few minutes of a training or TED talk, bringing in current research from the field, doing a guided meditation, or practicing a technique that we might use with our clients or in our groups. When clinical supervision feels heavy, we end with a closure script to help us settle, center ourselves, and leave the work in the space for further healing.

I like to run group therapy supervision as a parallel process to what group therapy can be like. I utilize some of the same techniques (bridging, taking risks, building authentic connection, processing rupture/repair, setting goals, etc.) when running group therapy supervision. I focus on exploring Highs/Lows, Wins/Fails, building trust, facilitating hope, encouraging cultural curiosity and cultural humility, and sometimes I sit back and observe the process. I model some of the group leader characteristics that I hope for them to learn and use in their work conducting group therapy. The more a supervisee feels supported and challenged in clinical supervision, the better outcomes for their clients in their groups.

The Group Contract

From the outset, I establish a contract with supervisees for our supervision group. These expectations include: regular attendance and participation, coming prepared to discuss cases/dynamics/challenges/successes, respecting confidentiality, and having a shared goal to learn together. I foster a warm and supportive atmosphere, where clinicians can be vulnerable and share their hopes and overwhelm with each other throughout their time together. Our primary goal is to become better group therapists.

Prior to leading groups in my practice, clinicians must have some knowledge about group work and some experience leading/coleading/or shadowing in groups. I encourage clinicians to shadow/or colead some of my groups and other more experienced group clinicians in my practice, so they can observe our styles and learn some basic techniques. Consent is gathered from group participants or their parents before this occurs. I also prompt my clinicians to do online training through AGPA, watch the GROUP YouTube show, listen to podcasts regarding group therapy, read about the topic, and participate in an experiential group process experience for therapists (for which I pay). We also explore their reflections on their own experiences in groups over the years—their family group, consult groups, training groups, book clubs, church groups, or their own group therapy experiences. They can begin participating in group therapy supervision before they get a group off the ground, so they can learn and become more immersed in challenges inherent to running effective groups.

Part of the group contract is to be regularly evaluated and open to feedback. Formal evaluations are important to enhance learning and professional development, as an opportunity to set goals and mediate challenges with the supervisee and promote an open dialogue regarding their clinical work and the supervisory relationship. I encourage clinicians to periodically offer their clients a Group Session Rating Scale to rate how they feel about group therapy. It's helpful to incorporate this feedback from clients and it's useful to me when writing evaluations and trying to assess clinical progress of clients and professional development of the supervisee (especially as I don't typically colead groups with my supervisees or have a one-way mirror to observe their work). I like to incorporate the Working Alliance Inventory and the Supervision Feedback Form to explore feelings about the supervisory relationship as well.

Stage of Learning of Participants

The supervisees have varied over the years in terms of their clinical experience, training in group therapy, self-awareness, and professional development. Some have been very "green"—with virtually no exposure or knowledge of group therapy, but with a willing attitude to learn. Some have been more seasoned and can jump into leading groups with more confidence. Some had a group therapy course in grad school, some had internship experience where they were exposed to group work, and some had no exposure whatsoever. I try to supplement their gaps in learning or experience and give them opportunities to shadow and further their understanding of leading groups. In reality, the best training truly comes from the opportunity to run or colead groups—such a rich learning environment when one is cast into the waters and has to figure out how to swim!

The Role of Group Supervisor of Group Psychotherapy

I have always taken an integrative approach to group therapy supervision. The supervisory models that feel natural to me include: a Developmental approach, a Psychodynamic approach, and the Person-of-the-Therapist approach. I have a strengths-based and culturally humble stance in my work with supervisees. I've been particularly drawn to the following ideas that guide my supervision of developing clinicians:

- We all grow. Supervision evolves as supervisees gain experience, competence, self-assurance, and self-reliance. The goal is for the supervisee to become less dependent on the supervisor over time.
- We are all impacted by the content and process in group therapy. It can be helpful to attune to affective reactions, defense mechanisms, transference, and counter-transference.
- Supervisees have the capacity to effectively develop as a therapist; supervisor can be viewed as a collaborator.

- The past and unconscious can influence here-and-now behavior, thinking, and choices.
- Clinical supervision should prepare the therapist to make active and purposeful use of who they are, personally and professionally, in all aspects of the therapeutic process. Use of whole self is encouraged.
- Group therapy supervision is a parallel process to group therapy. Supervisees should leave feeling validated, more inspired and supported, learn from hearing each other's experiences leading groups, feel less alone, and that they have a dedicated space to work on their own developmental goals.

Being a group leader is complex, nuanced, and requires much of the clinician to hold the space effectively for a group of clients. Being a group therapy supervisor is equally complicated and layered in its demands. It has helped me to think about three functions of group therapy supervision: Normative (management), Formative (learning), and Restorative (support). I view my primary role to provide the oversight of clinical performance of staff so that our clients receive the best care and outcomes. I feel that it is my legal, ethical, and clinical responsibility to review documentation, listen to case presentations, assist with timing of interventions, manage critical incidents and ruptures that can occur in groups, and aid with the development and modification of treatment goals. There are administrative responsibilities that I attend to in my role as well—marketing for our groups, selecting which staff to run which groups, and providing training opportunities.

It's important for me to ensure that there is effective communication within our supervision group, between supervisee-client, and the broader community in which we live that sends referrals to our practice. I am always attending to how the individual supervisees are developing over time, how the therapy group dynamics are progressing, and how our supervision group works together on the tasks at hand. I encourage sharing, risk-taking, flexibility, self-compassion, and patience. I strive to build their competence and their confidence, facilitate greater self-awareness, assist with skillful self-disclosure, and help them learn to remain emotionally regulated while leading groups.

Training Influences On My Development as a Group Therapy Supervisor

I attended Pepperdine University in the 1990s, majoring in sociology. From the beginning, I was interested in what happened *between people* more than I was interested in what happened *within a person*. I was fascinated by the study of human social behavior, social groups, and social systems—including factors like class, race, gender, and culture. I gained experience working with youth on probation, youth in low-income schools, homeless families, and foster youth. I went on to receive my Masters in Social Work at California State University, Long Beach. During that time, I was exposed to more in-depth learning of psychology, community organization, public policy, social institutions, child and family welfare, clinical social work, and group psychotherapy.

During my first year in graduate school, my field practicum experience was at a small community service agency. It was a rich learning experience where I was able to conduct individual therapy sessions and colead many group therapies. During my year, I co-led Gang Diversion Groups in an alternative school, Teen Mother Groups in a Catholic high school, Domestic Violence Victims' Groups, Child Abusers' Groups (for those parents involved in the public child welfare system), and Batterers' Treatment Groups. During this formative year, I was supervised and influenced by an Licensed Clinical Social Worker (LCSW) with a psychodynamic and systems perspective. I was drawn to depth, insight, how the unconscious shapes present behavior, self-awareness, how early life and relationships shape current functioning, and connections between individuals and their wider world. It was here that my love and appreciation of group therapy developed.

After graduation, I worked for three years in public child welfare with foster youth and their families. I worked to reunify families, testified in juvenile court, and helped children become adopted if they were not able to return to their birth families. I then began working as a clinical social worker at UCLA Neuropsychiatric Hospital in 2001, on the Child Inpatient Psych Unit and then the Adolescent Inpatient Psych Unit and Eating Disorders Unit. I was the family therapist assigned to the children on our units and occasionally I would get to lead the adolescent inpatient process groups. I was gaining my clinical hours during this time and it was an abundant environment to be in group supervision with other clinicians and to participate in daily "rounds" with the treatment team of doctors, nurses, clinicians, speech therapists, occupational therapists, and recreational therapists. I was exposed to cognitive behavioral therapy, psychodynamic perspectives, and family systems perspectives. I had a psychodynamically trained LCSW supervisor that was inspiring for me and continues to be a mentor to this day. It was during this time at UCLA that I became licensed and grasped the value of group supervision, training, and consultation.

In 2005, I started my own private practice primarily working with adolescents, young adults, and their families. In 2012, I found that I missed group work and that this was an area of need in our community so, I began offering adolescent process groups in my private practice. I earned my Certified Group Psychotherapy designation and have been active in the AGPA and Group Psychotherapy Association of Los Angeles over the years. My groups became popular and continue to be sought out today—my practice now offers seven different group therapy options for youth and young adults each week. I began to provide clinical supervision in 2013 as a field instructor for MSW graduate students. This led to me taking on my first associate in private practice in 2016 and my practice has now grown to a group practice with five associates and one licensed clinician. As my practice grew, and our group therapy offerings increased, I became more intentional around group therapy supervision. For my staff, I offer individual/triadic/group supervision and group therapy supervision for those running groups.

A Contextual, Ideographic, and Pragmatic Approach

Francis Kaklauskas

Structure, Frame, and Format of Group Psychotherapy Supervision

The contextual, ideographic, and pragmatic approach to group psychotherapy supervision developed from my varied clinical and supervisory experiences. While uncovering the ideal universal group method would be comforting, I found that flexibility and pragmatism were essential due to various commix factors: the embedding organization's theoretical approach, the unique composition of each group, and individual members' needs, identities, and histories (Kaklauskas & Nettles, 2019). Although many theories and evidence-based approaches have strengths in addressing specific goals, rarely were they a perfect fit for every group or individual.

Diverse identities, values, beliefs, histories, and cultural norms mark each group and its members. Crenshaw's (1991) work on intersectionality invites us to examine how we label and categorize individuals and collectives. Cultural histories, language, and power structures shape our field's taxonomies, and within any group identification, differences remain. While labels are unavoidable and often valuable, we must also examine their potential limitations. Postmodern pragmatist traditions encourage us to consider multiple lenses and acknowledge that our understanding of knowledge is unavoidably shaped by personal and cultural subjectivities (Rorty, 1991).

Over a century ago, William James (1890) introduced pragmatism to psychology and wondered if certainty was ever attainable in our field. He felt we could move toward increasingly accurate and beneficial understandings through continuous research informed by various methodologies, new theory building, and critical analysis. Data points can be examined for their specific relevance to the presenting situation, correspondence with other views, and consideration of potential confounds.

However, the group psychotherapy tradition has generally yet to centralize the pragmatic, contextual, and ideographic traditions. Psychology is often many years behind important cultural paradigms suggested by philosophy and art. At this point, the significant paradigmatic shifts proposed in language, process, and postmodern philosophies and art have only been explored in a very limited way by the group field. However, advances in global psychology and increased awareness of traditional and Indigenous healing practices and ways of knowing have expanded the possibilities for clinicians. However, group psychotherapy evolved from and has remained primarily grounded in the post-enlightenment modernist framework of explaining phenomena by seeking more universal and often reductionistic paradigms.

Currently, the sheer volume of models and research findings can overwhelm contemporary group psychotherapists. While each model provides vital guidance, each has been shaped, and perhaps limited, by their cultural zeitgeists (Kaklauskas et al., 2021). Each model can also be challenged with potential confounds and inevitable exceptions. Despite this postmodern dilemma of competing narratives and explanations, group clinicians and supervisors must choose how to proceed. We are invited to recognize the unavoidable filters embedded in our ideas and the complexity of our clients toward finding beneficial actions.

An argument can be made that faithfully conducting an empirically supported targeted model toward a specific outcome (e.g., symptom reduction) will be, in many circumstances, positively impactful. Others prefer staying closely aligned with one theoretical view. The contextual supervision model asks what may be missing within these paradigms and what other approaches or adjustments may be beneficial while not being deleterious. If some modification seems prudent, group leaders can take comfort in the overwhelming evidence of group psychotherapy effectiveness when conducted ethically with foundational group practices and principles (Hewitt & Liew, 2023; Whittingham et al., 2023). The supervision group is an excellent format for creatively addressing challenges while critically analyzing what approaches or modifications may increase beneficial outcomes and reduce the risks of ineffective or harmful impacts.

Group Contract

Contracts, built upon the work of Hobbes and other philosophers, have been critiqued for the classically liberal ideal of equality that may discount oppressive forces acting upon some societal positions (Mills, 1997; Pateman, 1988). The foundational understanding of *contracts* evolved from a culture with worldviews much different than our current contexts. *Contracts* can also be a signifier of binding legal or rigid moral obligations. *Agreements*, often used in group literature, represent wording that feels more collaborative, dynamic, and less authoritarian (Rutan et al., 2014). Agreements can be renegotiated to address a group's and even a specific member's needs.

Although these supervision groups have a clinical focus, members may share more about their personal lives than in other supervision formats. Clinical challenges, such as countertransference, may be seeded by the clinician's history or current life events. No specific structure is required to present cases, and variety is promoted. These groups often alternate between discussing a particular case and broader themes, such as boundaries, ethics, change processes, and the therapist's experience. While the content and even processes can be expansive, the general group structural agreements follow traditional practices. The groups meet for 85 minutes weekly or biweekly; confidentiality is required, and attention and focus are shared across all members over time. Often, the members stay in these groups for many years, and despite differences in identities and ideas, they experience the group as a supportive community.

Stage of Learning of Participants

While I have used similar supervision models in many agency and academic settings, I currently conduct private practice supervision groups. Members often have had some in-depth training from a specific tradition but eventually have felt limited with their current approaches and desire to understand the work from other perspectives. This model may be better suited for therapists with some clinical experience than those who would benefit from an introduction to foundational principles and common functional skills (Barlow, 2013). Membership requires emotional maturity, including curiosity rather than defensiveness, empathy, the ability to tolerate ambiguity and complexity, and personal, clinical, and cultural humility. A typical group composition may include individuals with backgrounds in existential therapy, social justice, modern analysis, gestalt, somatic approaches, and time-limited manualized approaches.

This model addresses two foundational supervision goals: client well-being and supporting supervisees' professional growth (Watkins et al., 2021). Group members may enter with different stated objectives, but often, clinicians' focus changes over time. The members aim to find ways of working constructively with their groups, but other topics include negotiating organizational dynamics and preventing burnout or examining future career paths. Over time, members broaden their leadership skills, get exposed to new ideas, and may clarify their clinical beliefs and values. Members often value the support and relational connections as much as any clinical guidance.

The Role of Group Supervisor of Group Psychotherapy

The supervisor's primary task is managing the group culture toward beneficial interactions (Rutan et al., 2014). Central leadership considerations include external boundary management of time, space, attendance, and fees. The leader reinforces the group's norms toward relevant interchanges addressing members' needs and desires. The group culture promotes engagement, honesty, and spontaneity within a safe enough space. The leader modulates and paces the group's intensity so productive interactions occur within the members' tolerance and match their development level.

The leader must intervene to prevent or address deleterious group events, such as scapegoating, groupthink, disrespect or mocking, task drift, and damaging personal or sociocultural enactments. The design allows for potential robust disagreements about a case or theory. Working proactively to prevent and repair ruptures is necessary. Generally, these groups grow comfortable hearing multiple perspectives and do not need a consensus.

A leader needs to appreciate the variety of group traditions and research findings. The leader also tracks the members' areas of interest and further development. Sometimes, the leader or another member may share a short article through an email forum for others to review and consider.

While as a leader, I continually have many thoughts, feelings, and related case examples in my mind, I generally try to turn the group's work over to the members. Almost always, a member will refer to the ideas in my mind, and the practice of members articulating their views is helpful for their self-development. The leader may need to be directive in introducing other indispensable perspectives or ensuring ethical work.

Brief Case Illustration

During the initial check-in, Azari reported wanting to avoid but knowing they had something they needed to investigate. At their agency, Azari leads LGTBQIA+ support/process groups and Acceptance and Commitment (ACT) groups through a contract with Vocational Rehabilitation. Azari identifies as nonbinary and comes from a lower socioeconomic history, but also acknowledges holding other privileged identities of being white, well-educated, and not having any significant disability.

Azari told us that at the start of a new ACT group, they introduced themself with their preferred pronouns and invited others to share what they felt comfortable disclosing. Immediately, Lan, who insists on being called Ram, remarked, "I've seen a lot of combat, and I don't want to be led by someone who is not a real man." While Azari had faced similar comments in the past, they felt unusually stung and frozen. After about a minute of silence, Azari asked for other introductions and then focused on explaining the therapeutic model and the group structure. After the group, Azari thought of many potential responses, felt terrible about freezing, and dreaded returning to the group.

Most of the supervision group immediately expressed anger and outrage toward Lan and his bias, ignorance, and aggressive behavior, and others reported times when they had frozen. Azari described Ram as about 50ish, very muscular and overweight with old clothes and a buzz cut. From the intake summary, Azari learned Ram's parents met during the Vietnam War. Ram identified as Vietnamese and Irish, without any disabilities, and had many entry-level jobs after his military service, but was currently unable to find employment.

While the supervision group tried to stay in emotional support, Azari requested clinical guidance. During supervision around identity differences, some pull may exist to avoid or simplify the complexity of the topic to prevent intense internalized experiences of discomfort, shame, and guilt (Hardy, 2016). Supervising members suggested client resistance and ambivalence and how new group members often enter through their old coping strategies. Other members hypothesized a spectrum of trauma responses and personality organization frameworks. Another noted that both Azari and Ram have oppressed identities, which may interfere and potentially be a bridge toward a therapeutic alliance.

As the supervision group talked and reflected on their experiences, we could see how concepts of projective identification may be present in both groups (Ogden, 2018). These ideas resonated the most with Azari and their interest in psychodynamic approaches. Projective identification postulates a therapist may similarly experience a client's repressed or disowned history. This process is simultaneously a primitive defense, a means of communication, a contagious object representation, and a potential pathway for healing. This idea provided a pragmatic framework for potentially understanding the personally atypical manner in which they were experiencing anger, avoidance, domination fantasies, and self-deprecating thoughts. Azari may have been invited to try to contain and metabolize Ram's feelings and schematic structures.

But what were the options? Some wanted Ram immediately removed from the group. Others foresaw scapegoating dynamics and wondered if a positive culture could ever be achieved. Azari could firmly restate the group agreements and behavioral expectations. Despite concerns about the sociocultural enactment of racial power, another member suggested calling Ram out explicitly in the group. Another member commented that our process felt like strategizing war plans. Perhaps social justice themes could be incorporated into ACT's focus on recognizing values. These options were to be balanced with the embedding agencies' goal to increase the client's basic skills and awareness, suggest additional referrals if needed, and successfully fulfill their joint contract.

Ultimately, despite some uncertainty and strong feelings, Azari wanted to continue to evaluate the situation and start the next session by following the manual and introducing mindfulness. Moving forward, Ram's behavior felt less toxic. He was generally quiet and remote, with occasional boasts about his courage and physical strength that Azari and the group didn't engage. More group therapeutic factors emerged in the group's process. After the penultimate group, Azari addressed Ram privately about his initial comment and overall participation. While Ram did not show great insight, he apologized and reported feeling bad about how he acted throughout the group. Azari felt positive about their clinical choices and work. However, other supervision group members explored the theoretical and personal reasons why they wished Azari worked differently.

Training Influences On My Development as a Group Therapist and Supervisor

In many ways, I followed a traditional path suggested by my mentors and outlined in group literature (Kaklauskas & Greene, 2019). Early in my career, I led various groups across divergent settings, including community mental health centers, recovery programs, academic institutions, and criminal justice settings. Concurrently, I rigorously studied the history group of theory and research and contrasted book knowledge with real-life experiences. From graduate school forward, I have been a member of several process and consultation groups. For the past 35 years, Dr. Robert Unger has been my primary supervisor and mentor. I was lucky to colead a group with him and learned from his creative, compassionate, and unique approach. While in one of his groups, I was also in a group with his partner, Helena Unger, for over a decade. Their impeccable boundaries contained the complexity of this experience, and each helped my growth in distinctive ways.

Throughout my career, I have witnessed clinicians who neglect personal therapeutic work create trouble for themselves and others. While I benefited tremendously from my varied group experiences, nothing compares to my 27-year demanding training analysis with Dr. Doloires Welber. As I tried to say everything, I learned so much about many things. Throughout this period, she also analyzed my partner. While not traditional, she taught us how to be collaborative teammates with each other and with others in our lives. We resolutely journeyed together through the storms of regression, incredulousness, and enactments. Beyond learning about my own, others' cultural unconscious pulls and patterns made the journey maturational toward greater empathy, gratitude, humility, emotional and cognitive flexibility, increased moral and relational awareness, and the courage to listen closely to oneself and others. Despite my broad and even antithetical interests, each mentor encouraged my unique path and supported my professional, personal, and cultural individuation processes. Each group clinician's path will likely be distinctive, contextual, pragmatic, and hopefully personally fulfilling and beneficial to others.

References

Barlow, S. (2013). *Specialty competencies in group psychology*. Oxford University Press.

Crenshaw, K. (1991). Mapping the margins: Intersectionality, identity politics, and violence against women of color. *Stanford Law Review, 43*(6), 1241–1299.

Hardy, K. V. (2016). Toward the development of a multicultural relational perspective in training and supervision. In *Culturally sensitive supervision and training* (pp. 3–10). Routledge.

Hewitt, P. L. & Liew, S. M. (2023). Enhancing group therapy outcomes with measurement-based care. In R. MacNair-Semands & M, Whittingham (Eds.), *Group psychotherapy assessment and practice: A measurement-based care approach*. Taylor & Francis.

James, W. (1890). *The principles of psychology* (vol. 1). Holt.

Kaklauskas, F. J. & Greene, L. R. (2019). Finding the leader in you. In F. J. Kaklauskas & L. R. Greene (Eds.), *Core principles of group psychotherapy: A training manual for theory, research, and practice* (pp. 182–197). Taylor & Francis.

Kaklauskas, F. J. & Nettles, R. (2019). Towards multicultural and diversity proficiency. In F. J. Kaklauskas & L. R. Greene (Eds.), *Core principles of group psychotherapy: A training manual for theory, research, and practice* (pp. 35–54). Allyn & Francis.

Kaklauskas, F. J., Olson, E. A., & Bustemante, K. L. (2021). A contemplative practice of large group process: Interdisciplinary contextual perspectives. In F. Kaklauskas, S. Nimanheminda, L. Hoffman, M Jack, & J. Perlstein (Eds.), *Brilliant sanity: Buddhist approaches to psychotherapy and counseling, Revised and Expanded* (vol. 1, pp. 57–82). University Professors Press.

Mills, C. (1997). *The racial contract*. Cornell University Press.

Ogden, T. H. (2018). The analytic management and interpretation of projective identification. In A. Alexandris & G. Vaslamatzis (Eds.), *Countertransference: Theory, technique, teaching* (pp. 21–46). Routledge.

Pateman, C. 1988). *The sexual contract*. Stanford University Press.

Rorty, R. (1991). *Objectivity, relativism, and truth: philosophical papers* (vol. 1). Cambridge University Press.

Rutan, J. S., Stone, W. N., & Shay, J. J. (2014). *Psychodynamic group psychotherapy*. Guilford.

Watkins Jr., C. E., Vîşcu, L. I., & Cadariu, I. E. (2021). Psychotherapy supervision research: On roadblocks, remedies, and recommendations. *European Journal of Psychotherapy & Counselling, 23*(1), 8–25.

Whittingham, M., Marmarosh, C. L., Mallow, P., & Scherer, M. (2023). Mental health care equity and access: A group therapy solution. *American Psychologist, 78*(2), 119–113.

A Psychoanalytic Object Relational Approach

Michelle A. Collins-Greene

The Structure, Frame, and Format of Group Therapy Consultation

I run a supervision group of 4–6 group therapists as part of my private practice. Members are from diverse settings such as university counseling centers, private practices and outpatient clinics and generally do not work with each other. They are self-referred based on our shared engagement in professional organizations such as the AGPA or the American Psychological Association.

Other than setting the frame (time, space, fees, agreements regarding attendance and participation), I am nondirective although I do suggest a structure in which members take responsibility for presenting material on designated dates. What they present is entirely up to them: the clinical material can range from a microanalytic moment of rupture and repair to a review of an entire session or an analysis of several sessions. They are free to present excerpts from audiotape recordings, read their clinical process notes taken after a session, or focus on a particular question, concern or dilemma they may be having about their group. They may send any material before the supervision session for the group to review with their comments or questions. Sometimes we view and review segments of videotapes of group sessions such as those found online or via AGPA video presentations. In addition, members are free to bring material about their personal lives as it relates to their clinical work.

The Group Contract

Much like establishing a contract at the start of a therapy group, I establish a set of agreements for supervisees in our supervision group, including regular attendance and participation and putting feelings into words not actions. I emphasize the importance of maintaining confidentiality about our group, both content and process, and individuals' participation in the group. I articulate the primary goal of our group; while emerging relationships among the participants and with me as supervisor may have the consequence of being therapeutic and social, the aim of our work is help each other become better group psychotherapists. For both conducting group therapy and supervision, I suggest that outside interactions be brought back to the group consultation. We are colleagues so multiple relationship situations are expected to occur.

Stage of Learning of Participants

The participants vary in terms of clinical experience, self-awareness, leadership development and foundational knowledge of group therapy, four independent domains that are not necessarily correlated. In my ongoing assessments, I have found that the supervisees often have considerable clinical experience but sometimes uneven mastery of group leadership skills including counter-transference awareness, as well as uneven foundational knowledge of group therapy including group developmental stages, levels of group process and anti-therapeutic group processes.

Role of the Group Supervisor of Group Psychotherapy

In my role as leader of a supervisory group, I attend flexibly to three primary levels of analysis: (1) the individual supervisees (particularly what, whether and how they are learning, including their resistances to learning, and their development as group leaders), (2) the therapy groups they are presenting (including the emotional climate and prevailing dynamics within the group and the nature and quality of the emerging relationships between and among the clients and their individual and collective ties to the supervisee-therapist), and (3) our supervision group (including members' commitment to the work, sense of safety for risk-taking and experimentation, the quality of the group processes, cohesiveness, and the working alliance between me as supervisor-leader and the supervisee-members).

As in leading group therapy, my role as leader of the supervision group involves tracking the levels and quality of interactions and ascertaining which level of process is most fruitful to promote, bring the group's attention to, allow to unfold, or interrupt to pause and reflect on. I make sure everyone has a chance to participate, encouraging those who participate frequently to bring in others, and those who patiently wait to participate to make room for themselves. I also encourage group members to relate to each other and respond to each other's material before I do. When I contribute, I attempt to relate the process or material to theory, validate or reflect upon each person's contribution, and offer that there's usually more than one way to view material. Even though I am nondirective and encourage as much participant involvement as possible, I believe part of my supervisory responsibility is to impart some didactic learning as it relates to the material at hand, and as much as possible to the development of each supervisee as a group therapy leader. Infrequently I will make an interpretation about counter-transference or their leadership style, but usually when asked or I perceive the person can make use of it or perceive how it might be relevant in that moment to their group.

In terms of monitoring and managing the group climate, I encourage tolerance, risk-taking, and especially the working through of shame, guilt or anxiety. I try to facilitate their developing a sense of confidence and comfort in offering their own unique point of view about what is being explored and then assess their capacity to hear feedback from others. Although sometimes the group tends toward drifting into an exclusive here-and-now process group, I do try to balance a focus on the here-and-now with a focus on their relationships to their therapy groups, usually by investigating parallel process.

The primary conceptual tool that I rely on in psychoanalytic object relations supervision is parallel process. This notion posits that dynamics within the therapy group—between the supervisee and their group, or among members in their group—can be reenacted within the supervisory group. Keeping parallel process possibilities in mind helps to generate hypotheses about what is happening in the therapy group.

More generally, viewing group phenomena through the lens of psychoanalytic object relations theory invites us to explore how early beliefs about self-in-the world and associated unconscious motivations, defensive needs, instinctual desires and wishes get deployed and enacted in the social field, whether it be in the therapy groups led by the supervisees, the supervisory group, or the relationships between the therapy and supervisory groups. Interpretation leading to insight into these developmentally early unconscious motivations and beliefs and how they may be unnecessary and maladaptive in the present is the main therapeutic change process in personality structure and evolution in psychoanalytic psychotherapy. The context of group therapy adds a therapeutic dimension not available in individual therapy, namely transferences and enactments toward fellow group members. This is true not only in the therapy group but also the supervision group. Competition for the leader, sibling rivalry, jealousy, and making judgments are all underlying motivations, sometimes conscious and other times not. In addition, other reactions in the supervisory groups such as feeling neglected by the leader or unworthy of the leader's attention, feeling inadequate compared to group members, arrogance, self-criticism, shame and embarrassment in relation to others are all potentially present for all members of the supervision group at different times and can be explored in the service of developing increased self-awareness necessary for competence in group therapy leadership. Transferences toward the consultant also are "grist for the mill," whether the consultant is viewed as all-knowing, incompetent, understanding, blind, abusive of power, or humble. In psychoanalytic consultation of group therapy in group all of these transferences, and counter-transferences, are considered valuable material for processing work that is considered relevant to the group leaders' development as a group therapist and their ability to lead groups productively, as well as to the supervision leader's development as a group supervisor and their ability to evolve as a supervisor.

Training Influences On My Development as a Group Therapy Supervisor

I attended McGill University during Donald Hebb's time, the 1970s, and so was first introduced to neurological and behavioral understanding of psychology. However, I was curious why Freudian theories were not taught and seemed devalued. I transferred to the University of Colorado at Boulder where I studied and conducted experiments in the cognitive psychology lab under Lyle Bourne. Here too I experienced primarily behavioral, experimental and neurological models. While these primarily cognitive models were a worthwhile knowledge base, I was still interested in integrating thought and emotion in human development and pursued clinical experience at an inpatient psychiatric institute on adult and adolescent units before going to graduate school in clinical psychology. During those three years, I learned and practiced psychoanalytic theory under the supervision of Linnea Carter who had trained at Menninger's. Much of the clinical work in these formative years was conducted in groups. Training and supervision of staff also occurred primarily in groups via the exploration of here-and-now group process with some individual supervision. It was a community mental health model and patient treatment usually lasted three to six months, and sometimes up to two years; this was the late 1970s. I found value in psychotherapeutic treatment there through group process and found psychoanalytic concepts helpful in promoting mental health. I did quite a bit of reading on my own during those three years of Kernberg, Mahler, Horney, Yalom and attended courses at Naropa and conferences, all with a focus on psychoanalysis, interpersonal and group psychotherapy. I also participated in my own psychotherapy with feminist, Marjorie Leidig, and in a psychotherapy group.

Though that first supervision in groups proved valuable, at times it seemed unnecessarily pathologizing of students and colleagues. Consultation, supervision, and evaluation was merciless and judgmental in analyzing staff members personalities and vulnerabilities, and used as evidence for promotion, or nonpromotion. Also having that first experience in an institutional, hierarchically organized, mental health setting made me aware of how administration could use psychoanalysis in service of power dynamics and gender bias. My experiences there led to my career-long commitment to a strength-based, egalitarian and affirming approach in my psychotherapy, supervision and consultation, while maintaining a psychoanalytic orientation.

I then attended the Institute of Advanced Psychological Studies at Adelphi, now called the Derner Institute, for graduate and postdoctoral degrees and certifications in psychoanalysis and psychodynamic psychotherapy, and joined the Eastern Group Psychotherapy Society for certification in group psychotherapy. Throughout my career I've been an active member of the AGPA and the Eastern Group Psychotherapy Society. Ronnie Levine served as my personal analyst and group therapist over all of those years and guided my invaluable experiential learning. As object relations theory matured, I found it helpful in understanding the relationships that developed in groups.

As an avid believer in the benefits of group psychotherapy that I have personally experienced that are above and beyond individual therapy, I have created therapy, consultation, and supervision groups in all of my inpatient, outpatient and private practice work. These include numerous consultation and supervision groups of interns and externs and colleagues in various hospital and community mental health settings. Currently, I enjoy leading a supervision group of group psychotherapists in my private practice.

An Interpersonal Approach to Working with Children and Adolescents

Tony L. Sheppard

The Structure, Frame, and Format of Group Therapy Consultation

For many years I have supervised graduate students from the School of Professional Psychology at Spalding University in my private practice, Groupworks Psychological Services. Students are placed with our practice for a year-long practicum experience that involves coleadership of groups with children and adolescents. Each of our groups is co-led by a psychologist and a graduate student. These groups are process oriented in nature and address three broad areas with regard to goals: (1) Improved Self-Regulation, (2) Improved Self-Concept and (3) Improved Interpersonal Skills. Our program is structured so that supervisees go from observing the group during the beginning phase of their experience to full coleadership as they progress.

Given that I supervise graduate students, the frame is one that naturally involves a power differential. In our initial supervisory meetings, this power differential is addressed as part of the contract. I invite students to consider this relationship and how it might impact their relationship to the group. My advice to students is twofold. Primarily, I frame the goal of their experience as one of finding their own style of being in groups. It is not the goal for them to learn to facilitate groups in the exact way that I do. In other words, I'm not there to tell them what they're doing right or wrong, but to guide them in being present in the group in a way that fits with their individual identities and style. Secondly, while the power differential between us is real, we must present to our group members as equals. It is important for the learning and development of our young group members that they view us both as authority figures, albeit benevolent ones. Inevitably, the progression of the supervisory relationship involves revisiting this, as group members will often attempt to place one group leader "over" the other with regard to their authority.

Graduate students receive two different types of supervision. First, they are supervised individually, which involves weekly hour-long meetings with me or one of the other psychologists. Secondly, they participate in group-based supervision with our entire staff of six psychologists and three graduate students. The individual supervision is focused more specifically on the clinician and their relationship to both the individual participants and the group as whole. Our group-based supervision takes more of a problem-solving approach to working with children and adolescents. Students present cases to the treatment team and we offer advice on how to improve the work with group participants and with the group-as-a-whole.

The Group Contract

The contract is of critical importance in both the individual and group supervision formats. Of primary importance is the honoring of students' intersecting identities. I believe that the foundation of honoring our members' identities is to begin with the supervisory relationship. Supervisees must feel empowered to be fully themselves in the context of the relationship. Research suggests that child and adolescent clinicians who self-disclose to their clients within reason are most effective. In support of this, I stress the student's sense of safety in learning. It is critical that students' intersecting identities be acknowledged and affirmed. Equally critical is the adherence to the highest of ethical standards with regard to boundaries in the student/supervisor relationship.

Part of our agreement is that students will share their countertransference reactions to group members and to the supervisor/coleader. This facilitates a deeper understanding of the relational dynamics in the group. Working with youth can bring up unique countertransference reactions that are often rooted in the clinician's own childhood or adolescence. Further, younger clients often have transferences emerge with group leaders that are complex. Given that students are asked to disclose in this manner, trust and safety in the context of the supervisory relationship is essential.

Another important aspect of the contract includes the time boundaries of supervision. Each student is expected to participate in two hours of supervision per week. Both students and the psychologist agree to the importance of time boundaries and of being fully prepared for supervisory sessions. Since there is no monetary cost associated with the supervision, this is not part of the contract.

Addressing Issues around Diversity, Equity, and Inclusion (DEI) in Supervision

Addressing issues around DEI is of utmost importance in my work. Our practice is one that is dedicated to creating an affirming space for our clients to grow and for our supervisees to learn. Further, this is particularly relevant in a model that emphasizes the personhood of the clinician. It is, as mentioned previously, essential for supervisees to feel that all aspects of their intersecting identities are seen and acknowledged by the supervisor. This includes sex, gender identity, sexual orientation, race, culture, ethnicity, body type, ability status, socio-economic status and other aspects of the person's identity. This is part of the initial contract discussions with supervisees. Of equal importance is the empowerment of the supervisee to bring any microaggressions that might occur to the attention of the supervisor or the supervisory team. This includes microaggressions that might occur in the context of the supervisory relationship and those that might occur in the group sessions. Processing these occurrences is important to the process of bringing one's full self into the work of psychotherapy.

Stage of Learning of Participants

Participants in supervision at Groupworks, being graduate students, present with varying levels of experience in group therapy. Most students have taken the group psychotherapy course in their program, so they have a foundational understanding of group dynamics. When students have not taken this course, they are encouraged to read our book *Group Psychotherapy with Children: Core Principles for Effective Practice* (Sheppard and Thieneman, 2024).

It is worth noting that many of our students have not had the experience of sharing their reactions to situations in the therapeutic and supervisory spaces. In some cases, they have actually been discouraged from doing so. Therefore, it is essential that we nurture students' willingness and sense of safety in doing this important work. Frequently, there needs to be some education about the importance of transference and countertransference in our work.

The Role of Group Supervisor of Group Psychotherapy

Since I typically supervise individuals at the beginning of their career as psychologists. I serve in several different roles. Among the roles that I consider to be important are mentor.

supervisor and role model. I take these roles and the responsibilities that accompany them as seriously as I take my work with group members in my groups. In these supervisory relationships, I'm representing the fields of psychology and group psychotherapy for my supervisees.

Being a mentor to my students involves providing them with a sense of their place in the worlds of psychology and group psychotherapy. I strongly encourage involvement in the AGPA through membership, E-learning events, and participation in AGPA's annual conference, "Connect." This serves the purpose of providing them with mentors and role models beyond myself. It is important that students find mentors and role models who best match their own intersecting identities as my identities often don't fully align with theirs.

Not only do the supervisees experience me in the supervisory role; as my group coleader, they will experience me in the clinical role of group leader. Given this, I serve as a clinical role model for my students. In short, they will see every action I take as the coleader of the group. My approach is rooted in mentoring students to find their own style of leadership; not merely to learn mine. The style of group leadership that I employ is one characterized by genuineness, immediacy and placement of the relationship with my client as having the utmost importance. This style might not be the one that my supervisees adopt for themselves. It is my role to mentor them in developing that style within the parameters of what is known to be effective about group psychotherapy.

In the supervisory role, I guide my supervisees to reflect upon their own experiences of the group and to utilize that in the service of helping group members to grow and change. I emphasize development of awareness of their own reactions to group members. We explore these countertransference reactions as a way of understanding our groups better. Employing Yalom's Social Microcosm Theory of Groups (Yalom & Leszcz, 2020), we look at how individuals impact each other, the group-as-a-whole and ourselves as a way of determining the path toward healthier relationships.

Training Influences On My Development as a Group Therapy Supervisor

I have had the honor of being trained by some outstanding mentors, supervisors and role models throughout my career. At the beginning of my training at Spalding University, I found people who embodied the quote from Harry Stack Sullivan, "We are all more simply human than otherwise." I was also fortunate to grow and develop in a program that valued the impact of relationships in psychotherapy. The interpersonal theories of Sullivan and Yalom & Leszcz had a profound impact on my understanding of the therapeutic process.

Connecting with the AGPA felt like a continuation of the training I received in graduate school. Training with Scott Rutan in group psychotherapy early in my career further solidified my belief in the power of the group modality and further reinforced my approach. That approach being one that is grounded in relational work that emphasizes the importance of exploration of relational factors being so powerful in supervision.

Finally, one of my mentors and supervisors, John James, PhD, told me something early in my career that had a tremendous impact on my thinking. John emphasized to me that the key to working with different populations with regard to chronological age is that one have a fundamental understanding of human development. That began the early shift in my career to focusing on children and adolescents. John's words have held true over time. Working from an understanding of the developmental trajectories of people's lives, in the context of their relationships, has been the foundation of my work and of my approach as a supervisor. Working with children and adolescents can often become very transactional in the sense that interventions lack a relational component. I believe that teaching youth how to form healthy relationships is foundational to our work with them. In order to do that, we must work relationally.

Notes

1 SCT's protocol for undoing anxiety starts by identifying the source of the anxiety (thought, feeling, or edge of the unknown). If anxiety is coming from a thought, the work is to reality-test the thought. If from a feeling, to make room for it. If from the edge of the unknown, to get curious (Agazarian, 1997).
2 "By centering we can calm the chattering that goes on in our brain and free ourselves from distracting thoughts. We become mindful. When we are centered, we can sit at the edge of the unknown with curiosity, explore our experience, comprehend as well as apprehend our context, turn on our researcher and observe and be aware of ourselves, our roles, and our history in context" (SCT Foundation Manual, 2011, p. 6).
3 Importantly in SCT, participants are discouraged from applying SCT with others until having completed the intermediate skills training intensive as SCT sees it as essential that members learn first to apply the SCT structure and protocols with themselves before applying it with others.

References

Sheppard, T. L. & Thieneman, Z. J. (2024). *Group psychotherapy with children: Core principles for effective practice*. Routledge.

Yalom, I. & Leszcz, M. (2020). *The theory and practice of group psychotherapy* (6th ed.). Basic Books.

Chapter 4

The Supervisory Relationship in Group Psychotherapy Supervision

Maria T. Riva

This chapter explores how to develop and nurture a productive supervisor–supervisee relationship. It also discusses how the supervisory alliance facilitates the supervision task of focusing on clinical data occurring in the psychotherapy group. The goal here is to inform and improve the treatment process and promote the clinical skills of the group psychotherapist. The chapter discusses the importance and benefits of a strong supervisory relationship along with methods for developing the relationship for the novice group psychotherapist as well as the novice supervisor. Additionally, this material is just as relevant for more experienced supervisors given that many are providing supervision without the benefit of formal education and training on the supervisory tasks, especially concerning the supervisory relationship. The chapter describes methods to achieve and sustain a positive supervisory relationship. The timing of different supervision techniques, the supervision agreement, stages of the supervisory relationship, models of supervision, and current research on the supervisory alliance are also covered.

The Importance of Supervisory Relationships for Group Psychotherapy

"Group psychotherapy is a commonly practiced, complex, and effective format of treating a wide range of presenting problems and client populations" (Riva & Erickson Cornish, 2018, p. 218). Research over many years has found group psychotherapy to be effective and, in some situations, more effective than individual psychotherapy (Burlingame et al., 2013). Unfortunately, even though the research on group psychotherapy has expanded over the past few decades, the supervision of group psychotherapy has received much less attention. With the benefits and growth in the utilization of psychotherapy groups in many settings (e.g., mental health agencies, high schools, college counseling centers, residential facilities for adolescents, Veterans Administration Hospitals, private practice, etc.), the need for competent group facilitators is critical, as is the supervision of these group leaders. Regrettably, many group leaders have had little training in facilitation, and equally disturbing is that many group leaders receive little to no supervision on their groups (Denton et al., 2019; Riva, 2014). Riva (2011) suggested that "it is typical that if supervision of groups is provided, the primary focus is on problematic clients and not on the group dynamics. Similarly, if the counseling group has co-leaders, minimal time is spent during the supervision session on the coleader relationship" (p. 370). This is an artifact that most group leaders and supervisors are first trained and supervised in individual therapy and supervision, and many are

DOI: 10.4324/9781003410621-5

from a psychoanalytic theoretical framework which prioritizes the individual, even in group therapy. Group dynamics, which include relationships not only with the leader but also between group members, and with the group-as-a-whole, are far more complex, and sometimes more subtle than those in individual treatment, and worthy of supervisory attention. There seems to be no dispute that supervision is a vital component of training group leaders. As Yalom and Leszcz (2020) noted, "supervision is the sine qua non in the education of group therapists" (p. 645). Due to the complexity of group psychotherapy compared to the individual format, these authors also asserted that it is at these intricate decision points "that a supervisor makes a valuable and unique contribution to the student therapist's education" (p. 645).

Characteristics of a Beneficial Supervisory Relationship

On the top of the list of essential ingredients of a productive supervisory relationship is a constructive alliance that focuses on the professional, ethical, and skill development of the group psychotherapist. The supervisor needs to demonstrate respect for the group leader and instill a sense of respect for the group facilitator's clients. Trust is a necessary feature of the supervisory relationship, which is developed across many interactions (Bernard & Goodyear, 2019). Setting the right climate for supervision includes a nonjudgmental approach which encourages openness on the part of the supervisee. Clarity and agreement of responsibilities of both the supervisor and the supervisee, that include the purpose, goals, objectives of the supervision, and the methods of evaluation, encourage a positive alliance (Yalom & Leszcz, 2020). A nonjudgmental environment and positive alliance with the supervisor also aid cohesiveness among supervision group members (if supervision is being done in a group) and provides modeling for group leaders to bring back to their groups.

Over 20 years ago, Nelson et al. (2001) pointed out that a strong supervisory relationship is *the* primary task of early supervision meetings. Building trust, reducing supervisee anxiety, and developing a robust connection within the supervisory relationship will help the supervisee hear corrective feedback which is a crucial aspect of supervision. Research suggests that supervisors have difficulty providing corrective feedback on supervisees more personal behavior (e.g., defensiveness or not taking responsibility) vs. feedback on specific skills such as sitting with silence or probing more deeply (Bernard & Goodyear, 2019; Hoffman et al., 2005). There is a well-documented inclination for those in evaluative roles to skirt providing negative feedback, which has been labeled the MUM Effect for remaining Mum about Unpleasant Messages (Rosen & Tesser, 1970; Scarff et al., 2019). Therefore, supervisors need to provide direct and honest feedback while being supportive in the service of supervisee competence and group member growth. A strong positive alliance and strength-based supervision is an important foundation before embarking on corrective feedback.

In a broad sequential structure called the Proctor Model of Supervision developed by Bridgid Proctor in 1986 (Proctor, 2010), the author described three elements of supervisory attention: normative (administration and configuration of supervision, such as the supervisory agreement), formative (focusing on group sessions and connecting material to theory and practice), and restorative (supporting the supervisee during challenging group dynamics and encouraging supervisee self-care). Yalom and Leszcz (2020) stated that "The most effective supervisors are able to tune in to the trainee, track the trainee's central concerns, capture the essence of the trainee's narrative, guide the trainee through clinical dilemmas, and demonstrate personal concern and support" (p. 647).

It is widely acknowledged that a strong supervisory relationship will assist in weathering relationship storms within supervision. The supervisory role is complex and often a challenging one where conflicts can and do arise from many root causes. Bernard and Goodyear (2019) describe four categories of supervisee–supervisor conflicts including "(a) a supervisor mistake or a miscommunication between the two, (b) normative processes, (c) interpersonal dynamics and expectations of the supervisee, and (d) cultural differences" (p. 94). Although these types of conflicts and their subsequent mending are often called "ruptures and repair" or "tears and repairs," most of the focus has been on the relationship between a therapist and client/patient (e.g., Safran et al., 2011). More recently, this literature has expanded to include ruptures and repairs in group psychotherapy (e.g., Marmarosh, 2021), and in group supervision of therapists-in-training (Watkins et al., 2015). Although therapy and supervision are distinct in many ways, the process for repairing a tear is similar. Steps for addressing ruptures in supervision include recognizing and acknowledging the rupture without defensiveness, listening carefully to the supervisee's feelings and perceptions of their experience (even if you do not concur), and have an open discussion by leaning into the description of the occurrence. The supervisor will want to show self-reflection and own any part they played in the rupture and offer a genuine apology. It is recommended that the supervisor consider what changes need to occur to the structure, policy, norms, etc. that will address some of the concerns. It will be vital for the supervisor to maintain a goal of strengthening the supervisory relationship and model for the supervisee how to have difficult conversations which can then provide an example of how the supervisee can repair ruptures with their clients (see Watkins, 2021 for an extensive discussion of rupture and repair in clinical supervision).

Supervisory Relationship vs. Psychotherapy Relationship

Although there are some similarities between a supervisory relationship and a psychotherapy relationship, there are major and important differences. In general, supervision requires much more structure, activity and direction on the part of the supervisor than in psychotherapy. What is *not* the role of the supervisor is to veer into providing therapy to the supervisee. Many beginning supervisors resort to using the same model and mode of doing supervision as they do psychotherapy. A supervisor can guide the supervisee's recognition and insight into the areas of learning and personality styles and even countertransference tendencies in the development of a good group therapist, as long as the supervisor does not fall into the role of psychotherapist with the focus on trying to cure or treat the supervisee's problems. For these types of problems, the supervisee may need to be referred to their own personal psychotherapy. Alonso (2000) advised "the supervisor has to listen with a clinician's ear and speak with a supervisor's mouth" and remain true to this boundary (p. 55). Similarly, McMahon (2014) described four guiding principles for supervisory relationships. They include "offering emotional presence and sensitivity, valuing both vulnerability and competence, offering knowledge and experience with humility, and developing a relationship to support continued personal and professional growth" (p. 333). Separating the supervisory alliance from the psychotherapy one is often difficult for early group leaders and one that modeling and training by the supervisor is typically necessary.

One area that is common in early supervisory sessions is the anxiety of the supervisee that can interfere with the supervisee's ability to facilitate their psychotherapy group and to openly present material to the supervisor. Supervisors who appreciate that novice group therapists operate better with clear expectations, an understanding of how they will be evaluated, and a focus on concrete skills will fare much better in the supervisory role. Much of the supervisory alliance literature concentrates on working in a dyad with supervisees who have individual clients. A great deal of this information can be generalized to supervision of group psychotherapy, yet the unique features of therapy groups add multiple layers to the supervisory process. Supervisors who can convey the message that anxiety about being in supervision, and about facilitating group psychotherapy is normal for early group therapists will help ease concern and deepen trust (Bernard & Goodyear, 2019).

Openness to Learning: A Collaborative Process

While it is recognized that the supervisory relationship is hierarchical, it must be emphasized that it is also a collaborative process. Most typically supervision is between one supervisor and one group psychotherapist, yet there are other models such as a supervisor with group coleaders, or a supervisor with several group psychotherapists. While the focus is on the supervisee's learning, it will benefit the relationship if both the supervisor and the supervisee have a learning stance that is open and nondefensive. This collaborative supervisory relationship requires a supportive and trusting bond and a supervisor who, even when providing supervision with a specific theoretical orientation, shows acceptance and curiosity of different theories, leadership styles, and the multitude of ways that group psychotherapists operate in a group. It requires the supervisor to be both supportive and constructively truthful in a way that is experienced by the supervisee as a learning/teaching moment and, at the same time, allows and even encourages different viewpoints and feedback from their supervisee(s).

Especially for early group leaders, supervisors need to appreciate the developmental levels of group facilitation. Research has shown that early group leaders think differently about their groups than those more experienced. Novice group leaders have been found to be more linear and use overly simplified knowledge structures compared to those with more experience (Kivlighan & Kivlighan, 2009; Kivlighan & Tibbitts, 2012). For example, Kivlighan and Tibbits (2012) identified both errors of commission and omission for early leaders' knowledge structures compared to the more experienced group leaders. As an example, trainees considered silences as bad (and often caused considerable anxiety) compared to leaders with more group experience, who saw silence as a positive opportunity. This study pointed to the developmental level of supervisees and how the supervisor can provide training based on their knowledge level. It is crucial for supervisors to acknowledge and normalize the high levels of anxiety and uncertainty felt by novice group leaders and to encourage them to express their feelings and concerns in a supportive supervisory relationship while at the same time helping them to increase their cognitive complexity.

Most of the obstacles to a good supervisory alliance have to do with the attitudes and use of the inherent hierarchical relationship by both the supervisor and supervisee. However, given that the supervisor is presumably in the more powerful position due to their institutional position, supposed greater expertise and knowledge, and their evaluative and gatekeeping function, it is their responsibility to steer the alliance and navigate factors that influence a positive or negative relationship. Supervisor attitudes that are vital for an effective supervisory relationship include treating the trainee with the same respect, compassion, empathy, and dignity that one would show a client (Yalom & Leszcz, 2020). Attitudes beneficial to the collaborative relationship on the part of the supervisee are openness to learning, nondefensiveness, respect, and confidence in the feedback given by the supervisor and their ability to evaluate this feedback.

Psychotherapy Supervision Formats

This section includes frequently used formats of supervision of group psychotherapy. Each format values the supervisory alliance, but the foci of relationship variables are somewhat different for each. They all teach concepts and skills to the group psychotherapist(s) concerning group psychotherapy and provide supervision in the service of client care. They also each have advantages and disadvantages in their practice. The most common format includes *supervision with one supervisor and one group psychotherapy facilitator*. In this format, the supervisor can address topics in depth given that the time is concentrated on one group leader. The downside is that the supervisor only obtains one view of the workings of the psychotherapy group compared to supervision with the coleaders, and unless the supervisor views videotapes or listens to audiotapes of the group, the information gained can be limited and biased. In this one-to-one format, attending to the supervisory relationship can be a major focus by monitoring and attending to interpersonal reactions between the supervisor and supervisee to make sure communication is open and clear. Additionally, the supervisor can pick up interpersonal patterns in the dyadic relationship that may be useful or detrimental to group leadership.

In a second format, *the supervisor provides supervision to the coleaders* of a psychotherapy group, sometimes called *triadic supervision*. Here the supervisor provides skill development to the coleaders and can focus on the coleaders' relationship with each other in the group. The downside of this composition can occur when there is competition between the supervisees, or widely varying skill levels, and less direct time that can be spent with each leader individually. An advantage is the opportunity to view in vivo the supervisees' interpersonal styles with each other and with the supervisor, and their leadership styles with the group, which provides more material for supervision.

Another alternative includes supervision where the supervisor conducts a group with several group psychotherapists, described as *group supervision of group psychotherapy*. This method allows the supervisor to provide training with several group leaders at once as well as the leaders can learn from each other's experience. This composition has many similarities with group psychotherapy such as developing trust in the group, setting norms, experiencing group dynamics, conflict, etc. This format allows for addressing similar dynamics in group supervision that occur in the supervisees' psychotherapy groups such as developing cohesion, setting clear norms, modeling group skills, and addressing parallel process. The drawbacks of group supervision of group psychotherapists are that there is much less time to respond to individual supervisee needs and, due to the multilayered material, with multiple group members with different levels of experience and diverse backgrounds, it takes a skilled supervisor that has a deep understanding and facilitation experience in both supervision *and* group dynamics.

One additional option is when a *supervisor coleads a psychotherapy group with their supervisee*. This method provides the supervisor with direct observation of the supervisee's skill as a group facilitator and can model effective leader behavior. Some unfavorable aspects of this method that might affect the supervisor–supervisee relationship are the possibility of a dual relationship depending on the supervisory alliance outside of coleading the group, or if the supervisor seizes more responsibility for the leadership, in effect, muting the supervisee. The supervisor needs to be sensitive to the supervisee's anxieties about the hierarchical relationship and be generous in the support of them.

Psychotherapy Supervision Structure

There are various ways to structure group psychotherapy supervision, depending on the level of supervisee knowledge of group psychotherapy and the theoretical orientation followed. What helps to set the structure is the use of a *supervisory agreement or contract* which is an agreement between the supervisor and supervisee about the essence of their relationship and what each person expects from the other that decreases the likelihood of misunderstanding. It requires supervisors to explicitly outline the requirements of both parties in a written agreement that generally entails the purpose of the relationship, tasks, roles, and their expectations. Other elements of supervisory agreements typically include the logistics such as how often supervision will occur, the days, times, and place of the meetings. It also is helpful to outline the evaluation processes; what client reports, notes, and other written documents will be required for supervisor review; and the methods of observing the supervisees clinical work (transcripts, videotapes, live group sessions, etc.). If there is a financial fee for supervision, that needs to be outlined as well. Having all of this spelled out is the normative aspect of supervision. It can provide security and transparency to the supervisee, thus enhancing trust and predictability in the relationship. Delineating accountability of both parties at the beginning of supervision goes a long way in providing a sound structure for the relationship to develop in. It can also be a demonstration that the supervisor is invested in "power with" rather than "power over" in the relationship.

One challenge for the supervisory alliance is the *power differential* that is inescapable within the supervisor–supervisee relationship. Supervisors teach skills and evaluate supervisee performance to name a few. Supervisors will need to recognize and address this power asymmetry directly with the supervisee. This hierarchical relationship has often been described as negative and it is certainly possible for supervisors to provide deficient or harmful supervision. Ellis et al. (2014) distinguished inadequate clinical supervision (e.g., does not allocate enough time for supervision) from harmful supervision (e.g., boundary crossing, sexual relationship with supervisee). In their sample, a staggering 90% of the 363 supervisees recounted at least one depiction of inadequate supervision, while 28% described harmful supervision. In the narratives of supervisees collected by McNamara et al. (2017), the authors found that the most common categories of harmful behavior were abuse of power, cultural discrimination, and public shaming. Yet, power inequality also can be viewed as positive, one that formalizes and facilitates the supervisory relationship. Having a good structural foundation in which it is evident that the supervisor's role is to empower and support the supervisee will foster a good relationship.

Another structural component of supervision is how the supervisee's clinical material will be observed and evaluated. There are several avenues for the supervisor to oversee the supervisee's facilitation of their psychotherapy groups including watching *videotapes*, listening to *audiotapes*, using a *one-way mirror*, conducting *role-plays* during supervision meetings, utilizing *coleadership* with the supervisee and supervisor leading a group together, and having the supervisee *report on their group*. Several group and clinical organizations require some form of direct observation which precludes supervisee self-report as the sole method. Discussing the supervisee's feelings, anxieties, and even positive anticipation about each of these methods can facilitate an open relationship. It is also important for the supervisee to know how, and to whom, the clinical material will be shown and evaluated.

Supervision Models from Theoretical Frameworks

There are several models of supervision that focus mostly on supervision of individual therapy. Bernard and Goodyear (2019) formulated a three-part classification of clinical supervision models that help to categorize them with similar foci. They include: (a) psychotherapy theory-based models that are centered on applying one theoretical approach, (b) developmental models that are focused on the complexities of the learning process for supervisees across the developmental spectrum, and (c) supervision process models that typically take a step back to observe the supervision process itself (p. 46). Each of these three umbrellas have multiple models subsumed underneath. For example, psychotherapy theory models include psychodynamic, humanistic relationship, cognitive-behavioral, systemic, feminist, constructivist (narrative and solution focused), and integrative (see Bernard & Goodyear, 2019). Some of the most common are included below. For more information about other models, please see Bernard and Goodyear (2019), and the chapter on Contemporary Approaches to Group Psychotherapy Supervision in this manual.

Psychotherapy-Based Models

Psychodynamic Supervision

Psychotherapy-based models reflect the theoretical orientation of the supervisor. The oldest model of supervision has its nucleus in psychoanalytic theory. Sarnat (2010) discussed four areas that supervisors must foster to develop supervisee competence. They include first, viewing the relationship with clients and with the supervisor as the "crucible of psychotherapy change" (p. 23). Second is the ability to self-reflect and use the self in interactions with the client. Third, Sarnat describes using assessment and diagnoses from a psychodynamic orientation, and the fourth is using psychoanalytic interventions consistent with the theory.

In the article "The supervisory alliance and the training of psychodynamic group psychotherapists," Kleinberg (1999) provided six domains for a supervisor to consider. They include clinical skills, knowledge of psychodynamic theory, knowledge of group dynamics theory, self-reflective capacity, consultation skills, and the capacity to be supervised. Challenges to the supervisory alliance often fall into the supervisees' capacity to: (a) present the process of group treatment accurately, (b) articulate the necessary emphasis for supervision, (c) being nondefensive in response to the information and comments by the supervisor, (d) willingness to try suggestions, (e) ability to consider connections between their psychotherapy group and the supervisory group, (f) capacity to monitor what has been learned during the supervision sessions and revise goals as needed, (g) know when to get personal treatment when blocks to learning occur, and (h) able to consider one's own learning style and communicate it in supervision. Several of these domains directly relate to the supervisory alliance. For example, the third domain addresses supervisee nondefensiveness and the fourth point refers to the supervisee being willing to try suggestions. Both of these domains require a supportive supervisory relationship that allows for honesty from the supervisee and one where the supervisor encourages the supervisee to take risks.

The description by Kleinberg (1999) of the supervisory alliance suggests a more cognitively complex psychotherapist than a novice one. All the points described above are goals for the supervisor to help develop a skilled and experienced therapist. For group psychotherapists, one goal would be to recognize (and appreciate) the multidimensionality of group psychotherapy. Here the supervisor can point to diverse avenues that a group therapist might take. Responding in a concrete manner complicates discussions of intricate group dynamics, self-awareness, and other foci in supervision. Additional struggles in the supervisory relationship transpire when supervisees have excessive anxiety about conducting group psychotherapy, have conflicts with authority, and feel shame about making mistakes. For Kleinberg, each of these points anticipate growth over time. Several current concepts about supervisory relationships derive from psychoanalytic and psychodynamic theory, including the supervisory alliance, parallel process, transference, countertransference, and resistance.

Parallel Process

Parallel process is a concept directly from psychodynamic theory and hence psychodynamic supervision. It occurs within the relationship with the supervisor and supervisee(s), or among members in group supervision of group therapy. Parallel process in supervision "occurs when (1) the therapist brings the interaction patterns that occur between the therapist and client(s) into supervision and enacts the same pattern but with the therapist trainee in the client's role, or (2) the trainee takes the interaction pattern in supervision back into the therapy session as the therapist, now enacting the supervisor's role" (Tracey et al., 2012, p. 330). These researchers found support for bidirectional parallel process and point the way to study this phenomenon quantitatively. Searles (1955) first coined the term "reflection process" and defined it as occurring when the supervisee unconsciously communicates their clients' concerns in the relationship with the supervisor. As an example, the client talks urgently with their therapist with rapid speech, and then in supervision, the therapist presents the information to the supervisor in a pressing and frenzied manner. Bernard and Goodyear (2019) state that at times, the supervisee may become aware of the parallel process by having the supervisor point it out but at other times, using role-plays or using motivational interviewing strategies help the supervisee explore what might be occurring beneath the surface of these reactions. In the above example, the group client may be talking rapidly to impress the group therapist or acting out a need for the therapist's attention in competition with other group peers. Another possibility is that the group client perceives their problem to be extremely urgent and the supervisee responds to this urgency. Without awareness, the supervisee may have similar underlying motivations vis-à-vis the supervisor. The usefulness of exploring the interaction is to identify and become aware of underlying motivations of clients that the therapist might otherwise overlook, or not allow themselves to identify with it if it causes shame.

Transference

Transference has been noted for years in group psychotherapy and in supervisory relationships. As early as 1895, Freud described transference as attitudes that are *transferred* from client to therapist that are "earlier attitudes toward important figures in the client's life" (Yalom & Leszcz, 2020). This same interaction can occur within the supervisory alliance such as when a supervisee, who feels that their parents were withholding information from them, is frustrated with the supervisor who is characterized as "not giving me all of the answers I am looking for." Identifying transference in the supervisory relationship can often open up a more reality-based relationship and unblock opportunities for learning. At these junctures it is important that the supervisor use it in the service of improving the supervisory relationship and the work of supervision, and not resort to doing therapy with the supervisee. Transference can also occur between and among supervisees in group supervision. When supervisees can become aware of these transferences in their relationships in supervision, they can also be used to illuminate parallel processes with their group members.

Countertransference

Countertransference occurs when the supervisee has an intense reaction to a group member that often stems from a past relationship rather than the actual behavior of the client such as when their reaction mirrors a conflict they had with their sibling or parent years earlier. The intensity of the supervisory relationship can result in the supervisor also being susceptible to *countertransference* reactions with supervisees. These reactions are the supervisor's unconscious and conscious emotional responses to a supervisee that are based on the supervisor's own past experiences. A supervisor has a duty to monitor these reactions to ensure they can be worked through adaptively, in a way that avoids undue harm to supervisees or clients. At times they may need to obtain consultation with a colleague or process it in their personal therapy (Falender & Shafranske, 2021, p. 206).

In their 2011 article, Counselman and Abernethy review and provide guidance on countertransference reactions in the context of group therapy and include various affective reactions that a supervisor may experience including over-identification with the supervisee, attraction to the supervisee, or ethnocultural issues, anger, and shame. They also discuss other affective reactions that can be present because of family of origin dynamics, particularly in a group supervision environment. For instance, the supervisor may dispense criticism to supervisees the way they experienced criticism in their family, alternatively if a supervisor was shamed for mistakes, they might fear evoking shame with their supervisee and avoid any negative feedback to the supervisee. Feelings of jealousy or grief could arise in a situation where a supervisee is in a similar life situation, such as if a supervisee becomes pregnant while a supervisor is similarly trying to begin a family. Counselman and Abernathy (2011) present a decision-making tool and support strategies to guide supervisors in ethically managing such responses. Some methods for dealing with countertransference in the supervisory relationship are to openly discuss it with the supervisee, listening carefully to the supervisee's emotions and respond sensitively to them, use self-disclosure when appropriate, and uphold professional boundaries. Additionally, discussing countertransference with supervisees can help supervisees become more open in the supervision sessions about their own countertransference and how it might be affecting relationships and treatment in their groups. It is important for the supervisor to help their supervisee distinguish between subjective countertransference, that which derives from the supervisee's unresolved issues, and objective countertransference, which is the supervisee's direct response to their clients' behavior. Distinguishing what is objective will provide a significant source of clinical data for the group therapist to understand their group members.

Resistance

Resistance in supervision can occur for several reasons such as supervisee defensiveness, shame, and anxiety. Resistance can occur in supervision when the supervisee responds defensively to a perceived threat. When feeling threatened, counselors in supervision seek coping strategies to reduce their anxieties. Some of these strategies interfere with the process of learning and may be seen by the supervisor as resistance. The various forms of resistant behavior might include describing only positive case summaries, being late for supervision, asking a lot of questions to deflect looking at supervisory material, dismissing every suggestion ("Yes … but"), etc. (Liddle, 1986). It also can manifest in behaviors akin to leaving out important data from the psychotherapy group, readily agreeing with the supervisor to avoid a discussion, and missing supervision sessions. In each of these situations, it is the responsibility of the supervisor to assist the supervisee in recognizing and modifying their reactions. These components by themselves are complex in individual supervision yet the supervisor must consider the multidimensionality of each of them when exploring with a supervisee the functioning of their several member psychotherapy group. Sometimes resistance can become contagious in a group so that the whole group unconsciously engages in it so that it becomes a group norm. For example, cancelling because of ostensibly real-life circumstances becomes acceptable. Often the group therapist, or even the supervisor is unconsciously co-opted into the resistance, typically called "colluding." Scapegoating is another example typical of groups that do not want to explore their own issues that they see in the scapegoated member.

Projection, Projective Identification, and Internalization

Projection, projective identification, and internalization are three other related relational mechanisms that occur both in the supervisory relationship and in group processes. *Projection* refers to a person's behavior when they project a quality onto another person that they are not aware or conscious of that they possess themselves. *Projective identification* is a little more complicated and similar to projection in that a person unconsciously identifies with an aspect of the other but imputes the other as owning or enacting the quality in their interpersonal context. It involves two prongs: projection: a person attributes a characteristic to another person and the other person internalizes those projected qualities (identification). *Internalization* can be an unconscious taking in and accepting a projection and believing it is one's own. For example, someone might be accused of being a liar by a lying person who doesn't realize they lie, or if they do, disavows it. Meanwhile, the accused person figures they must be a liar. This can particularly happen in parental situations, and in situations of unequal power such as the supervisory relationship. Internalization of values and interpersonal behavior also occurs by being around others, as in children taking on parent's behaviors. It's also the vehicle of acculturation.

Cognitive-Behavioral Supervision

Another commonly used psychotherapy-based model is cognitive-behavioral therapy (CBT) supervision. The strengths of CBT supervision approaches revolve around focusing on observable behavior. These include teaching specific skills and eliminating maladaptive behavior. Developing skills include teaching how and when to apply them and honing them with methods such as roleplaying and shaping. Supervisors use learning theory to identify and teach behaviors much as they would use CBT in clinical practice. Liese and Beck (1997) set out an agenda for each supervisory meeting. These include a check-in time in the beginning of the meeting followed by setting an agenda concerning goals for the session, underscoring learning aspects from earlier sessions and previous therapy clients discussed in supervision, reviewing homework assignments and progress made between sessions, ranking the items on the agenda for the work of the current meeting, allocating new homework, providing a summary of the session and formative feedback, and encouraging questions and feedback from the supervisee. Similarly, Cummings et al. (2015) described three "supervision processes that should be used at each meeting: agenda setting, encouraging trainee problem-solving, and formative feedback" (p. 158). Some specific techniques used in CBT supervision include identifying behavioral skills that are specific, measurable, achievable, realistic, and time-limited, addressing irrational or unhelpful cognitions, shaping (i.e., successive approximation), problem-solving, roleplaying, feedback, homework assignments, and audio- and videotape review. CBT supervision often includes a check-in that is employed as a link between earlier supervision sessions, setting an agenda for the supervision session and prioritizing the importance of those agenda items, reviewing homework and assigning new homework, providing a summary of the supervision meeting and communicating formative feedback, and obtaining feedback from the supervisee including questions and comments (Bernard & Goodyear, 2019). Although CBT often is seen as focusing only on skill development and not on the relationship between the supervisee and the supervisor, several authors have affirmed the need for a strong and positive supervisory alliance (e.g., Newman & Kaplan, 2016).

Developmental Models

One model, the Integrated Developmental Model (IDM; Stoltenburg et al., 1998; Stoltenberg & McNeill, 2010), developed for individual supervision, describes characteristics of supervisees, suggesting that early supervisees (Level 1) are highly motivated, dependent on the supervisor, and self-preoccupied making it difficult to focus on the client. Stoltenberg et al. (1998) stated that at the beginning level, "their evaluation of self-performance is often guided by a perception of accuracy in faithfully performing a given technique" (p. 19) or doing what is correct. Their high motivation, although positive, can cause the early trainee to seek the "best" way to provide therapy, a rather rigid view. The authors describe supervisory strategies at this early level as giving support and encouragement, specific and concrete suggestions and advice, an initial focus on theory to practice, and helping the supervisee pivot from attention on themselves to that of the clients. Regarding the self and other awareness structure, for example, a novice supervisee holds all of the messages they have been taught in their head about how to conduct group psychotherapy, such as "don't be defensive, listen carefully to what is said, and note the nonverbal behavior." These messages are often overwhelming for an early group therapist which makes it difficult to hear their group members, therefore they regularly miss opportunities to be empathic and connect group member comments. Supervisees at this level also are commonly confused as they learn that there is not a "right" way to do most techniques. It is certainly easier to believe that there is one way, or that there is a right way. Learning that there are diverse ways of providing group psychotherapy can cause confusion and uncertainty but can also help to move the supervisee to a deeper level (Level 2). A strategy to reduce the supervisee's belief that there is only one "right answer" is for the supervisor to provide several alternatives to different scenarios.

Using the same three characteristics discussed in Level 1, Level 2 therapists are described by Stoltenberg et al. (1998) as moving from a self-focus to more attention on the client, motivational levels that are more changeable based on the perceived success of the therapist, and therapists becoming less dependent on the supervisor. Their motivation fluctuates between being confident and insecure/confusion. In this level, supervisors can provide conceptual interventions that suggest several ways to conceptualize a client's behavior. They can also begin to allow for less structure and explain more complex topics such as transference and countertransference. In Level 2, the supervisor can decrease the amount of structure given which will encourage more autonomy from the supervisee, and allow the supervisee to generate many options as they move from concrete or more simplistic case conceptualizations.

Level 3 therapists continue to develop their skills and become more independent, with high motivation, and are able to self-evaluate both their strengths and weaknesses in an honest way and see evaluations and assessments as strategies for growth. Supervision moves to being more collegial at Level 3, as supervisors help develop supervisees' own clinical orientation. With the supervisees' increased flexibility and awareness, supervisors can encourage supervisees to incorporate their "self" in their therapy. This focus on self deepens the supervisory relationship and the richness of discussion (Stoltenberg et al., 1998).

Stoltenberg and McNeill (2010) also outline the development of supervisors that mir-rors many of the components of early supervisees. These authors described Level 1 super-visors as "either highly anxious or somewhat naïve ... focused on doing the right thing and are usually highly motivated ... They tend to apply fairly mechanistic approaches to supervisory talks and may take a strong 'expert' role" (p. 201). Alternatively, it is also typical for some early supervisors that they may approach the supervisory alliance from a collegial view, feeling uncomfortable being an "expert." Early supervisors most often use the theory that they used when they were in supervision. It takes some maturity and confidence as a supervisor to become open to alternative theoretical orientations and to begin developing their own style. They naturally become both more active in supervision and more able to support the strengths of the supervisee, even if they are different from those of the supervisor. Understanding the development of the trainee and the supervisor provides an opportunity to match appropriate skills and encourage growth to a more complex level.

Process Models

The Discrimination Model (Bernard 1979, 1997), categorized as a process model, was cre-ated to aid early supervisors to make cognitive discriminations among the many options they had of how to engage and proceed with their supervisee. The model addresses the *Roles* of the supervisor related to the supervisory relationship that include teacher, counselor, and consultant. This model emphasizes two main focal points for the supervisor to consider, each with three components. The supervisor needs to attend to the *Foci* that point to specific skill development of the supervisee including: intervention, conceptualization, and balan-cing their personal style while holding clear boundaries that involve counter-transference. This pan-theoretical model is commonly used with early supervisors due to its "parsimony and versatility" (Bernard & Goodyear, 2019, p. 46). These models were mostly devised for supervision of individual therapy, yet they also can guide supervisors when supervising group psychotherapists.

The Common Factors Model

A more recent model is the Common Factors Model that describes specific characteris-tics that are thought to span all models. Watkins (2017) discussed 50 features that encom-pass nine areas. The main areas include genuineness and warmth, supervisory alliance, self-reflection, and providing feedback. Supervision, then, would address some of these recurrent components with the supervisee while modeling them with the supervisee such as providing quality feedback and being genuine and warm even when giving difficult com-ments. Although this model and others were designed for individual therapy and individual supervision, these same common factors can be found in group psychotherapy supervision.

The Multicultural Orientation Framework

A model that specifically addresses multicultural interactions in psychotherapy, as well as group therapy, is the Multicultural Orientation Framework. As with other models, the super-visory relationship is key to addressing diversity and multicultural interactions. Multicultural conversations can often be complex and delicate. Supervisors will want to approach the conflict by addressing it rather than ignoring or minimizing it. The model was developed to integrate multicultural competencies with research on psychotherapy process (Davis et al., 2018, Watkins et al., 2022). The focus for group leaders and for supervisors is on three prongs which are cultural humility, cultural opportunities, and cultural comfort. This framework initially concentrated on individual psychotherapy, yet has been expanded to include interactions in group psychotherapy (e.g., Kivlighan & Chapman, 2018; Riggs et al., 2020; Watkins et al., 2022). Cultural humility calls for the group psychotherapist to have an accurate sense of their strengths and particularly their limitations, void of a sense of self-importance. This stance allows the group therapist to respond collaboratively and nondefensively to material that is unclear or unknown to them. The other two pillars of the framework are cultural opportunities and cultural comfort. Cultural opportunities are occasions when a group member raises cultural values, beliefs, or other information that can be explored by the group leader. Regarding cultural comfort, if a group leader possesses ease toward cultural conversations and with cultural others, they will be able to explore the raised material in more depth.

These same three prongs relate to the supervisory relationship as cultural components come up in all psychotherapy groups and in supervisory interactions and often provoke anxiety for the group facilitator as well as the supervisor. Yet, it is known that supervisors have difficulty providing negative feedback to their supervisee(s), particularly when it is related to personal characteristics (e.g., defensiveness, rigidity). Supervisors will want to address the conversation in a humble manner, such as admitting when they lack knowledge on the topic, with the goal of opening up the dialog (and not ignoring it) and modeling moving into rather than away from the conversation. Encouraging reflection and discussion will provide a model for supervisees to use with their group psychotherapy members. If supervisees have limited experience with these sometimes highly charged conversations, they need to gain additional training outside of the supervision meetings.

Microaggressions in group therapy are interactions that are often highly charged and should be addressed in supervision. Lefforge et al. (2020) and others have provided training models for addressing microaggressions in group psychotherapy. Without attention to addressing and repairing these microaggressions, ruptures can occur. Watkins et al. (2015) addressed the need to apologize as one intervention for repairing ruptures. Although this seems common sense, apologizing also requires the group leader (and/or the supervisor) to acknowledge the microaggression and be able to show humility for their error.

Stages of the Supervisory Relationship

Much like group psychotherapy, the supervisory relationship develops through stages. In the early stage, supervisors and supervisees are learning about each other, what supervision will be like, and the expectations for each other. Similar to group psychotherapy, this first stage is critical in the development of trust. The supervisory written agreement is an anchor to begin setting the stage for the work ahead. Much of this chapter has focused on the working stage of supervision that includes skill development and professional development of the supervisee.

The stage that is rarely discussed is termination of the supervisory relationship. Most research in psychotherapy has discussed premature termination, which is an important focus but, in this section, planned termination is the focal point. Like termination in psychotherapy, supervisees and supervisors can have a range of thoughts and emotions about termination. Supervisors may wonder if they did enough to launch the supervisee. Supervisees may feel unprepared to move on to their next phase or even feel abandoned by the supervisor as it might bring up personal reactions from an earlier time. Some strategies will benefit the ending of the supervisory relationship. Several authors discuss critical components of termination in group psychotherapy (e.g., Corey et al., 2014; Gladding, 2015) which are just as relevant for ending the supervisory relationship. These authors talk about addressing unfinished topics, reviewing goals and successes, preparing the group therapist for potential future difficulties, and making room for the feelings of both members about the relationship ending. If supervision has been a place where strong trust has been developed, it can also be productive to discuss the strengths and weaknesses of the supervisory relationship.

Conclusion

There is little debate that the supervisory alliance is an essential (some suggest *the* essential) component in group psychotherapy supervision. A strong alliance will provide the building blocks for the development of trust which will provide a foundation for the supervisee to increase their skills in group psychotherapy, focus on their professional development, and deliver competent therapy in a group. Supervision of group psychotherapy is multidimensional requiring supervisors to be knowledgeable and adept in both supervision *and* group psychotherapy. There are many models and methods for providing supervision for group psychotherapy yet all need to attend to the supervisory relationship, establish the goals between (or among) the supervisee, and articulate the tasks that will be accomplished. It seems clear that one strategy for clarity is a contract or agreement that outlines the responsibility of the supervisor and the supervisee. What continues to need additional attention is not only the supervisory relationship in general, but also the theory, practice, and especially research on specific ways for the supervisor to move novice group leaders to competent group leaders. It will be helpful to begin to pinpoint specifically what components in the supervisory relationship can promote this process.

References

Alonso, A. (2000). On being skilled and deskilled as a psychotherapy supervisor, *The Journal of Psychotherapy Practice and Research, 9*(1), 55–61.

Bernard, J. M. (1979). Supervisor training: A discrimination model. *Counselor Education and Supervision*, 19, 60–68.https://doi.org/10.1002/j.1556-6978.1979.tb00906.x

Bernard, J. M. (1997). The discrimination model. In C.E Watkins, Jr. (Ed.), *Handbook of psychotherapy supervision* (pp. 310–327). New York, NY: Wiley.

Bernard, J. M. & Goodyear, R. K. (2019). *Fundamentals of clinical supervision* (6th ed.). Pearson.

Burlingame, G. M., Strauss, B., & Joyce, A. S. (2013). Change mechanisms and effectiveness of small group treatments. In A. E. Bergin & S. L. Garfield (Eds.), *Handbook of psychotherapy and behavior change* (4th ed., pp. 640–689). ResearchGate.

Corey, M. S., Corey, G., & Corey, C. (2014), Groups: Process and practice (9th ed.). Belmont, CA: Brooks/Cole.

Counselman, E. F. & Abernathy, A. D. (2011). Supervisory reactions: An important aspect of supervision. *International Journal of Group Psychotherapy, 61*(2), 196–216. https://doi.org/10.1521/ijgp.2011.61.2.196

Cummings, J. A., Ballantyne, E. C., & Scallion, L. M. (2015). Essential processes for cognitive behavioral clinical supervision: Agenda setting, problem-solving, and formative feedback. *Psychotherapy, 52*(2), 158–163. https://doi.org/10.1037/a0038712

Davis, D. E., DeBlaere, C., Owen, J., Hook, J. N., Rivera, D. P., Choe, E., Van Tongeren, D. R., Worthington, E. L., & Placeres, V. (2018). The multicultural orientation framework: A narrative review. *Psychotherapy, 55*(1), 89–100. https://doi.org/10.1037/pst0000160

Denton, L. K., Gross, J. M., & Rogers, D. L. (2019). Factors contributing to the status of group programming at psychology internship sites. *International Journal of Group Psychotherapy, 70*(1), 89–116. https://doi.org/10.1080/00207284.2019.1686387

Ellis, M. V., Berger, L., Hanus, A. E., Ayala, E. E., Swords, B. A., & Siembor, M. (2014). Inadequate and harmful clinical supervision: Testing a revised framework and assessing occurrence. *Counseling Psychologist, 42*(4), 434–472. https://doi.org/10.1177/0011000013508656

Falender, C. & Shafranske, E. (2021). *Clinical supervision: A competency-based approach* (2nd ed.). American Psychological Association. https://doi.org/10.1037/0000243-000

Gladding, S. (2015). Group: A counseling specialty (7th ed.). Upper Saddle River, NJ Pearson.

Hoffman, M. A., Hill, C. E., Holmes, S. E., & Freitas, G. F. (2005). Supervisor perspective on the process and outcome of giving easy, difficult, or no feedback to supervisees. *Journal of Counseling Psychology, 52*(1), 3–13. https://doi.org/10.1037/0022-0167.52.1.3

Kivlighan III, D. M. & Chapman, N. A. (2018). Extending the multicultural orientation (MCO) framework to group psychotherapy: A clinical illustration. *Psychotherapy, 55*(1), 39–44. https:// doi.org/ 10.1037/pst0000142

Kivlighan Jr., D. M. & Kivlighan III, D. M. (2009). Training related changes in the ways that group trainees structure their knowledge of group counseling leader interventions. *Group Dynamics: Theory, Research, and Practice, 13*(3), 190–204. https://doi.org/10.1037/a0015357

Kivlighan Jr., D. M. & Tibbits, B. M. (2012). Silence is mean and other misconceptions of group counseling trainees: Identifying errors of commission and omission in trainees' knowledge structures. *Group Dynamics: Theory, Research, and Practice, 16*(1), 14–34. https://doi.org/10.1037/a0026558

Kleinberg, J. L. (1999). The supervisory alliance and the training of psychodynamic group psychotherapists. *International Journal of Group Psychotherapy, 49*(2), 159–179. https://doi.org/10.1080/00207 284.1999.11491579

Lefforge, N. L., Mclaughlin, S., Goates-Jones, M., & Mejia, C. (2020). A training model for addressing microaggressions in group psychotherapy. *International Journal of Group Psychotherapy, 70*(1), 1–28. https://doi.org/10.1080/00207284.2019.1680989

Liddle, B. J. (1986). Resistance in supervision: A response to perceived threat. *Counselor Education and Supervision, 26*(2), 117–127.

Liese, B. S. & Beck, J. S. (1997). Cognitive therapy supervision. In C. E. Watkins Jr. (Ed.), *Handbook of psychotherapy supervision* (pp. 114–133). Wiley.

Marmarosh, C. L. (2021). Ruptures and Repairs in Group Psychotherapy: From Theory to Practice. *International Journal of Group Psychotherapy, 71*(2), 205–223. https://doi.org/10.1080/00207 284.2020.1855893

McMahon, A. (2014). Four guiding principles for the supervisory relationship. *Reflective Practice, 15*(3), 333–346. https://doi.org/10.1080/14623943.2014.900010

McNamara, M. L., Kangos, K. A., Corp, D. A., Ellis, M. V., & Taylor, E. J. (2017). Narratives of harmful clinical supervision: Synthesis and recommendations. *The Clinical Supervisor, 36*(1), 124–144. https://doi.org/10.1080/07325223.2017.1298488

Nelson, M. L. & Friedlander M. L. (2001). A close look at conflictual supervisory relationships. *Journal of Counseling Psychology, 48*, 384–395.

Newman, C. F. & Kaplan, D. (2016). *Supervision essentials for cognitive-behavioral therapy* (Clinical Supervision Essentials Series). American Psychological Association.

Proctor, B. (2010). *Supervision: A co-operative exercise in accountability, enabling and ensuring.* Leicester National Youth Bureau and Council for Education and Training in Youth Work.

Riggs, T., Kivlighan III, D. M., & Tao, K. W. (2020). Problematic systems: Applying a multicultural orientation framework to understand "problematic members." *Professional Psychology: Research and Practice, 51*(3), 278–283. https://doi.org/10.1037/pro0000277

Riva, M. T. (2011). Supervision of group counseling. In R. K. Conyne (Ed.), *The Oxford handbook of group counseling* (pp. 370–382). Oxford University Press.

Riva, M. T. (2014). Supervision of group leaders. In J. Delucia-Waack, C. R. Kalodner, & M. T. Riva (Eds.), *Handbook of group counseling and psychotherapy* (2nd ed., pp. 146–158). Sage.

Riva, M. T. & Erickson Cornish, J. (2018). Ethical considerations in group psychotherapy. In M. M. Leach & E. R. Welfel (Eds.). *The Cambridge handbook of applied psychological ethics* (pp. 218–238). Cambridge.

Rosen, S. & Tesser, A. (1970). On reluctance to communicate undesirable information: The MUM effect. *Sociometry, 33*(3), 253–263. https://doi.org/10.2307/2786156.

Safran, J. D., Muran, J. C., & Eubanks-Carter, C. (2011). Repairing alliance ruptures. *Psychotherapy, 48*(1) 80–87. https://doi.org/10.1037/a0022140

Sarnat, J. (2010). Key competencies of the psychodynamic psychotherapist and how to teach them in supervision. *Psychotherapy: Theory, Research, Practice, Training, 47*(1), 20–27. https://doi.org/10.1037/a0018846

Scarff, C. E., Bearman, M., Chiavaroli, N., & Trumble, S. (2019). Keeping mum in clinical supervision: Private thoughts and public judgements. *Medical Education, 53*(2), 133–142. https://doi.org/10.1111/medu.13728

Searles, H. F. (1955). The informational value of the supervisor's emotional experiences. *Psychiatry: Journal for the Study of Interpersonal Processes, 18,* 135–146.

Stoltenberg, C. D. & McNeill, B. W. (2010). *IDM supervision: An integrative developmental model for supervising counselors & therapists* (3rd ed.). Routledge.

Stoltenberg, C. D., McNeill, B. W. & Delworth Stoltenberg, U. (1998). *IDM supervision: An integrated developmental model for supervising counselors and therapists.* Jossey-Bass.

Tracey, T. J. G., Bludworth, J., & Glidden-Tracey, C. E. (2012). Are there parallel processes in psychotherapy supervision? An empirical examination. *Psychotherapy, 49*(3), 330–343. https://doi.org/10.1037/a0026246

Watkins Jr., C. E. (2017). Convergence in psychotherapy supervision: A common factors, common processes, common practices perspective. *Journal of Psychotherapy Integration, 27*(2), 140–152.

Watkins Jr., C. E. (2021). Ruptures and rupture repair in clinical supervision: Some thoughts and steps along the way. *Clinical Supervisor, 40*(2), 321–344. https://doi.org/10.1080/07325223.2021.1890657

Watkins Jr., C. E., Hook, J. N., DeBlaere, C., Davis, D. E., Wilcox, M. M., & Owen, J. (2022). Extending multicultural orientation to the group supervision of psychotherapy: Practical applications. *Practice Innovations, 7*(3), 255–267.

Watkins Jr., C. E., Reyna, S. H., Ramos, M., & Hook, J. N. (2015). The ruptured supervisory alliance and its repair: On supervisor apology as a reparative intervention. *Clinical Supervisor, 34*(1), 98–114. https://doi.org/10.1080/07325223.2015.1015194

Yalom, I. D. & Leszcz, M. (2020). *The theory and practice of group psychotherapy* (6th ed.). Basic Books.

Chapter 5

Multiculturalism and Diversity in Group Psychotherapy Supervision

Envisioning Justice, Equity, Diversity, and Inclusion

Michele D. Ribeiro, Salaheddine Ziadeh, J. Joana Kyei, Rita M. Rivera, and Kun Wang

Introduction

The group psychotherapy field has become increasingly sensitive and attuned to the role of cultural influences on the psychotherapy process and the movement toward collective action against inequitable and oppressive structures. As a result, there is a need for supervisors of group psychotherapy, and their supervisees, to increase their awareness and responsiveness to the role of culture and society and the need to advance social justice in the work (supervision, training, research, and practice). Along with a strong foundation of group psychotherapy theory, principles, and practice, a multicultural model that integrates JEDI is foundational to all aspects of mental health and group psychotherapy, including supervision. This chapter invites practitioners to incorporate an ecological and liberation psychology framework into the supervision of group psychotherapy practice.

As mental health inequities within the US and globally continue to be reckoned with, particularly within minoritized populations (e.g., racial and ethnic minorities, those from lower socioeconomic backgrounds, those with disabilities, and transgender people), group therapy is increasingly regarded as a hopeful and viable treatment option for engaging with these inequities (Whittingham et al., 2023). As group therapy becomes more central and accessible, so then does the need to elevate cultural diversity competence and humility in group psychotherapists (Abernethy, 2024). Hence, the need for equally fluid and flexible supervision of group work.

Ecological frameworks (Bronfenbrenner, 1979; APA, 2017a) that center JEDI are essential in the growing landscape of group psychotherapy supervision. Liberation psychology not only promotes a multicultural orientation but also places social justice and transformation at its core through the use of psychological approaches in understanding and addressing oppression among individuals and groups (Bulhan, 2015; Comas-Díaz & Torres Rivera, 2020; Martín-Baró, 1994). A specific training model, the Public Psychology for Liberation Training Model (Neville et al., 2021), calls for transforming psychology as a discipline and widening its lens to be more inclusive of justice and anti-oppression in all aspects of training. At the same time, Riva and Smith (2024) set the imperative for the psychology profession to further the guidelines for practice to expand and include the group supervision milieu. Thus, a supervision model of group psychotherapy that incorporates JEDI with the aim toward liberatory practices would set the stage for advancing ethical practice and a socially engaged science for the public good.

DOI: 10.4324/9781003410621-6

Group psychotherapy and supervision of group have long been relegated to the periphery despite the abundant use of groups in various clinical settings and the recent recognition of group psychology and group psychotherapy as a Specialty within the American Psychological Association (Whittingham et al., 2021). Supervision of group psychotherapy is by no means simple, in part because of the multiple levels and elements that need to be considered and managed. One aspect of this complexity is the multiple levels through which group dynamics can be examined. Traditionally, groups have been examined and explored at a minimum of three levels: individual (or intrapsychic), interpersonal, and group-as-a-whole. More recently, another level has been added: the socioecological context (e.g., Bemak & Chung, 2004). This context includes the impact that race, sexual orientation, class, and other social identities have on individuals, interpersonal interactions, and the group-as-a-whole. In this vein, Luke and Kiweewa (2010) speak of a "supra-group" level, which refers to external systemic forces impacting a therapy group (Goodrich & Luke, 2011, p. 25). For example, when the group is predominantly comprised of heterosexual members (or assumed to be), members may favor heteronormative ways of discussing relationships, to the detriment of same-sex relationship themes. In this example, the supra-group level reinforces heterosexism (which is an oppressive system) versus being inclusive of lesbian, gay, bisexual, pansexual, and other sexual minority relationships as well. Thus, awareness of the socio-ecological level would invite a more inclusive discussion on the full continuum of genders and sexual orientations.

A multicultural model of group psychotherapy supervision is the professional practice of teaching, mentoring, modeling, and guiding therapists leading or coleading therapy groups that integrates *critical consciousness* and ethically negotiates power, privilege, marginalization, and social justice within an ecological framework (APA, 2017a). Freire (2000) developed the notion of critical consciousness and defined it as the ability to analyze and act on social, political, and economic inequalities. Ecological frameworks speak to the layers of influence on an individual. These layers include the family, community, religious institutions, politics, and media that guide internal thoughts, values, and beliefs throughout a person's life and their life as member in a psychotherapy group. Thus, attention to diversity and the dynamics at play is warranted from all involved with a group: the supervisor, supervisee(s), and members of the therapy group(s).

Liberation as Foundational

The liberation training model (Neville et al., 2021), although created for psychology training, in general, fits well within the group psychotherapy and supervision of group psychotherapy milieu. This model, when adapted, is particularly useful as it offers guidelines for supervisors of group therapists, to focus on facilitating healthy interpersonal relationships necessary for group therapy, empowered supervisory relationships, bidirectional learning and knowledge in the supervisory relationship, and incorporating ethics and equity at all levels of group therapy practice and supervision. A JEDI-integrated supervision of group psychotherapy model builds upon the liberation training model by accentuating the following as vital:

1. healthy interpersonal relationships that focus on a level of trust and support for learning and collaboration between the supervisor and supervisee(s) and between the supervisee(s) and individual members of their group/group-as-a-whole;
2. empowered supervisory relationships that apply strengths-based approaches in providing feedback during supervision of group therapy that is culturally attuned;

3. bidirectional/cocreational understanding and learning that is maintained between supervisor and among supervisees and the group members;
4. practicing ethical decision-making within supervision of group psychotherapy (see Dalal, 2023; Brabender & MacNair-Semands, 2022); and
5. advocating for health equity that addresses bias, inequities, and social justice within group therapy settings (see Miles et al., 2021).

To approach justice and equity requires supervisors to craft the supervision milieu as an opportunity to expand or challenge Euro-centric practices/structures (Hopson, 2024). This can be done by exploring and appreciating the diversity of identities that interplay at all supervisory and group levels. Acknowledging social identities (Hays, 2008; Ribeiro, 2020), both similar and different within the therapy group and within the supervisory relationship, begins to create opportunities for integrating diversity dialogues (Bemak & Chung, 2019) into all aspects of psychological practice.

Group work is "founded on principles inherent in collectivistic cultures that adhere to interdependence, mutual cooperation, collaboration, harmony, and sharing" (Bemak & Chung, 2004, p. 34). The value systems of these collectivistic cultures are rooted in social networks of family and community and make up the majority of the world's populations, including the US in its historical and current immigration context. The group is a social microcosm of the larger society in which each member lives (Yalom & Leszcz, 2020). In fact, Rigg et al. (2020) go on to say, "Therapists who are able to identify these systemic influences and verbalize their observations using a group-as-a-social-microcosm perspective are thus more likely to create a space for members to speak directly about how their social identities and life experiences are playing out within the group" (p. 280). Coupled, with the social microcosm, is the idea of cultural maps (Falicov, 2014), on an individual and collective level. Cultural maps are the histories and social identities that influence how a person interacts with another person, all of which can influence dynamics within a group and thus supervision. Families and society influence who we are, how we think and at times how we behave. Supervision provides an opportunity to examine these larger, interpersonal, and internal forces that create more material to examine (Miller Aron & LeFay, 2024). For example, a supervisor was coleading a process group with an intern. One of the group members who came from a rural area in the state shared how she didn't feel she belonged in higher education. Upon inviting this client to unpack this belief with the group, the client shared more of her social identities including coming from a low socioeconomic background (she noted being considered "white trash" growing up) and being 20 years old and a mother. In response to these personal disclosures, two others in the group shared their own vulnerabilities of feeling like they also didn't belong. Further, they shared how much more they respected this client for being at the university. In supervision, the coleading intern processed her own countertransference that resonated with her lower-class status. Exploring this within supervision allowed her to not over-identify with the client while also holding empathy for the challenge that the client and the intern herself were facing. Later groups allowed for more unpacking of the harmful stereotype of "white trash."

Identities are complex, fluid, and intersectional in nature and have different salience and impact depending on the context. Table 5.1 provides a reflective exercise for both supervisor and supervisee in attending to the interplay and impact that social identities can have on the therapy group and within the supervisory relationship. Bringing this into the supervisory relationship at the beginning of the supervisory relationship could invite implicit thoughts and feelings about these issues to be more explicit and more readily available for exploration.

Table 5.1 JEDI Group Facilitation and Social Identities Matrix

Social Identity (SI)	Which SI(s) do you think about the most as a group (co)leader/ supervisor?	Which SI(s) do you think about the least as a group (co)leader/ supervisor?	Which SI(s) has an effect on your decision-making as a group (co) leader/ supervisor?	Which SI(s) give you power and privilege in society/ in the group?	Which SI(s) have the greatest effect on how your group members/ supervisee see(s) you?	Which SI(s) will you need to attend to in order to work from a JEDI orientation?
Age and generational influences						
Developmental Disability						
Disability Acquired Later in Life						
Religion/Spirituality						
Race						
Ethnicity						
Socioeconomics						
Sexual Orientation						
Indigenous Heritage						
National Origin and Language						
Gender						
Body Size						
Education Level						
Other:						

This exercise could be revisited within the supervision milieu as issues arise both explicitly and implicitly within the therapy group.

The Role of Culture

Multiculturism with its diverse worldviews is woven into all human and group interactions, including those arising in the therapy group. But, until recently the mosaic of identities has largely been neglected in the consulting room (Abernethy, 2024; Kleinberg, 2012; Shah & Kosi, 2012). In fact, the entire field of mainstream psychology in the US has long reflected a hegemony characterized by a worldview and narrative dubbed as Western, Educated, Industrialized, Rich, and Democratic (WEIRD) (Muthukrishna et al., 2020), representative only of a small portion of the human population. Adams et al. (2018) went on to report that such a narrow and exclusive framework privileges specific ways of knowing, being, and doing as natural, normative, and progressive that when unacknowledged becomes a norm of practice rather than a privileged and biased worldview. This is not only true within individual clinical practice but also within the history of group psychotherapy which has roots within a psychoanalytical frame.

Tummula-Narra (2004) notes that "a major challenge to multicultural training is the lack of access to supervisors and mentors who come from culturally and racially diverse backgrounds and/or familiar with multicultural perspectives" (p. 301). According to the APA (2021), there continues to be huge disparities in racial demographics within the psychology workforce, where White psychologists make up the majority (80.85%), and racially minor-itized populations trail significantly behind. Specifically, Hispanic (7.95%), Black/African American (5.08%), Asian (3.28%), people of other racial groups (2.68%), American Indian/Alaska Native (0.13%) and Native Hawaiian/Pacific Islander (0.03%), populate the other 20% in the workforce. Even within the American Psychological Association's division of group psychology and group psychotherapy (Division 49) there are only 11.2% of total membership who identify as "People of Color" or multiracial/multiethnic (APA, 2024), up from 5.2% in 2016 (APA, 2016). Fong and Lease (1997) expressed serious concern regard-ing racial disparities in supervision and identified four kinds of challenges that White group therapy supervisors faced when trying to supervise through a culturally sensitive lens: unin-tentional racism, power differential dynamics, establishing trust in building a supervisory alliance, and communication. Tummala-Narra (2004) adds that White supervisors' resist-ance to talking about race and culture in supervision negatively impacts supervisees of color, as the feedback from supervisors tends to be "rooted in a limited dominant-culture perspective despite good intentions" (p. 304). With few guidelines for supervision of group therapy, supervisors had much latitude to unconsciously and at times explicitly focus on the figure (e.g. the group, the individual) rather than the ground (e.g. race, culture, socio-economics, etc.), where so much material can be left unexamined and thus undiscussed.

In 1999 and 2012, the Association for Specialists in Group Work developed and adopted the Principles for Diversity-Competent Group Workers (Haley-Banez et al., 1999) and the Multicultural and Social Justice Competence Principles for Group Workers (ASGW, 2012), respectively. These guidelines set a precedent that culture and diversity issues and dynamics need to be integrated into all aspects of group psychotherapy practice, research, training, and supervision. This shift into making the implicit explicit was strengthened by a competency-based clinical supervision model (Falender & Shafranske, 2004, 2017) and invited clinical, conceptual and empirical efforts to investigate the role of culture in group therapy (APA, 2019; ASGW, 2012 Kivlighan III et al., 2019; Kivlighan & Chapman, 2018; Kaklauskas & Nettles, 2020; Miles et al., 2023). Ongoing work now continues to address power and priv-ilege (Rigg et al., 2020) and how these play out in the group therapy setting.

The ongoing ethical practice in building cultural competence (Rousmaniere et al., 2019) which includes naming and leveraging power dynamics is reinforced in the litera-ture (DeAngelis, 2023; Ellis et al., 2014; Falender et al., 2014). To be sure, the supervisor–supervisee relationship is uneven in terms of power (due to accountability and professional stature among other things). As a result, this supervisory relationship needs to be culti-vated with tact and cultural humility, particularly as it relates to multicultural issues and factors that can undermine the relationship. Shifting this power differential can at times strengthen the supervisory alliance and, paradoxically, empower both parties to better address difference and diversity issues. By collaboratively discussing such matters as "emotional equals" in the relationship, for instance, supervisors can move the power paradigm from "power over" their supervisees to "power with" them (Rousmaniere & Ellis, 2013; Rousmaniere et al., 2019, p. 123). The notion of power with assumes that des-pite the supervisor being an expert on group theory, the supervisee is the expert on their own experience. Further, centering JEDI in supervision aligns with the ethics of practicing beneficence and non-maleficence; justice and advocacy (APA, 2017b; NLPA, 2020), and lessening microaggressions. Microaggressions can occur when issues aren't discussed or when collusion around the status quo or just silence around dynamics are reinforced (Miles et al., 2021). Ethical guidelines emphasize doing no harm whether as a super-visor toward the supervisee, or in their role as group leader, and in seeking socially just interventions if insensitivities occur around marginalized identities in group or when speaking of others outside of the group.

Healthy Relationships: Centrality of the Supervisory Relationship

A good supervisory relationship is central to supervision's success (Nelson & Friedlander, 2001; Rousmaniere et al., 2019), and JEDI is central to the success of the supervisory relationship of group psychotherapy. This centrality is reflected in the *Supervision Guidelines of the American Psychological Association* (APA, 2015) and recent literature on group supervision (Riva & Smith, 2024). Specifically, the second guideline of APA calls on supervisors to work toward a "respectful supervisory relationship" with their supervisees and to "facilitate [their] diversity competence" (APA, 2015, p. 15). The fourth guideline prompts supervisors to develop their multicultural knowledge, model advocacy, and promote change in how diversity is discussed and attended to in the context of therapy practice. In this vein, Falender and Shafranske (2017) recommend that supervisors attend to "multiple multicultural identities" from the outset of supervision. This includes the exploration of different worldviews and avoidance of incorrect assumptions, since these can strain or rupture the supervisory relationship.

The JEDI-integrated supervisor adopts a stance of respect, interest, and openness with the supervisee and constantly monitors the strength of the supervisory alliance. In the case of a strain or rupture, the supervisor moves to repair the relationship, considering steps to move forward. And, since any supervisory work that promotes or hinders cultural humility can ripple through to the supervisee–client relationship and therapy work, the supervisor should always consider the impact of discussing the supervisee's diversity issues with the supervisee and, by extension, the supervisee–group dynamics. Such matters need to be broached sensitively, with attention to timing, content, and current alliance strength, for supervisory interventions to succeed and to maintain a good supervisory relationship. In managing the supervisory relationship, the supervisor must take into consideration the supervisee's cultural norms, especially normative social behaviors in the context of relationship (Rousmaniere et al., 2019). This cannot be established, however, without knowing the supervisee's level of acculturation (Schwartz et al., 2010) and cultural identifications in the context of familial heritage (Rousmaniere et al., 2019; Yoon et al., 2011). Therefore, the competent supervisor makes no quick assumptions about the supervisees' cultural identities and differences related to privilege or oppression based identity and strives instead to access that knowledge respectfully and collaboratively, to better understand and manage the supervisory relationship.

Empowered Learning: Readiness

JEDI-integrated group therapy supervision integrates socialization processes (Harro, 2000) related to identity and identity development with the goals and issues that group members are coming to group therapy for. Thus integration, not just the acknowledgment, is foundational and necessary (Tummala-Narra, 2004).

Since oppressive systems, bias, and stereotyping uphold systems of dominance and cause harm to everyone, including supervisees and their group members (Fernandes & Lane, 2020; Hook et al., 2018), supervisors have an ethical responsibility to understand context within the environments they are supervising. For instance, supervisors from more individualistic cultures who provide supervision in more collectivistic cultures will need knowledge of the political, cultural, and organizational contexts (i.e., the use of supervisory authority, and decision-making in the clinical supervision process). They also need an awareness of how professional practices (such as clinical expertise, professional roles, and supervisory interactions) and personal characteristics affect the supervisory relationship (see Tsui et al., 2014). For example, in providing supervision for a therapist from Guatemala, an ecological framework would be necessary. It would entail learning how the supervisee was impacted by the country's history, including the lengthy war which resulted in the genocide of the indigenous Maya. A deeper understanding of the culture would additionally entail the subsequent forced silencing of public mourning and reparations for affected families and communities (Rohr, 2012). On another systems level, the supervisory relationship could also entail awareness of the transference of this culture of trauma and mistrust in the therapeutic group and supervisory relationships; and knowledge of the boundaries or lack thereof given to supervision by the organizations providing care. A supervisor couldn't know all of this at the onset but acknowledging even some of these dynamics would allow the supervisee to be seen within their cultural context. Being seen can help build a sense of holding and safety in the supervision. Anne McEneaney (personal communication, May 25, 2023), who provides extensive international supervision across various countries, additionally recommends that supervisors understand the premise that most supervisees from more collectivistic cultures respect the teacher's authority and may think asking questions or disagreeing challenges that authority and therefore should not occur. Helping the supervisee(s) to develop a new understanding that sharing their own perspectives and experiences will enrich the process of supervision is critical. Equally important is acknowledging and exploring that the supervisor and supervisee may have differing views of authority and feelings about challenging authority and that their goal in supervision is to navigate these differences of learning and teaching and practice. Understanding and containing these differences as normal and acceptable is crucial to supervision.

Another area is within the supervisory needs of international students of color training in the US, who are often wrongly assumed to be similar in personality to those of minoritized US populations. Keeping in mind, that international students even from the same country can be vastly different from each other because of other identity markers (i.e., SES). While both subgroups share some similarities, the literature highlights that international supervisees from collectivist cultures are generally oriented toward teaching styles in which the instructor, and by extension the supervisor, assumes the role of "expert to be listened to," in contrast to Euro-American teaching styles that favor interactive engagement from students (Akanwa, 2015; Rao, 2017; Smith & Khawaja, 2011; Yildirim, 2017). Such differences can strain the supervisory process, in terms of expectations, and cause stress to international trainees that is likely to increase if the supervisor fails to adapt their supervisory style. The following personal account (JJK) reflects how providing a supportive environment for the trainee can move supervisor and supervisee alike into the zone of growth and inclusivity.

> As an international trainee in the US, I remember how stressful my first year of clinical training was, especially in a group supervision context. I was expected to participate in a manner wholly foreign to me (i.e., by expressing my opinion even if it contradicted the expert supervisor's perspective). In my culture, contradicting an expert amounts to a disrespectful challenge of an authority figure in public. Although my anxiety gradually decreased as I progressed with my training, it had proved challenging. If this difference in style of supervising/ learning could have been named and explored, however, I could have experienced an easier transition to the stark differences in style and values. An invitation to discuss would have also modelled an attitudinal openness of hearing what I, the supervisee, might need in that particular context as well.

When in a supervision group, supervisees who represent marginalized identities may also experience interpersonal isolation which can have a negative impact on their clinical work (Kiteki et al., 2022; McKinley, 2019; Pendse & Inman, 2017; Sangganjanavanich & Black, 2009). International students (in graduate psychology programs in the US) who are less acculturated to US culture have also reported having lower counseling skills self-efficacy and weaker supervisory work alliances (Nilsson & Dodds, 2006). Supervisors can gradually adapt their role from that of the technical expert to a role in which they become more collaborative over time. Supervisors can also lessen supervisees' interpersonal isolation by making space for supervisees to contribute to the supervision process using more of an affective (in contrast to a cognitive) mode of processing in supervision.

For example,

I (JJK) was in an AGPA annual meeting supervision workshop with a first-time attendee from China who conveyed his confusion over being asked to verbally share his associations to the material being presented. The facilitators however were quick to model multicultural orientation in action as they asked this group member about his experiences in supervision in his home country and invited him to share what would be helpful for him in the current group. This member shared how he had used his emotional intuitive understanding in his home country during a supervision meeting. In hearing his experience, I (JJK) and my cofacilitator encouraged him to use his emotional intuition with us as well when discussing the case, we had offered. Attuning to his needs as a supervisee, connecting to a cultural value and norm of his, enriched group process as it acknowledged the unique strengths and perspectives of each group member.

Another area of power imbalance is within linguistic competence. Sometimes supervisees (e.g., bilingual) have more linguistic variability in their skill sets than their supervisors (e.g., monolingual). Case in point, one of the present writers (R.R.) was on internship. The center sought out a Spanish-speaking supervisor to maximize and ethically support the intern's ability to provide services in Spanish to clients seeking this language diversity offering. But what happens if no supervisor at the center could provide supervision in Spanish and/or doesn't understand the nuances of language enough to guide particularly a beginning therapist? Then both supervisee and clients would be deprived of this advantage, given the effectiveness of conducting therapy in the client's native language (Smith et al., 2011). Moreover, ethical issues may emerge in the context of differential linguistic competence regarding treatment, such as when supervisees disagree with their supervisors about specific uses of language or the broader issue where a supervisee knows more in terms of language but less in terms of therapy. When the supervisory relationship is strong, disagreements can be worked through easier. The supervisor and supervisee can negotiate the difference with more respect and understanding for the other's perspective.

Given the large number of linguistically diverse populations especially in certain areas of the US, language becomes a necessary addition to mental health service provision. Training programs and sites could center liberation practices by prioritizing language accessibility as part of their commitment to comprehensive clinical training. By ensuring that multilingual trainees have the necessary resources to develop their skills in different languages, a more inclusive and patient-centered healthcare environment can be created, along with ensuring ethical training and practice.

Reciprocal Knowledge

At the onset of supervision, the supervisor must clearly communicate that diversity issues, anti-oppression, and liberation will be an integral part of the supervision and thus invite the supervisee(s) to identify and explore these issues as they emerge, be it in treatment, the supervisory relationship, or the supervision group. In parallel, the supervisee actively participates in this process from a position of transparency and openness (to learning) by bringing up pertinent JEDI-integrated themes; and discussing and processing them in their respective contexts (i.e., treatment, supervisory relationship, and supervision group). The dominant spirit is one of understanding and mutual growth. This is done in a respectful and collaborative space that is secured and promoted by the supervisor. Throughout, a primary consideration is the readiness of the stakeholder(s) to engage in and make sense of such conversations (e.g., in terms of developmental stage or timing). For example, early in the supervisory relationship, psychological resistances and defenses against receiving feedback may emerge due to shame and/ or anxieties of not knowing "enough" either related to technique or diversity-related issues. Supervisors can model cultural humility by owning that they will not know everything there is to know about group, dynamics, and culture so it is fair to say that the supervisee won't know everything as well. Encouraging an openness to feedback can lessen resistances and defenses.

One way to initiate an atmosphere of openness to exploring diversity issues within supervision is to have a one-day cultural autobiography session that entails sharing a journey of salient social identities and life experiences. This sharing of identities and the current relationship to them can set the stage for ongoing discussions and examination within the therapy groups, the supervision group, and/or the supervisor–supervisee dyad. Naming these identities and integrating them throughout the supervisory experience, allows the supervisor to share awareness and limitation in worldview when processing with the supervisee(s) and the material they present regarding their groups. The session can be structured with a series of questions such as the following adapted from the Counseling and Psychological Services (2018) at Oregon State University. Such an exercise sets the stage for more open conversations between the supervisor and supervisee, including how to engage in diversity-related topics within supervision and the group therapy context as well. Below are some items to consider in the autobiography reflection and process.

1. Describe your family of origin including information on: (a) composition/members (parents, siblings, birth order, etc.); (b) ethnic identity; (c) sociocultural background (class); and (d) neighborhood. Do you consider your family of origin/yourself upper, middle, or lower socioeconomic class? What meaning do you attach to this label? What family stories or narratives inform your understanding of your roots?
2. What is your first recollection about your ethnicity, race, class, sexual orientation, religious/spirituality, etc. (a) How did you come to realize your current identity? (b) How did you come to identify with any group and to learn that there are "others" different from you? Who were (are) defined as "outsiders" and "insiders" by your family or group? Do you recall "journeying out of your own world" or "entering the mainstream?"
3. Who were your playmates and friends when growing up? Today? Who lived in your neighborhood? Who was a "desirable" friend to bring home? How did you select your dates (if you dated), roommates, mates? Sexual taboos? Does this relate to ethnicity, class, or race? If yes, how?
4. Can you relate your education aspirations and/or choice of job/profession to the aspirations of your group (e.g., your race, class, gender identity, sexual orientation)? Optimism vs. pessimism about these aspirations?

5. What do you think about the current socialization (e.g., how gender roles are defined and how they may or may not be related to your ethnic, class, gender, sexual, or racial identity) of children into your groups? Who is the head of the family, should women work, what is the role of men/women/nonbinary/trans within your cultural group?
6. How do you perceive the relative power position(s) of particular individuals and families as related to their social class, race, and/or ethnicity? How do these individuals and/or groups vary in political power and decision-making authority? What are the attitudes toward the government and the role of the state? How would you relate this to the way social services are delivered and their accessibility?
7. What groups or individuals were influential to you during your formative years? Why was this? Does this relate to your culture at all?
8. How would you want to define your role as a group therapist considering your thoughtful answers to the above questions?
9. Given your answers above, what do you see as the main barriers for you when working from a JEDI-integrated framework within group psychotherapy and supervision? What are your main resources/personal attributes that can assist working within a JEDI framework?

Critical Ethical Consciousness: Microaggressions/Microinvalidations

Microaggressions refer to subtle yet consistent verbal or nonverbal psychosocial messages that take the form of insults, slights, or offenses—whether intentional or unintentional—that communicate hostile, derogatory, or negative feelings and attitudes directed toward others often solely based on their marginalized group membership (Pierce, 1970; Sue et al., 2007). Such negative experiences regularly occur in group therapy (Kivlighan et al., 2021; Miles et al., 2021; Ribeiro, 2020; Harris, 2024). The ethical work is to process and repair such ruptures. But, as the literature suggests, they often are unaddressed and/or unprocessed, due to group discomfort, group composition and dynamics or an inability to manage success-fully (Belcher Platt, 2017). In a recent survey of racial ethnic minoritized clients (N = 71), in therapy groups conducted across various university counseling centers, 80% of Latine/Hispanics reported experiencing at least one racial microaggression. The majority (69%) of multiracial participants reported the same occurrence—specifically, 67% Asian/Asian Americans and 53% African American/Blacks (Kivlighan et al., 2021). Research also shows microaggressions to be a regular occurrence in supervision (Hird et al., 2001; Leary, 2000). Often supervisors have been identified as missing the mark with their supervisees and/or downplaying the harm that can be caused by not naming/acknowledging them when they occur. The literature suggests that supervisors who work toward naming and apologizing for such microaggressions are seen as safer and are more accepted than those who ignore them or adopt a "sweep under the rug" approach (Kivlighan et al., 2021).

Given the above research findings, supervisors need to play an active role in addressing and managing microaggressions. A JEDI-integrated approach can assist in reducing such occurrences, through the practice of cultural humility (Tervalon & Murray-Garcia, 1998) and openness to difference. Moreover, supervisors could use cultural opportunities as entry points to difficult topics and gradually optimize their cultural comfort with diversity themes (Owen et al., 2011).

An example of a JEDI-integrated approach with the practice of cultural humility, entailed a supervision group where a beginning group therapist, Nancy (pseudo name), disclosed her sexual orientation as pansexual during a cultural autobiography exercise. Later this same therapist, Nancy, and her coleader, Michele (who was also her supervisor of group supervision), cofacilitated a process group in which there was one gay, nonbinary, Chinese

American graduate student member; one Latina, nontraditional age, female student who disclosed never having had sex before; one White, female, Veteran, nontraditional, heterosexual undergraduate student; one multiracial Asian/White graduate student; one international, South African, heterosexual, female grad student; and one White, heterosexual, nontraditional undergraduate male presenting with an invisible disability. The group began a discussion around dating and dating apps and soon the discussion quickly took a heteronormative bend regarding relationships. Nancy at one point offered the comment "dating apps are not just between opposite sex partners" but seemed to pause after this. Michele reinforced that dating was not just between a woman and a man, and asked the group to consider widening their views. Group members agreed but the topic went back to sharing straight dating trends. Without inviting more process around the heteronormative culture during the group, the group continued without further acknowledgment, and then ended with the leaders unintentionally colluding with the focus on male/female dating as the norm. After the group, Nancy and Michele discussed the useful comment that Nancy had made and the failure by Michele to ask the group for further reflection when heteronormativity returned in the group. Nancy and Michele discussed the microinvalidation by not facilitating more process around gay experiences and formulated a plan to revisit at the next group. Later that week, during the supervision group, Michele invited the three group therapists in the supervision group to share updates on their group facilitation and any struggles/successes. Nancy, the cofacilitator with Michele, opened up with her disappointment in her own process of withholding her authentic self/shared gay identity with another member in our group who was also gay. Michele owned her part in colluding with silence and invited the supervision group to unpack the parallel process of Nancy's family and what was potentially recapitulated in the group with this parent, Michele, who failed to validate the member and ultimately Nancy. The group therapists in supervision with Michele were able to process some of the dynamics within the group and the marginalization that occurred despite Nancy making an attempt to address it. After processing within the supervision group, Nancy and Michele discussed revisiting and correcting the harm and, the following week, they brought back the issue into the group. This corrective experience allowed for all members to unpack the heteronormativity from the week prior, which led another member to share her experience of being with another woman; a disclosure she had not shared the week prior. The nonbinary gay member also spoke up about their experience, in all likelihood as a result of the two facilitators inviting deeper processing.

As cultural opportunities arise, a supervisory approach rooted in cultural humility and comfort can go a long way (Kivlighan et al., 2021). In the same vein, supervisory reflectiveness could create the necessary space to identify and manage a microaggression when it occurs. To train and motivate such a reflectiveness, a number of attributes seem necessary. We highlight them next.

Tripartite Model

The tripartite model was first proposed within the multicultural counseling movement, with its three core dimensions of "knowledge," "skills," and "awareness" (KSA) (Chu et al., 2016), to map out therapist–client interactions. This same model has been applied to group work and multicultural supervision (Goodrich & Luke, 2011). Specifically, multicultural group supervision requires academic preparation, awareness of cultural power differentials, and the skills to navigate cultural difficulties (e.g., microaggressions) as they occur within the supervisory relationship and/or in the context of therapy (e.g., parallel process). A fourth component of *attitude* is also necessary when integrating a liberatory and JEDI framework.

Watkins and colleagues (2019) underlined the primacy of "attitude" in their proposed multi-cultural orientation to supervision (MCO-S), with a set of key attributes that include being oriented toward learning and growth, lessening fears of making mistakes, and creating equitable environments that shift away from pain and struggle to more joy and healing (Gonsalvez & Crowe, 2014). This equates to a supervisory stance that would "orient" the supervisor in multicultural work toward humility, opportunity, and self-awareness.

Evaluation: Assessing Learning and Practical Skills

While the attitudinal attributes set the tracks for supervision to move forward, its success still requires a set of practical skills such as supervisee performance and assessment of supervisory outcome. In a JEDI-integrated context, these same skills necessitate additional honing and should be practiced with awareness, humility, and constant monitoring of outcome. Any assessment of group therapy facilitation outcomes should involve the supervisee, in part because a supervisee's experience cannot be entirely accessible to the supervisor without the former. In this vein, equity and inclusion outcome evaluation is necessarily dialogical. Evaluation occurs after a period of time where learning can take place (e.g., usually after at least eight to ten group sessions). A supervisor would have met weekly with the supervisee, and if the supervisor is coleading with the supervisee, preferable 30 minutes before and after each group to discuss these aspects of learning that the evaluation is assessing. The following are sets of questions, adapted from the Counseling and Psychological Service (2010a, 2010b) of Oregon State University to assess mutuality in evaluative growth and processes that integrate a JEDI and liberatory model. These evaluations can be given at various intervals of a supervisee training and can be further adapted based on need.

The first set in Table 5.2 solicits the *supervisor's evaluations of group therapy competencies of supervisees* with a focus on multicultural competence (MCC) and it includes some comments/questions (adjacent to some of the items) to guide an understanding of how a beginning group therapist/trainee can be evaluated. Items include:

The next set of items solicits the *supervisees evaluations of the supervisor if serving as a cofacilitator with the supervisee* of the group. A Likert scale can be utilized with descriptions of what constitutes a 1–5 rating.

____ 1. Is able to establish a working alliance with the trainee *that acknowledges safety in the context of any difference (e.g., power, gender, race).*

____ 2. Clearly communicates and negotiates coleadership responsibilities (e.g., note writing) *including what aspects of culture (e.g., defer to authority, harmony vs. confrontation) might inform their leadership.*

____ 3. Clearly communicates own work style and anticipated structure of the group, *including the aim of coleadership to be focused on equitable decision-making and power in facilitating the group.*

____ 4. Consistently spends time processing each group session *to include dynamics related to diversity issues (i.e., power differentials, microaggressions/invalidations) as they emerge within the group.*

____ 5. Challenges and supports the trainee to experiment with new skills/behaviors *that feel culturally congruent to them.*

____ 6. Prioritizes the working relationship with the supervisor and addresses conflict as necessary.

___7. Shows ability to explore the supervisee's personal experiences that may influence the group experience.

___8. Helps the supervisee build confidence around identifying and managing diversity issues within group.

___9. Gives timely and appropriate feedback to *the supervisee regarding their multicultural competencies.*

___10. Accurately assesses the trainee's strengths and areas for growth *with regard to cultural diversity and humility in group.*

___11. Invites feedback about *supervisee as a coleader and the sociocultural identities that informed their cofacilitation.*

___12. Provides useful alternatives for intervening in group sessions *including those based on multicultural sensitivity and humility.*

___13. Provides useful conceptualizations about group dynamics *in the context of diversity.*

___14. Addresses ethical issues as necessary *including those related to multicultural work.*

___15. Encourages the exploration of individual and group differences from a multicultural perspective.

A liberatory and JEDI-integrated model of supervision, optimized with the attitudinal attributes of conscientiousness, reflectiveness, and relationality, is likely to positively impact both supervisee performance and supervision outcome. A supervisor can invite a supervisee to share, but the latter might not respond if trust in the relationship is hampered or cultural humility is lacking (i.e., attitude value attributes are not present). A culturally sensitive and aware space may be a necessary, but not sufficient, condition for safety and expression in supervision. Therefore, the supervisory space requires more than assurance of safety but also the necessary attitudinal attributes (e.g., openness to feedback) on the part of the supervisor. Keeping all of these practices in mind, we now move to the various ways supervision can occur in terms of models, followed by modalities in which they occur.

Models

Several models have been proposed to provide guidance for supervisors within a group supervision context (i.e., one supervisor with three or more supervisees). When we look at the ecological approach, we must look beyond what is explicit (supervisor, supervisee, group-as-a-whole, members of the group) and understand levels of systems that include the administrative, institutional, cultural, national, political, and global. When we expand to include these levels, the material we are working with becomes more in tune with the multiple systems within the larger global society and with the dynamics that parallel this larger context, consciously or unconsciously at times, in therapy groups and group supervision. Three of these models of supervision of group psychotherapy are described below, along with their advantages and limitations. Supervisors are encouraged to assess which model may function well for their setting and the type of supervision they offer.

The Supervision of Group Work Model

The Supervision of Group Work (SGW) model was adapted from the "discrimination model" (Bernard, 1979) and applied to group work supervision with the intent to promote diversity competence (Okech & Rubel, 2007). A main strength of the SGW model is that it facilitates the

Table 5.2 Evaluation: Group Therapy Competencies of Supervisees by Supervisor

Likert scale score	Supervisor's evaluation	Commentary on item
1–5 (low to high level of competency)	Prescreens and selects appropriate group clients *keeping in mind composition as it pertains to the diversity of membership.*	Does the supervisee understand the impact on an individual group member and group dynamics when they identify as an "only" in the group, particularly if the person holds a marginalized identity (e.g., only one female, only one BIPOC, only one trans-identified member, only one male, etc.). When is it advisable to have two or more of the same social identities when forming a group during the prescreening? Is it ok to have a group of people who may be the only one with a specific identity (e.g., race, gender, culture) or better to have an affinity group who share a particular salient social identity (e.g., race, gender, or sexual orientation)?
	Establishes clear group norms and the parameters of the group process *while taking into consideration cultural and diversity variables.*	A group norm can be naming that safety can be experienced differently in group depending on their experience of marginalization and privilege within this context and society.
	Designs and implements specific intervention strategies for the group, *including how to manage microaggression/invalidations as they occur.*	Identifying at pregroup meeting and at the onset of the group that microaggressions will occur, and our goal is to name them and work through the impact rather than focusing on the intent of the person who committed the hurt.
	Assesses and identifies multicultural group dynamics and interactions among group members (i.e., *Is able to assess and name how power and marginalization may play out between members, between leader(s) and member(s), and intrapersonally.*)	Does the intern discuss in supervision, when dynamics such as privileged members possibly talk more or over others with less social identity privilege (i.e., white male talks over a white female).
	Assesses the benefits and value of the group for individual participants *in the context of practicing conversations related to differences in life experiences and social identities.*	A comment by the group therapist could be, "having a group of members with varied life experiences allows us a broader understanding of each other and how to have intergroup dialogue regarding these differences."
	Effectively manages termination issues of group counseling *while taking into account the differential impact on group members in the context of their culture.*	Asking the questions "How are endings handled within your family of origin? Does culture influence endings in your family?"
	Develops and maintains an effective working relationship with a coleader *around diversity issues.*	Discusses issues regarding cultural differences and power and how these interplay with the group members and the coleader dyad.

(Continued)

Table 5.2 (Continued)

Likert scale score	Supervisor's evaluation	Commentary on item
	Maintains appropriate and timely documentation of group therapy cases.	Are cultural aspects of group members highlighted within record keeping when appropriate?
	Integrates issues of diversity/ multiculturalism in groups *at the onset during the pregroup meeting to the termination phase of group.*	
	Practices within standards and ethical guidelines, *including the multicultural guidelines within an ecological context.*	
	Utilizes group theory and research *including research based on diverse populations and dynamics such as the importance of diversity dialogues in group psychotherapy.*	

integration of "awareness of self, awareness of client's worldview, and diversity-appropriate interventions with the individual, interpersonal, and group-as-a-whole dimensions of group work" (Okech & Rubel, 2007, p. 245). Following the discrimination model, the SGW model attends to and promotes supervisees' skills of conceptualization, intervention, and personalization; yet, it surpasses the former by going beyond the individual and interpersonal spheres to that of group interaction (Okech & Rubel, 2007). The SGW model also prescribes the use of specific supervisor roles (i.e., teacher, counselor, and consultant) in a balanced way that also suits the developmental needs and experience level of supervisees (Bernard, 1979; Okech & Rubel, 2007; Rubel & Okech, 2006).

A practical advantage of the SGW model is its trans-theoretical application. It can be used by supervisors from different therapeutic orientations (Constantine, 2001). A conceptual advantage of the SGW model is its compatibility with the MCC framework (Okech & Rubel, 2007). Specifically, the awareness, knowledge, and skill domains of MCC align nicely with the personalization, conceptualization, and intervention foci of the SGW model (Okech & Rubel, 2007). One shortcoming of the SGW model, however, is the limitation of its scope to three levels of examination (i.e., individual, interpersonal, and group) and neglect of the socio-ecological context in which they are all immersed.

LGBTQ Responsive Model for Supervision of Group Work

An important consideration in supervision of group psychotherapy is that of the supervisory role (i.e., teacher, counselor, consultant) which is most suitable to drive home the intervention. Further, the supervisor should decide which competency domain (i.e., knowledge; awareness; skills; attitude) to work on with the supervisee. Such is the contention of Goodrich and Luke (2011) in their LGBTQ Responsive Model for Supervision of Group Work (RMSGW). The model, illustrated with a special focus on the LGBTQ client population, is based on a systematic approach to SGW, where "each group system level (e.g., intrapersonal) is conceived as a point of entry for the supervision. Further, the supervisor determines the area of MCC (e.g., awareness) in which the supervisory content occurs, and then selects the most effective supervisory role (e.g. teacher role-supervisor will spend time teaching a theoretical concept) through which to deliver the supervisory intervention" (Goodrich & Luke, 2011, p. 24). The cognitive mapping that comes from the systematic approach is a strength of the model in that it includes the socio-ecological. Conversely, the model has a major shortcoming, which it shares with the other two models presented. None have been empirically evaluated. Nonetheless, they are still useful in that they provide conceptual and procedural guidance that is scarce in the field of group work supervision.

Multicultural Orientation in Group Supervision

Expanding on the MCC model, Owen and colleagues proposed a framework for understanding the interplay of the cultural worlds (e.g., perspectives, beliefs, values) of therapists and clients in treatment (Davis et al., 2018; Owen et al., 2011). The framework called "multicultural orientation" (MCO) is largely relational and requires an empathic attunement on the part of the therapist to the cultural world of the client (Owen et al., 2011).

The MCO can be applied to all treatment modalities (e.g., individual; group) (Kivlighan & Chapman, 2018) and has three components: cultural humility, cultural comfort, and cultural opportunities. Each of these constructs has a specific meaning. All, however, are interdependent and may be described as attitudinal inasmuch as they reflect an intentional orientation to context. Cultural humility involves an attitudinal openness to the client's cultural world as well as an introspective examination of one's own elements (e.g., cultural identity and history) and contributions (e.g., assumptions) in the context of culture. Such a "humility," with which one meets and treats cultural phenomena, opens up a space for meeting the other unhinged by biases and distortions—be they regarding oneself or another—and thus facilitates the encounter (Hook et al., 2013). Yet, in interaction, difficult feelings may arise despite one's position of openness and reflectiveness as one anticipates, engages in, or reels from a culturally charged conversation (Watkins et al., 2019). In the context of MCO, this level of unease is subsumed under the construct of "cultural comfort." To be sure, the discomfort can occur on either end of the interaction or both. If the discomfort is activated in the supervisor, seeking consultation/training outside of the supervisory relationship is imperative rather than seeking it from the supervisee. If the discomfort is in the supervisee, the hope would be that the supervisor sets the stage in supervision to ask when they sense discomfort or the supervisee or client alludes to discomfort. This checking in can help build relationship and further the supervisory alliance. For this reason, the timing of a culturally pertinent conversation is critical to its success. In this vein, we can speak of missed or seized opportunities.

Formats of Multicultural Group Psychotherapy Supervision

There are many formats in which supervision of a psychotherapy group can be offered, including (1) supervision of a solo group therapist, (2) supervision of a junior therapist by the senior group therapist of a therapy group they facilitate together, (3) supervision of two cotherapist supervisees leading a group, (4) supervision of multiple solo therapists leading separate groups, and (5) supervision of multiple pairs of cotherapists leading separate groups. This section will highlight these formats and identify critical elements to keep in mind to successfully integrate a JEDI and an ecological framework into any of the various structural arrangements of group supervision. An important aspect of this is also recognizing how supervision is being conducted, whether in person or via an online platform.

As technology continues to pervade the therapeutic landscape, it offers a unique platform for group therapists and group members to connect across geographical areas (Lin et al.,

2021; Shklarski et al., 2021; Weinberg, 2020) while also challenging class and/or ability-related issues (i.e., access-related). Group therapists encounter a broader spectrum of cultural backgrounds, beliefs, values, and experiences among their group members. Though enriching, such a diverse therapeutic context mandates an in-depth understanding of multicultural issues to ensure a culturally responsive and effective therapy. Some of these issues are technical and include captioning and the limits of the online platform for real time transcription, and the captioning errors that occur as a function of language difference or for people who are hard of hearing. Furthermore, group accessibility is magnified in telehealth services, as internet bandwidth can vary extensively based on the socioeconomics of a member as well as their country's internet infrastructure. Keeping these equity issues in mind, we now turn to the ways supervision can be conducted.

Setting norms at the beginning of supervision is key and this includes the JEDI-integrated points we have been discussing throughout this chapter. The supervisor creates the frame for the supervisee to grow and learn, as will the supervisor as they work with the supervisee in supporting their facilitation of the therapy group.

Supervision of a Solo Group Therapist

There are two core foci in the supervision of a group therapist: teaching foundational and functional competencies on how a group therapist responds to their group, and the relational part between supervisor and supervisee, often referred to as the supervisory alliance. In teaching group therapy techniques, inevitably, the supervisor will know the theory and will contribute to the supervisees learning and development. However, in the latter relational part of supervision, the supervisor needs to go beyond content and theoretical knowledge to their relationship with the supervisee. One critical aspect of this relationship is power differential. As noted in previous sections of this chapter, analyzing power is an important first step in creating an equitable orientation. The supervisor's acknowledgment that how they understand the world is not superior and acknowledging the supervisee's experiences as equally informed, assists in moving a supervisee toward an *empowerment* outcome. An example of how this could happen is in simply naming the power differences not just in the inherent supervisor–supervisee dyad but going deeper in terms of how identities (marginalized and privileged) may manifest. Below are some recommendations for supervisors to address in the context of power as they start a new supervisory relationship:

1. Name the power differential that is inherent in the traditional supervisor–supervisee relationship, where the supervisor serves as teacher of techniques and practice. This naming by the supervisor, due to the rational authority within any system, sets the stage for open dialogue including teaching and learning on more classical therapeutic dynamics such as transference, resistance, defense structures, and psychopathology through the context of cultural lenses. Beyond cultural awareness and optimal attitudinal attributes, the JEDI-integrated supervisor needs knowledge and awareness skills—which are necessary to address and tackle emerging issues, such as bias, microaggressions, and discrimination. As cultural sensitivity is necessary for a supervisor to detect a culturally pertinent signal, it is also critical to know how to interpret it and then manage it correctly. This requires knowledge and experience and a strengths-based approach to how feedback is offered. Absent knowledge or experience, a dialogical space still can prove useful inasmuch as it provides access to the supervisee's cultural experience and knowledge. Another supervisory issue in the context of cultural awareness is that of seeing cultural elements that aren't in the supervisory space. This may be due to overgeneralization, projection,

transference and/or counter-transference, and, thus, reflects a supervisory failure to accurately capture what is emerging in supervision. People who may share similar identities are still individuals with different personalities and histories. Persons and cultures should not be confused, given within-culture variability (Norcross & Popple, 2017). Supervisors need to check their assumptions, lest they fall prey to perceptual assumptions, stereotypes and biases when processing issues with the supervisee and/or about the group members. Ultimately, when in doubt, seek clarification (as a supervisor) in a curious rather than accusatory tone.

2. Consider completing sections or a full cultural autobiography (as described previously) that creates a structure for colearning about each other (supervisor–supervisee). Completing an autobiography as a supervisor and modeling vulnerability around social identities provides a foundation for openness and curiosity as the dyad gets to know each other in the service of the supervisee's group that they are facilitating. Salient identities will be highlighted by both which can naturally lend itself to a similar process with the group participants. This sets the stage for an integration of identities into problem identification, therapy goals, and what supports and/or gets in the way of healing goals that brought group members into the group therapy milieu.

3. The supervisor must also know how to manage multiple dynamics, through humility and apology when harm occurs, in any of its forms: microaggression, microinvalidation, stereotyping, and/or making incorrect assumptions (Watkins et al., 2022). Discuss with the supervisee the potential for microaggressions/microinvalidations, and how as the supervisor one would want to know how comments may be experienced by the supervisee. Also encourage the motivation to learn and work through them if/when they occur. Stating that invariably microaggressions occur can ease both parties into accepting at times the inevitable while still inviting dialogue on how they can work to repair and/ or understand the implications of what prompted the microaggression in the first place. Any given apology should match the severity of the offense (see Watkins et al., 2015) and leave room for the rupture to heal and repair, ideally with due time and attention.

4. Encourage a discussion that invites an examination of supervisor's identities that can interface with the supervisee's identities, both in terms of what identities are marginalized and what identities have more privilege within the cultural context in which the work is being done (see Table 5.1). Intersectionality shows a myriad of identities where individuals can hold privilege and/or oppression rather than a fixed representation of someone. Again, discussing what each person is aware of in themselves and others can invite and strengthen this process in the group milieu.

5. Continue to check in regularly on how the supervisee is feeling in terms of the supervision they are receiving, specifically in terms of focusing on cultural learning and skills within either the group sphere or the supervision dyad.

6. Work toward cultural humility as a supervisor and supervisee.

7. Show willingness to work through discomfort. Supervisors need to model how to address an error, a real or perceived microaggression. The supervisor learns to address conflict/ harm in a direct and caring way to open up dialogue, rather than shutting down, tiptoeing around them, or negatively reacting to them. This recourse provides a viable alternative to seeking out the highest administrator, thus allowing both parties to work through ruptures instead of evading them. However, if unresolvable, the supervisor can provide a colleague's name in case the supervisee doesn't feel their needs are being met within the supervision relationship. The supervisee needs to know who to go to if unhealthy dynamics persist within the supervisory dyad. Processing with the supervisee

to allow for a healthy transition and termination, as appropriate, is key to positive growth and development both on personal and professional levels.

Supervision of a Supervisee by a Supervisor Who Also Serves as the Senior Group Therapist

This type of supervision is quite common and involves the supervisor assuming the dual role of cotherapist and supervisor of the supervisee. This type is most utilized when the supervisee is in training or newer in the group psychotherapy field. In this arrangement, the challenge for the supervisor is related to equity, as the supervisor will likely be more skilled than the supervisee, as was the case in previous section, but now the supervisor is cofacilitating the group and not just providing outside supervision of the group from the trainee's perspective. Here, the supervisor has the added ability to leverage power as a cotherapist. Discussing ways to leverage power usually has to do with how active or responsive a seasoned clinician will be in a therapy group versus a less skilled clinician. Thus, assigning specific group process skills to leverage activity in group, is a great way to empower the trainee as they get more comfortable with the group context and experience. An example of dividing up skills is having the supervisee take on more structured components of the group, such as opening and closing group sessions. This will allow group members to see more shared leadership and equity in managing power.

Supervision of Two Cotherapist Supervisees Leading a Group

In this supervision arrangement, a dyad is being supervised (i.e., the group's cofacilitators). The supervisor must be attentive to dynamics that govern dyadic interactions and pay special attention to equity and power imbalances in the supervisory space. This is central in and of itself and also necessary inasmuch as it could reflect inequitable coleadership of the therapy group. This is both enriching and requires more astuteness to name the growing complexity and opportunity that arise involving two coleaders (as the supervisees) and one supervisor. The complexities could include differences in gender and race, and how one may or may not take a more active leader role, for instance as a result of internalized dominance or marginalization around these identities. Depending on acculturation and/or socialization, coleaders may feel positive toward the cofacilitator, or devalued/invisible if privilege plays out in the group. And even if the coleaders feel comfortable with how they are coleading, assessing group members' responses to which leader takes on more leadership is important as there may be transferences at play from the clients' perspectives. In addition to considering the recommendations delineated in the previous section on a single supervisee–supervisor dyad, a supervisor could benefit from the following recommendation:

1. Encourage a discussion that invites an examination of privileged and marginalized social identities of supervisor and supervisees. The supervisor could encourage an unpacking of the interplay of social identities (again of marginalization and privilege) in terms of cultural opportunities that will also avail themselves with the coleadership dyad and further with the diversity of identities of the group members. Inevitably, people who are diverse in terms of gender, race, ability, age, etc. will come to colead groups and get supervised. The key thing is to bring out these dynamics into the supervision and therapy group so everyone can understand and process pertinent behaviors and choices, both conscious and unconscious (e.g., does the White male group leader speak more in the

group to members than the Black female group leader?). Putting thoughts and feelings into words allows everyone (cotherapists, the supervisors, and group members) to talk about what they notice rather than let behaviors play out unconsciously (i.e., I notice as a Black female cotherapist, my White male cotherapist and I have to be conscious about sharing space equally in our coleadership. I wonder what the group has noticed in our leadership roles). Ideally, this reflective identification and examination of pertinent material will be conducted within the psychological/supportive/psychoeducational context in which the work is being done.

Supervision of Multiple Solo Therapists Leading Separate Groups

This type of supervision is also known as group supervision of group psychotherapy. The most salient aspect of this supervision arrangement is that it involves the supervision of an actual group (i.e., the cofacilitators). Here we have a living system (group of cosupervisees) with multiple cultural maps at interplay, with each informing their and their group's socialization processes and experiences. Moreover, the dynamics in this type of supervisory relationship, though more complex, actually provides more material and richness as the supervisees can offer multiple perspectives that a single supervisor might be limited in offering. This model can encourage the therapists to look at their strengths and weaknesses in leadership, how to support and disagree with how each might facilitate, how to respond to issues differently based on the social identities each may hold, etc. The supervisor will want to focus on the group dynamics also within the supervision group. In addition to the above, there are other dynamics to examine. The following exemplify how to conduct such examination:

1. Name the opportunity to explore parallel processes from the various groups the supervisees are leading to that of the supervision group the supervisees/group leaders may be enacting as well. (The notion that group is a social microcosm becomes even more relevant as the mix of identities and experience levels of the supervisees become apparent.) Create space for the supervisor to discuss how the socio-ecological issues from outside are playing out in the supervision group and/or therapy groups being discussed.
2. Note and acknowledge the differences in experiences of the supervisees and how their individual needs of learning about cultural aspects and diversity within the group may differ. Process how supervisees will negotiate the differing needs.
3. Invite discussion at various points in the supervision group on whether supervisee members are getting their needs met, while at the same time noting the interplay of dynamics related to the various identities of the supervisees to each other and the supervisor/consultant leading the supervision group.
4. Overtly use stages of group development to guide the stages of development of the supervision/consultation group in terms of forming, norming, storming, performing and the varying degrees of termination. Safety is a key issue here inasmuch as members who hold marginalized identities may not feel as comfortable speaking to processes, especially if the supervisor hasn't named the differences in power, via identities the supervisor/supervisees hold. Group therapists are also advised to assess for within group differences and process them as related concerns arise.

Supervision of Multiple Pairs of Cotherapists Leading Separate Groups

Structurally, this constellation of supervisees features dyads (i.e., pairs of cotherapists) grouped together for the purpose of supervision. It is comparable to the previous arrangement (i.e., multiple therapists facilitating different groups), albeit with dyads instead of solo therapists being supervised. In other words, the constellation is that of a group, but this group consists of paired units (i.e., cotherapists) instead of individual members (i.e., solo therapists).

Given its complexity and the lack of literature regarding its supervision, this group structure may appear at first impervious to simple practice recommendations. Indeed, definitive guidelines are yet to be drawn regarding this form of supervision. Until this milestone is reached, supervisors can arguably benefit from the conceptualization of this structure as a group made of dyads, and draw on pertinent recommendations. In short, this complex structure requires attention to all the factors discussed in the previous supervision arrangement sections, with a special attention to diversity dynamics between the various coleaders (i.e., dyads facilitating the same group, and between them and their counterparts in supervision) as well as the implications on group membership and their various identities. Although this type of supervision group is rather rare, it is important to name since group training has been established as a group specialty within APA and this raises the probability more therapists may seek training and supervision to guide their group practice.

Concluding Remarks

JEDI-integrated supervision of group psychotherapy requires supervisors to deepen the interchange in supervision to include the complexity and fluidity of social identities as they interface with the issues that supervisees and their group clients will naturally need to negotiate. Missed opportunities due to fear or lack of knowledge/skills by the supervisor dampens the social justice framework which itself calls us to be advocates for change for our supervisees and the groups they (co)lead. On a clinical level, this fear or lack of knowledge can also impair group cohesion, which in turn can impair supervisory outcome as well as clinical outcome. It also overlooks an important component of individual members psychological and personality development. Cross-cultural considerations within a socio-ecological framework necessitate group psychotherapy supervision to overtly examine and discuss the myriads of interactions shaped by socioeconomic, political, and demographic trends in any society today (APAa, 2017; Bemak & Chung, 2004; Clauss-Ehlers et al., 2019).

JEDI-integrated supervision that seeks liberatory change, is a reemerging science. In the present chapter, we sketched some of its principles, methods, and models, so that practitioners can put them to use whenever practicing and supervising with others in their group psychotherapy work. At the core of supervision of group psychotherapy is a relational and liberational approach that intersects with empirical inquiry to provide useful and equitable knowledge, the kind that helps people work and grow together. As highlighted throughout, JEDI-integrated multicultural supervision requires foundational competencies (i.e., attitudinal) in addition to practical skills, awareness, and knowledge. The centrality of the supervisor–supervisee relationship in supervision of group psychotherapy, is keenly tied to the practices of reflectivity, conscientiousness, and ongoing betterment to supervisory work.

Beyond foundational competencies, we provided in the present chapter an overview of frameworks and models that could explicitly guide JEDI-integrated supervision—namely, the SGW model, the LGBTQ RMSGW and the MCO framework as applied to supervision, which all need ongoing research to validate effectiveness. We also addressed specific challenges likely to arise in JEDI-integrated supervision (e.g., microaggressions) and how to manage them, in addition to those pertaining to ethics, use of telehealth services, and cross-national work. Explicit guidance on supervision, broken down by modality, was offered through point-by-point recommendations. Further, since practice cannot be optimized without rehearsal and reflection, we provided some practical tools (e.g., social identity table, cultural autobiography exercise, and evaluation examples) often outlining experiential learning exercises that can be integrated or expanded upon depending on the needs of your context and setting.

The authors' efforts to capture and explain a liberatory model that integrates JEDI throughout the supervision of group psychotherapy, parallel our attempts to understand the work we do to advocate for the well-being of others. Just as all group psychotherapy work is embedded in an ecology of diversity and change, our supervision of these group processes must therefore advance just as our systems do.

References

Abernethy, A. D. (2024). *Addressing diversity dynamics in group therapy: Clinical and training applications.* Routledge.

Adams, G., Kurtis, T., Gómez, L., Molina, L. E., & Dobles, I. (2018). Decolonizing knowledge in hegemonic psychological science. In N. N. Wane & K. L. Todd (Eds.), *Decolonial pedagogy: Examining sites of resistance, resurgence, and renewal* (pp. 35–53). Springer.

Akanwa, E. E. (2015). International students in western developed countries: History, challenges, and prospects. *Journal of International Students, 5*(3), 271–284. https://doi.org/10.32674/jis.v5i3

American Psychological Association. (2015). Guidelines for clinical supervision in health service psychology. *American Psychologist, 70*(1), 33–46. https://doi.org/10.1037/a0038112

American Psychological Association. (2016). Demographic characteristics of Division 49 members by membership status 2016.

American Psychological Association. (2017a). Multicultural guidelines: An ecological approach to context, identity, and intersectionality. www.apa.org/about/policy/multicultural-guidelines.pdf

American Psychological Association. (2017b). Ethical principles of psychologists and code of conduct (2002, amended June 1, 2010 and January 1, 2017). www.apa.org/ethics/code/ethics-code-2017.pdf

American Psychological Association. (2021). Data tool: Demographics of the psychology workforce. www.apa.org/workforce/data-tools/demographics

American Psychological Association. (2024). Demographic characteristics of Division 49 members by membership status 2024.

APA Task Force on Race and Ethnicity Guidelines in Psychology. (2019). Race and ethnicity guidelines in psychology: Promoting responsiveness and equity. www.apa.org/about/policy/guidelines-race-ethnicity.pdf

Association for Specialists in Group Work. (2012). Multicultural and social justice competence principles for group workers. https://psycnet.apa.org/record/2012-28712-005

Association for Specialists in Group Work. (2021). ASGW guiding principles for group work. / www.researchgate.net/publication/354767821_Association_for_Specialists_in_Group_Work_Guiding_Principles_for_Group_Work

Belcher Platt, A. A. (2017). Racial-cultural events and microaggressions in group counseling as perceived by group counseling members of color. ETD Collection for Fordham University, AAI10607840. https://research.library.fordham.edu/dissertations/AAI10607840

Bemak, F. & Chung, R. C.-Y. (2004). Teaching multicultural group counseling: Perspectives for a new era. *Journal for Specialists in Group Work, 29*(1), 31–41. https://doi.org/10.1080/01933920490275349

Bemak, F. & Chung, R. C.-Y. (2019). Race dialogues in group psychotherapy: Key issues in training and practice. *International Journal of Group Psychotherapy, 69*(2), 172–191. https://doi.org/10.1080/00207284.2018.1498743

Bernard, J. M. (1979). Supervisor training: A discrimination model. *Counselor Education & Supervision, 19*, 60–68.

Bernard, J. M. & Goodyear, R. K. (2019). Fundamentals of clinical supervision (6th ed.). Pearson.

Brabender, V. & MacNair-Semands, R. (2022). *The ethics of group psychotherapy: Principles and practical strategies.* Routledge.

Bronfenbrenner, U. (1979). *The ecology of human development: Experiments by nature and design*. Harvard University Press.

Bulhan, H. A. (2015). Stages of colonialism in Africa: From occupation of land to occupation of being. *Journal of Social and Political Psychology, 3*(1), 239–256. https://doi.org/10.5964/jspp.v3il.143

Chu, J., Leino, A., Pflum, S., & Sue, S. (2016). A model for the theoretical basis of cultural competency to guide psychotherapy. *Professional Practice: Research and Practice, 47*, 18–29.

Clauss-Ehlers, C. S., Chiriboga, D. A., Hunter, S. J., Roysircar, G., & Tummala-Narra, P. (2019). APA multicultural guidelines executive summary: Ecological approach to context, identity, and intersectionality. *American Psychologist, 74*(2), 232–244. https://doi.org/10.1037/amp0000382

Comas-Diaz, L. & Torres Rivera, E. (2020). *Liberation psychology: Theory, method, practice and social justice*. American Psychological Association.

Constantine, M. (2001). Multicultural training, theoretical orientation, empathy, and multicultural case conceptualization ability in counselors. *Journal of Mental Health Counseling, 23*, 357–372.

Counseling and Psychological Services. (2018). *Internship seminar on diversity*. Oregon State University.

Counseling and Psychological Services. (2010a). *Supervisor's evaluation of group therapy competencies of supervisee*. Oregon State University.

Counseling and Psychological Services. (2010b). *Evaluation of group co-leader's supervision by supervisee*. Oregon State University.

Dalal, F. (2023). The ethics of supervision: Reciprocity, emergence and prefiguration. *Group Analysis, 56*(1), 62–80. https://doi.org/10.1177/05333164211050756

Davis, D. E., DeBlaere, C., Owen, J., Hook, J. N., Rivera, D. P., Choe, E., Van Tongeren, D. R., Worthington, E. L., Jr., & Placeres, V. (2018). The multicultural orientation framework: A narrative review. *Psychotherapy, 55*(1), 89–100. https://doi.org/10.1037/pst0000160

DeAngelis, T. (2023). Increasing supervisor savvy around culture, race, and identity. *American Psychological Association's The Monitor, 54*(1), 34. www.apa.org/monitor/2023/01/culturally-responsive-supervision

Ellis, M. V., Berger, L., Hanus, A. E., Ayala, E. E., Swords, B. A., & Siembor, M. (2014). Inadequate and harmful clinical supervision: Testing a revised framework and assessing occurrence. *Counseling Psychologist, 42*, 434–472. http://dx.doi.org/10.1177/0011000013508656

Falender, C. A. & Shafranske, E. P. (2004). *Clinical supervision: A competency-based approach*. American Psychological Association. https://doi.org/10.1037/10806-000

Falender, C. A. & Shafranske, E. P. (2017). Competency-based clinical supervision: Status, opportunities, tensions, and the future. *Australian Psychologist, 52*(2), 86–93.

Falender, C. A., Shafranske, E. P. & Falicov, C. J. (2014). Diversity and multiculturalism in supervision. In C. A. Falender, E. P. Shafranske & C. J. Falicov (Eds.), *Multiculturalism and diversity in clinical supervision: A competency-based approach* (pp. 3–28). American Psychological Association. https://doi.org/10.1037/14370-011

Falicov, C. J. (2014). *Latino families in therapy* (2nd ed.). Guilford.

Fernandes, C. & Lane, W. D. (2020). Best practices in multicultural supervision in counseling. *Journal of Counseling Research and Practice, 6*(1), article 4. https://doi.org/10.56702/UCKX8598/jcrp0601.4

Fong, M. L. & Lease, S. H. (1997). Cross-cultural supervision: Issues for the White supervisor. In D. B. Pope-Davis & H. L. K. Coleman (Eds.), *Multicultural counseling competencies: Assessment, education and training, and supervision* (pp. 387–405). Sage.

Freire, P. (2000). *Pedagogy of the oppressed*. Continuum. (Original work published 1970.)

Gonsalvez, C. J. & Crowe, T. P. (2014). Evaluation of psychology practitioner competence in clinical supervision. *American Journal of Psychotherapy, 68*, 177–193.

Goodrich, K. M. & Luke, M. (2011). The LGBTQ responsive model for supervision of group work. *Journal for Specialists in Group Work, 36*(1), 22–40. https://doi.org/10.1080/01933922.2010.537739

Haley-Banez, L., Brown, S., Molina, B., D'Andrea, M., Arrendondo, P., Merchant, N., & Wathen, S. (1999). Association for specialists in group work principles for diversity-competent group workers. *Journal for Specialists in Group Work, 24*(1), 7–14. https://doi.org/10.1080/01933929908411415

Harris, D. J. (2024). Identifying and working through racialized enactments in group psychotherapy. In A. D. Abernathy (Ed.), *Addressing diversity dynamics in group therapy: Clinical and training applications* (pp. 7–24). Routledge.

Harro, B. (2000). The cycle of socialization. In M. Adams, W. Blumenfeld, R. Castañeda, H. Peters, & X. Zúñiga (Eds.), *Readings for diversity and social justice: An anthology on racism* (pp. 15–21). Routledge.

Hays, P. (2008). *Addressing cultural complexities in practice: Assessment, diagnosis, and therapy* (2nd ed.). American Psychological Association.

Hird, J. S., Cavalieri, C. E., Dulko, J. P., Felice, A. A. D., & Ho, T. A. (2001). Visions and realities: Supervisee perspectives of multicultural supervision. *Journal of Multicultural Counseling and Development, 29*(2), 114–130. https://doi.org/10.1002/j.2161-1912.2001.tb00509.x

Hook, J. N., Davis, D. E., Owen, J., Worthington Jr., E. L., & Utsey, S. O. (2013). Cultural humility: Measuring openness to culturally diverse clients. *Journal of Counseling Psychology.* https://doi.org/10.1037/a0032595

Hook, J. N., Watkins Jr., C. E., Davis, D. E., Owen, J., Van Tongeren, D. R., & Ramos, M. J. (2018). Cultural humility in psychotherapy supervision. *American Journal of Psychotherapy, 70*(2), 149–166.

Hopson, R. (2024). The work of overcoming racism/white supremacy in group. In A. D. Abernethy (Ed.), *Addressing diversity dynamics in group therapy: Clinical and training applications* (136–151). Routledge.

Kaklauskas, F. J. & Nettles, R. (2020). Towards multicultural and diversity proficiency. In F. J. Kaklauskas & L. R. Greene (Eds.), *Core principles of group psychotherapy: An integrated theory, research, and practice training manual* (pp. 25–45). Routledge

Kiteki, B. N. (2022). "A big part is to address the elephant": International counseling trainees' experiences in clinical supervision in the United States. *Journal of Counselor Preparation and Supervision, 15*(3), 10. https://digitalcommons.sacredheart.edu/jcps/vol15/iss3/10

Kivlighan, D. M. & Chapman, N. A. (2018). Extending the multicultural orientation (MCO) framework to group psychotherapy: A clinical illustration. *Psychotherapy, 55*(1), 39–44. https://doi.org/10.1037/pst0000142.

Kivlighan III, D. M., Adams, M. C., Drinane, J. M., Tao, K. W., & Owen, J. (2019). Construction and validation of the multicultural orientation: Inventory–group version. *Journal of Counseling Psychology, 66*(1), 45–55. https://doi.org/10.1037/cou0000294.

Kivlighan III, D. M., Swancy, A. G., Smith, E., & Brennaman, C. (2021). Examining racial microaggressions in group therapy and the buffering role of members' perceptions of their group's multicultural orientation. *Journal of Counseling Psychology, 68*(5), 621–628. https://doi.org/10.1037/cou0000531

Kleinberg, J. L. (Ed.). (2012). *The Wiley-Blackwell handbook of group psychotherapy.* Wiley. https://onlinelibrary.wiley.com/doi/10.1002/9781119950882.ch33

Leary, K. (2000). Racial enactments in dynamic treatment. *Psychoanalytic Dialogues, 10*(4), 639–653.

Lin, T., Stone, S. J., Heckman, T. G., & Anderson, T. (2021). Zoom-in to zone-out: Therapists report less therapeutic skill in telepsychology versus face-to-face therapy during the Covid-19 pandemic. *Psychotherapy, 58*(4), 449–459. https://doi.org/10.1037/pst0000398

Luke, M. & Kiweewa, J. M. (2010). Personal growth and awareness of counseling trainees in an experiential group. *Journal for Specialists in Group Work, 35*, 365–388. https://doi.org/10.1080/01933922.2010.514976

Martín-Baró, I. (1994). *Writings for a liberation psychology.* Harvard University Press.

McEneaney, A. (May 25, 2023). Personal communication.

McKinley, M. T. (2019). Supervising the sojourner: Multicultural supervision of international students. *Training and Education in Professional Psychology, 13*(3), 174–179. http://dx.doi.org/10.1037/tep0000269

Miles, J. R., Anders, C., Kivlighan III, D. M., & Belcher Platt, A. A. (2021). Cultural ruptures: Addressing microaggressions in group therapy. *Group Dynamics: Theory, Research, and Practice, 25*(1), 74–88. https://doi.org/10.1037/gdn0000149

Miles, J. R., Strauss, B. M., & Greene, L. R. (2023). Process measures. In R. MacNair-Semands & M. Whittingham (Eds.), *Group psychotherapy assessment and practice: A measurement-based care approach* (pp. 83–119). Routledge.

Miller Aron, C. & Lefay, S. (2024). Hidden diversity: The invisible oppressor of classism. In A. D. Abernethy (Ed.), *Addressing diversity dynamics in group therapy: Clinical and training applications* (91-104). Routledge.

Muthukrishna, M., Bell, A. V., Henrich, J., Curtin, C. M., Gedranovich, A., McInerney, J., & Thue, B. (2020). Beyond western, educated, industrial, rich and democratic (WEIRD) psychology: Measuring and mapping scales of cultural and psychological distance. *Psychological Science, 31*(6), 678–701. https://doi.org/10.1177/0956797620916782

National Latinx Psychological Association. (2020). Ethical guidelines of the National Latinx Psychological Association. *Journal of Latinx Psychology, 8*(2), 101–111. https://doi.org/10.1037/lat 0000151

Nelson, M. L. & Friedlander, M. L. (2001). A close look at conflictual supervisory relationships: The trainee's perspective. *Journal of Counseling Psychology, 48*(4), 384–395. https://doi.org/10.1037/0022-0167.48.4.384

Neville, H. A., Ruedas-Gracia, N., Lee, B. A., Ogunfemi, N., Maghsoodi, A. H., Mosley, D. V., LaFromboise, T. D., & Fine, M. (2021). The public psychology for liberation training model: A call to transform the discipline. *American Psychologist, 76*(8), 1248–1265. https://doi.org/10.1037/amp 0000887

Nilsson, J. E. & Dodds, A. K. (2006). A pilot phase in the development of the international student supervision scale. *Journal of Multicultural Counseling and Development, 34*(1), 50–62. https://doi.org/10.1002/j.2161-1912.2006.tb00026.x

Norcross, J. C. & Popple, L. M. (2017). *Supervision essentials for integrative psychotherapy*. American Psychological Association.

Okech, J. E. A. & Rubel, D. (2007). Diversity competent group work supervision: An application of the supervision of group work model (SGW). *Journal for Specialists in Group Work, 32*(3), 245–266. https://doi.org/10.1080/01933920701431651

Owen, J. J., Tao, K., Leece, M. M., & Rodolfa, E. (2011). Clients' perceptions of their psychotherapists' multicultural orientation. *Psychotherapy, 48*, 274–282.

Pendse, A. P. & Inman, C. (2017). International student-focused counseling research: A 34-year content analysis. *Counseling Psychology Quarterly, 30*, 20–47. https://doi.org/10.1080/09515070.2015.1128395

Pierce, C. (1970). Offensive mechanisms. In F. Barbour (Ed.), *The Black seventies* (pp. 265–282). Porter Sargent.

Rao, P. (2017). Learning challenges and preferred pedagogies of international students: A perspective from the USA. *International Journal of Educational Management, 31*(7), 1000–1016. https://doi.org/10.1108/IJEM-01-2016-0001

Ribeiro, M. D. (Ed.). (2020). *Examining social identities and diversity issues in group therapy: Knocking at the boundaries*. Routledge.

Rigg, T., Kivlighan III, D. M., & Tao, K. W. (2020). Problematic systems: Applying a multicultural orientation framework to understand "problematic members." *Professional Psychology: Research and Practice, 51*(3), 278–283. https://doi-org.oregonstate.idm.oclc.org/10.1037/pro0000277

Riva, M. T. & Smith, R. D. (2024). Beyond the dyad: Broadening the APA supervision guidelines to include group supervision. *Psychotherapy, 61*(2), 161–172.

Rohr, E. (2012). After the conflict: Training of group supervision in Guatemala. In J. L. Kleinberg (Ed.), *The Wiley-Blackwell handbook of group psychotherapy* (1st ed., pp. 517–545). John Wiley and Sons. https://onlinelibrary.wiley.com/doi/abs/10.1002/9781119950882.ch26

Rousmaniere, T., Bernard, J. M., & Goodyear, R.K. (2019). Multicultural supervision. In J. M. Bernard & R. K. Goodyear (Eds.), *Fundamentals of clinical supervision* (6th ed., pp. 117–140). Pearson.

Rousmaniere, T. G. & Ellis, M. V. (2013). Developing the construct and measure of collaborative clinical supervision: The supervisee's perspective. *Training and Education in Professional Psychology, 7*(4), 300–308. https://doi.org/10.1037/a0033796

Rubel, D. & Okech, J. E. A. (2006). The supervision of group work model: Adapting the discrimination model for supervision of group workers. *Journal for Specialists in Group Work, 31*, 113–134.

Sangganjanavanich, V. F. & Black, L. L. (2009). Clinical supervision for international counselors-in-training: Implications for supervisors. *Journal of Professional Counseling: Practice, Theory & Research, 37*(2), 52–65. https://doi.org/10.1080/15566382.2009.12033860

Schwartz, S. J., Unger, J. B., Zamboanga, B. L., & Szapocznik, J. (2010). Rethinking the concept of acculturation: Implications for theory and research. *American Psychologist, 65*(4), 237–251. https://doi.org/10.1037/a0019330

Shah, S. A. & Kosi, R. (2012). Diversity in groups: Culture, ethnicity and race. In J. L. Kleinberg (Ed.), *The Wiley-Blackwell handbook of group psychotherapy* (pp. 667–680). John Wiley & Sons.

Shklarski, L., Abrams, A., & Bakst, E. (2021). Will we ever again conduct in-person psychotherapy sessions? Factors associated with the decision to provide in-person therapy in the age of Covid-19. *Journal of Contemporary Psychotherapy, 51*(3), 265–272. https://doi.org/10.1007/s10879-021-09492-w

Smith, R. A. & Khawaja, N. G. (2011). A review of the acculturation experiences of international students. *International Journal of Intercultural Relations, 35*(6), 699–713. https://doi.org/10.1016/j.ijintrel.2011.08.004

Smith, T. B., Rodríguez, M. M. D., & Bernal, G. (2011). Culture. In J. C. Norcross (Ed.), *Psychotherapy relationships that work: Evidence-based responsiveness* (pp. 316–335). Oxford University Press. https://doi.org/10.1093/acprof:oso/9780199737208.003.0016

Sue, D. W., Capodilupo, C. M., Torino, G. C., Bucceri, J. M., Holder, A. M. B., Nadal, K. L., & Esquilin, M. (2007). Racial microaggressions in everyday life: Implications for clinical practice. *American Psychologist, 62*(4), 271–286. https://doi.org/10.1037/0003-066X.62.4.271

Tervalon, M. & Murray-Garcia, J. (1998). Cultural humility versus cultural competence: A critical distinction in defining physician training outcomes in multicultural education. *Journal of Health Care for the Poor and Underserved, 9*(2), 117–125.

Tsui, M. S., O'Donoghue, K., & Ng, A. K. (2014). Culturally competent and diversity-sensitive clinical supervision: An international perspective. In C. E. Watkins Jr. & D. L. Milne (Eds.), *The Wiley international handbook of clinical supervision* (pp. 238–254). John Wiley & Sons. https://doi.org/10.1002/9781118846360.ch10

Tummala-Narra, P. (2004). Dynamics of race and culture in the supervisory encounter. *Psychoanalytic Psychology, 21*(2), 300–311.

Watkins Jr., C. E., Hook, J. N., Owen, J., DeBlaere, C., Davis, D. E., & Van Tongeren, D. R. (2019). Multicultural orientation in psychotherapy supervision: Cultural humility, cultural comfort, and cultural opportunities. *American Journal of Psychotherapy, 72*(2), 38–46. https://doi.org/10.1176/appi.psychotherapy.20180040

Watkins Jr., C. E., Reyna, S. H., Ramos, M. J., & Hook, J. N. (2015). The ruptured supervisory alliance and its repair: On supervisor apology as a reparative intervention. *Clinical Supervisor, 34*(1), 98–114. https://doi.org/10.1080/07325223.2015.1015194

Watkins Jr., C. E., Toyama, S., Briones, M., Gaskin-Cole, G., Zuniga, S., Yoon, J., Hwang, H., Hasan, F., Doty, D., Harker, J. R., Hook, J. N., Wang, C. D. C., & Wilcox, M. M. (2022). Multicultural streaming in group psychotherapy supervision: Orientation to and preparation for culturally humble practice. *American Journal of Psychotherapy, 75*(3), 129–133. https://doi.org/10.1176/appi.psychotherapy.20210021

Weinberg, H. (2020). Online group psychotherapy: Challenges and possibilities during Covid-19: A practice review. *Group Dynamics: Theory, Research, and Practice, 24*(3), 201–211. https://doi.org/10.1037/gdn0000140

Whittingham, M., Lefforge, N., & Marmarosh, C. L. (2021). Group psychotherapy as a specialty: An inconvenient truth. *American Journal of Psychotherapy, 74*(2), 60–66. https://doi.org/10.1176/appi.psychotherapy.20210016

Whittingham, M., Marmarosh, C. L., Mallow, P., & Scherer, M. (2023). Mental health care equity and access: A group therapy solution. *American Psychologist, 78*(2), 119–133.

Yalom, I. & Leszcz, M. (2020). *Theory and practice of group psychotherapy*. Basic Books.

Yildirim, O. (2017). Class participation of international students in the USA. *International Journal of Higher Education, 6*(4), 94–103. https://eric.ed.gov/?id=EJ1150774

Yoon, E., Langrehr, K., & Ong, L. Z. (2011). Content analysis of acculturation research in counseling and counseling psychology: A 22-year review. *Journal of Counseling Psychology, 58*(1), 83–96. https://doi.org/10.1037/a0021128. PMID: 21142352.

Chapter 6

Ethical and Legal Considerations in Supervision of Group Psychotherapy

Maria T. Riva, Stephanie McLaughlin, and Michelle A. Collins-Greene

This chapter addresses the ethical and legal considerations in the supervision of group psychotherapy. The first section highlights the ethical and legal elements that are expected from a supervisor of group psychotherapy. It provides supervisors with an introduction to relevant ethics guidelines and resources. The second section concentrates on ethical dilemmas that frequently occur around ethical codes and guidelines, the responsibilities of the supervisor to address them, and ways that supervisors might respond to those often-complex dilemmas. Because it is necessary but not sufficient for group therapists and supervisors to be aware of their professions' codes of ethics and federal and state laws, this chapter also discusses decision-making processes and practical applications to help supervisees develop a professional ethical attitude.

Competencies and standards specific to ethical supervision of group psychotherapy leaders continues to evolve and lack empirical research. For this reason, material provided here is guided by three main sources. The first is the ethical foundations of group therapy provided by Barlow (2012, 2013) and Brabender and MacNair-Semands (2022). The second source is the ethics of individual psychotherapy supervision (APA, 2025, Falender et al., 2014), and the third is writings and observations of best practices of ethics of group therapy supervision.

Legal and ethical concerns have some variations, and it is incumbent upon the supervisor, and supervisee, to become aware of the country, state, and local expectations where they are practicing. The first variation is *jurisdiction*—state or country laws and ethics; the second is *professional disciplines and organizational codes of ethics* (e.g., for psychology, social work, counseling, psychiatry), and the third area of potential divergence is related to the *setting* (e.g., university counseling centers, schools, Veteran's Administration Hospitals, mental health agencies, private practice, etc.).

Jurisdiction: State or Country Laws and Ethics

From a legal perspective the group treatment that supervisors oversee is in accordance with their own state and federal laws, and the requirements of their state's licensing board. Supervisors and facilitators of group psychotherapy pay attention to the pertinent legalities and documentation requirements while also minding the ethical and moral principles.

Instilling an ethical attitude entails supporting the supervisee to abide by legal, state and national ethics codes, not solely to avoid penalties and reparative work but also to help group psychotherapists live up to the highest practice standards to protect patient and trainee welfare, and positively benefit society (Knapp et al., 2023). For example, when completing informed consent, regardless of whether it occurs for a group psychotherapist that is bringing a new member into their psychotherapy group, or for a supervisor deciding on a new

DOI: 10.4324/9781003410621-7

supervisee to join individual or group supervision, the group leader or supervisor ensures that the new member(s) fully understand the process and its potential impact as opposed to solely getting a signature on a consent form to fulfill a legal contractual requirement.

Jurisdiction has become noteworthy with the increased use of telehealth which makes rendering services easy across state lines. The state in which a group therapy professional is licensed constitutes legal authorization to practice counseling, psychology, psychiatry, and social work, for the people of that state only. Licensing and credentialling serves the function of assuring and protecting clients in each state where their group therapist meets the requirements that were set by that particular state to practice. In the case of a complaint of misconduct by a client or patient, that state's Office of Professions (as in Connecticut) or the State Department of Education (as in New York) adjudicates and has the authority to suspend, revoke, or put on probation the license for ethical misconduct. Some states do have reciprocity with other states. States may also vary on specific training requirements; for example, an increasing number of states have specific supervisor training requirements (e.g., continuing education courses), of which to be aware.

Since states can specify particular training and supervision requirements, supervision required for a license must be carried out by a supervisor licensed in that state. For this reason, it's important to establish whether the relationship will be supervisory in nature as opposed to consultative as they carry different professional, ethical, and legal responsibilities. In brief, in *supervision* the supervisor takes responsibility not only for the supervisee (group leader) but the members of the psychotherapy group as well. In *consultation*, the consultant gives guidance but does not have responsibility for the services ultimately rendered by the group leader or accountability for the group members. Consultation usually occurs with already licensed and insured group leaders (Brabender & MacNair-Semands, 2022; Falender & Shafranske, 2021). Supervision per se is usually for university students and those requiring supervision for academic or licensing and certification requirements. Consultation can be conducted across state lines and internationally if it is not used for licensing in a particular state. National and international associations of group therapy (e.g., AGPA and its affiliates) allow consultation to count for necessary hours toward certificat on (e.g., the CGP).

Aside from laws about training, most states have mandates about who and what needs to be reported in cases of child abuse—physical, sexual, and neglect. As well, Californ a's 1976 Tarasoff Act set precedence for the "duty to warn" if a client or patient (or supervisee) expresses credible intent to physically injure another person or oneself. These laws are the major exceptions to the overarching tenets of psychotherapy confidentiality. These are sensitive areas that unsettle and often present dilemmas for leaders of group therapy (and individual therapy) and cause them to rely on knowledgeable supervision. It's helpful for supervisors to be familiar with the word of law in their state and the exact procedures for making such reports, since it does vary from state to state. As well, it is often a clinical assessment skill to determine exactly what behavior or verbal report on the part of the client/patient that does meet criteria for reporting, a matter that should be discussed in supervision.

Association and Organizational Guidelines

Ethics codes are formulated by large professional organizations such as the American Psychological Association (APA) and American Counseling Association (ACA). Some ethics codes address group psychotherapy, while others address supervision (mostly supervision of individual therapy). If codes are violated, the organization adjudicates. However, these organizations defer to state licensing jurisdictions which make them enforceable by state law as well. If one is working in a litigious or adversarial environment, such as marital and custody battles, or child abuse, domestic abuse, trauma recovery from abuse, suicide, or even attempting to collect a debt, it's possible for an angry or dissatisfied client to challenge one's license. These situations are outside the purview of this manual, but if a therapist or supervisor finds themselves involved in court matters for a client, it's strongly advisable to get special supervision as well as legal counsel to discern the best ethical way to handle the case for the client while protecting oneself. Professional insurance is vital for the supervisor and supervisee and can help pay legal costs if that unfortunate situation arises. The APA has several "best practices" documents on these special situations. Additionally, obtaining additional training in the diagnosis and therapy of these groups can allay, safeguard, and ensure against potential ethical mistakes and unintended harm.

Association Ethics Guidelines for Group Psychotherapy

The APA Code of Ethics (2017) only briefly addresses roles, responsibilities, and confidentiality for group therapy. It states that "when psychologists provide services to several persons in a group setting, they describe at the outset the roles and responsibilities of all parties and the limits of confidentiality" (Standard 10.03). Also, related to confidentiality, the ACA Code of Ethics (2014) states: "In group work, counselors clearly explain the importance and parameters of confidentiality for the specific group" (B.4.a). The ACA Code addresses three other group specific areas of ethical judgment—screening, goal setting, and do no harm, stating that "counselors screen prospective group counseling/therapy participants. To the extent possible, counselors select members whose needs and goals are compatible with the goals of the group, who will not impede the group process, and whose well-being will not be jeopardized by the group experience" (A.9.a). The code continues by saying, "In a group setting, counselors take reasonable precautions to protect clients from physical, emotional, or psychological trauma" (A.9.b). A division of ACA, the Association for Specialists in Group Work (ASGW), provides some ethical standards and best practice guidelines specific to group treatment and give considerably more direction for group leaders and supervisors of group formats. They have several pertinent documents. The *ASGW Best Practice Guidelines* (2007) outlines the best practices for planning a group (e.g., identifying the type of group, what resources are needed), best practices for conducting the group (e.g., group competencies needed, evaluation of outcomes), and best practices in group processing (e.g., attending to diversity with sensitivity, use of an ethical decision-making model in response to ethical challenges). Another ASGW document is the *Professional Standards for Training Group Workers* (2000), which outlines the objectives for core training that includes coursework, knowledge, skills, and the experiential component for training competent group workers, and a higher level of specialization guidelines that provides more in-depth training. A third ASGW document, *Multicultural and Social Justice Competence Principles for Group Workers* (Singh et al., 2012) is also relevant. All three of these materials provide guidance to the group psychotherapist as well as pointing the supervisor to areas of competence needed by those who conduct group work.

Other organizations also provide guiding material such as the *Clinical Practice Guidelines for Group Psychotherapy* from the AGPA (currently under revision). It incorporates research findings that inform practice guidelines. A collaboration between AGPA and the International Board for Certification of Group Psychologists (IBCGP) contributed the *AGPA and IBCGP Guidelines for Ethics* (2002) which serves as a model for group therapists' ethical behavior

Table 6.1 Association Ethics Codes and Standards Relevant to Group Psychotherapy.

- **ACA Code of Ethics (2014)**
  www.counseling.org/docs/default-source/default-document-library/ethics/2014-aca-code-of-ethics.pdf
- **ASGW (ACA Division)**
  Professional Standards for the Training of Group Workers (2000)
  Multicultural and Social Justice Competence Principles for Group Workers (2012)
  ASGW Guiding Principles for Group Work (2021)
      www.asgw.org/resources/guiding-group-work
- **American Group Psychotherapy Association (AGPA)**
  AGPA and International Board for Certification of Group Psychotherapists Guidelines for Ethics (2002)
      www.agpa.org/home/practice-resources/ethics-in-group-therapy
  AGPA Clinical Practice Guidelines for Group Psychotherapy (2007)
- **APA**
  www.apa.org/ethics/code
  www.apa.org/practice/guidelines
- **APA Division 49: The Society of Group Psychology and Group Psychotherapy**
  www.apa.org/about/division/div49
  Division 49 Specialty Council
      www.apadivisions.org/division-49/leadership/committees/group-specialty (2018)
- **American Board of Professional Psychology**
  The American Board of Group Psychology (2024)
      https://abpp.org/specialists/ethics-education-consultation/
- **National Association of Social Workers (NASW)**
  NASW Code of Ethics (includes 2021 highlighted revisions to Code)
      www.socialworkers.org/About/Ethics/Code-of-Ethics/Code-of-Ethics-English
- **International Association for Group Psychotherapy and Group Processes (IAGP)**
  https://iagpforum.emnuvens.com.br/revista/ethical-standards

and outlines the responsibility to the client along with professional standards. One additional practice resource includes the Association for the Advancement of Social Work with Groups (AASWG) that published the *Standards for Social Work Practice with Groups* (2005). Similar to other documents it addresses core values and knowledge, pregroup planning and recruitment, and has a focus on group work practice for the beginning, middle, and ending phases of group work.

The recent publication on ethics in the AGPA Group Therapy Training and Practice series by Brabender and MacNair-Semands (2022) outlines several existing ethics codes and professional guidelines relevant to *group psychotherapy*. Some of these include how to respond to the context of the group-as-a-whole, address group silence, and respond to microaggressions, all which are complex aspects in training group leaders to ethically respond to their group members.

All the aforementioned guidelines are not legally regulatory but provide ethical guidance for the group leader at different levels of planning and conducting a group. The codes listed in Table 6.1 primarily focus on group psychotherapy ethics and not on supervision ethics per se; however, supervisors will want to be aware of these codes and encourage their supervisee's adherence to them.

Codes of Ethics and Standards of Practice for Supervision of Group Psychotherapy

Important preconditions for supervisors of group psychotherapists are knowledge of ethics related to group psychotherapy, as well as psychotherapy supervision. Table 6.2 contains ethical codes by associations related to supervision. It points to the Ethics Codes that center on supervision ethics which are based on individual supervision of individual psychotherapy but relevant to supervisors of group therapy.

In their recent publication on ethics, Brabender and MacNair-Semands (2022) not only outlined the ethics codes for group psychotherapists, but they also highlight guidelines for *supervision of group psychotherapy* in their chapter 6. Table 6.2 points to the Ethics Codes that center on supervision ethics which are most often individual supervision of individual psychotherapy but often relevant to supervisors of group therapy. Brabender and MacNair-Semands's guidelines provide direction for professional behavior, such as screening of group participants and informed consent. They acknowledge that many early supervisors are not prepared to address ethical dilemmas and that an early vital task of supervisors is to develop supervisees who are ethically minded.

With the complexity of multiple relationships in group therapy, there is an increased potential of ethical dilemmas that the supervisor oversees. As an example, the promise to group members of confidentiality can be assured (except in risk of harm) on the part of the group leader but is not entirely possible to enforce between group members even when group members agree to it. The *Association of State and Provincial Psychology Boards Supervision Guidelines* help guide the development of supervision requirements for students pursuing licensure as health service psychologists. The newly approved APA Guidelines for Clinical Supervision in Health Service Psychology (APA, 2025) have increased the focus a bit more on supervision ethics in groups (although much of the information is directed to group supervision), the guidelines do make it clear that in a group, supervisors will want to develop strong relationships with each member and also foster a strong working alliance among the group members which will help to decrease ethical violations. For counselors, the Association for Counselor Education provides guidelines in Best Practice in Clinical Supervision (ACES, 2011) where multiple aspects of the supervisory relationship are addressed including informed consent, goal setting, diversity, and advocacy considerations.

Another example of ethical standards for supervision is the ASGW *Professional Standards for the Training of Group Workers* (2000) which describes specifications for training in group

Table 6.2 Ethics Codes and Standards Relevant to Clinical and Counseling Supervision.

- **American Psychological Association Guidelines for Clinical Supervision in Health Service Psychology** (APA, 2015; 2025)
  www.apa.org/about/policy/guidelines-supervision.pdf
- **ACA**
  Standards for Counseling Supervisors (1990)
    https://acesonline.net/wp-content/uploads/2018/11/ACES-Standards-for-Counseling-Supervisors-1990.pdf
- **American School Counseling Association (ASCA, 2022)**
  The School Counselor and School Counselor Supervision (2022)
    www.schoolcounselor.org/getmedia/44f30280-ffe8-4b41-9ad8-f15909c3d164/EthicalStandards.pdf
- **National Association of Social Workers (NASW)**
  Best Practice Standards in Social Work Supervision (2013)
    www.socialworkers.org/Practice/NASW-Practice-Standards-Guidelines/Best-Practice-Standards-in-Social-Work-Supervision
- **ASGW (ACA Division)**
  Professional Standards for the Training of Group Workers (2000, updated 2021)
    www.tandfonline.com/doi/full/10.1080/01933922.2021.1950882
- **AGPA**
  www.agpa.org/home/practice-resources/dei-tf-resources/supervision-training-resources

work for supervisors and graduate training programs. This document outlines levels of training in group work that begin with required skills (Core Training Standards), such as theories of group work, principles of assessment of group functioning, observing and identifying group process, along with several other skills. These core skills set the foundation for more advanced skills (Specialization Guidelines) that are related to being able to demonstrate specific skills beyond observing and identifying them (see the ASGW Professional Standards). Ethical practice includes operating at the highest level of competence within one's discipline.

Each profession, whether it be psychology, psychiatry, social work, or counseling formalizes competencies, standards, and ethics of therapeutic practice which include training and supervision. While the *APA Guidelines on Supervision* (2015; 2025) and the American Counseling Association (ACA, 2014) are excellent sources for supervision of individual therapy, it should be kept in mind that these codes minimally address facilitators of psychotherapy groups.

Processes to Support Ethical Supervision Practice

Competency as an Ethical Standard

Gaining competency in supervision and group therapy is becoming an ethical standard. Recently, there has been a stronger focus on group psychotherapy supervision although ethics codes and legal requirements do not yet exist specifically for supervision of group psychotherapy. The reference list identifies some relevant articles and research on supervision of groups (marked with *). The APA Group Specialty Council defined education and training competency standards during efforts to have group psychology and group psychotherapy recognized as a specialty in psychology (Barlow, 2012, 2013; Brown & Lefforge, 2023; Kaslow et al., 2009; Rapin, 2014). The APA Commission for the Recognition of Specialties and Proficiencies in Professional Psychology (CRSPPP) formally recognized Group Psychology and Group Psychotherapy as a specialty practice in 2018. The specialty includes an education and training taxonomy that establishes training and supervision expectations at different stages. The specialty's established competencies also include training psychologists in ethics and legal standards and policies for group psychotherapy.

Based on a review of existing literature, there are several ways a supervisor can promote an effective, high quality supervisory experience for group psychotherapy guided by professional ethics, law, and other professional guidelines. Although pinpointing psychotherapy rather than group psychotherapy, APA Supervision Guideline (2025) Domain A states that supervisors "seek to attain and maintain competence in the practice of supervision," and "obtain requisite training in knowledge, skills, and attitudes of clinical supervision, are skilled and knowledgeable in competency-based models, and in developing and managing the supervisory relationship/alliance" (p. 10). The following practices are likely to increase the ethical conduct of trainees and the ethical practice of clinical supervision.

Informed Consent

Best practices would suggest the use of a supervision contract or agreement. Falender and Lee (2015) described a contract as a crucial component of the *Supervision Guidelines* stating:

> The supervisor contract is essentially an informed consent document that is a formalization of the supervisory relationship. During the process of collaboratively developing the contract, the supervisor engages the supervisee through discussion of supervisee and supervisor's expectations, standards, roles, and responsibilities and setting-specific regulations.
>
> (p. 39)

One example of a supervision contract can be found in the Resources section of *The Fundamentals of Clinical Supervision* (Bernard & Goodyear, 2019, pp. 315–317) and a reciprocal supervision agreement (pp. 318–319) that includes the responsibilities of both parties can be found in the same section.

A competency-based approach to supervision aligns learning goals, curriculum, training, evaluation, and outcomes, and improves accountability of the supervisory process so that the desired outcome (an effective supervision experience where the supervisee achieves the expected competencies) occurs. The use of a supervision contract or agreement within this competency framework helps establish the responsibilities and expectations of both parties and intentionally focuses on how data on these competencies will be gathered (e.g., videotaping), methods for feedback, and more. There is also a focus in this approach on effectively working through remediation in a methodical way when there are problems of professional competence. The contract aids in ensuring that ethics guidelines are addressed, including protecting the well-being of patients and the supervisees, and having an adequate framework for evaluating trainee performance (*APA Ethics Guidelines*, 2017).

Evaluation, Feedback, and Problems with Professional Competence

It is vital for supervisees to receive constructive feedback and offer resources to grow and develop, particularly in university settings. When a supervisee falls short of competency-based expectations, clear benchmarks with timelines need to be outlined so that there is an opportunity for the supervisee to obtain competency. Typically incorporated in this approach is a system where the supervisor and supervisee receive feedback (both formative and summative), including the supervisee's perspective on how the supervision is helping them develop their specified competencies. The Group Specialty Council (Barlow 2012, 2013; Brown & Lefforge, 2023; Kaslow et al., 2009; Rapin, 2014) has made the important contribution of defining competencies at various levels of professional training in group specialty programs, which will be a key part of helping programs track the progress of supervisees and can be utilized within a competency-based approach to supervision.

Supervisors, in general, are committed to training and supporting their supervisees. It is a distressing situation when a supervisor has to address a supervisee who has a problem of professional competence (PPC). Shen-Miller et al. (2015) stated, "PPC include difficulty acquiring or maintaining developmentally appropriate levels of skill, functioning, attitudes, and/or ethical, professional, or interpersonal behavior in functional or foundational domains in one or more settings" (p. 162). Complications can arise for supervisors when a trainee avoids or explicitly refuses to engage in educational or clinical work that would help them develop required ethical competency. One framework to consider when addressing such complicated encounters is the Ethics Acculturation Model (EAM; Knapp et al., 2013). EAM suggests, "the task of becoming a psychologist involves understanding new professional values and integrating them with preexisting moral values derived from one's own ethical heritage" (p. 372). This process is described as similar to the acculturation of immigrants to a new country and the variations in how they accept, adopt, and internalize the norms of their new country and culture and alternately adhere to those of their country of origin. Depending on their personal values, supervisees will vary in ways they adopt, accept, and integrate the ethics and social roles of their profession. Integration is considered the most effective stance, where supervisees know and follow the laws, regulations, and standards governing their professional practice while also knowing and having a focus on adhering to the values of their origin. Responding to the responsibilities of the supervisor in addressing a PPC, Kaslow et al. (2007) articulated it as follows:

Supervisors must rise to the occasion in terms of creating, communicating, and sustaining, a safe growth-enhancing climate in which their supervisees can learn optimally to conduct therapy more and more completely. At the same time, supervisors have a very real responsibility to spot serious problems and deficits in their supervisees' performance, to address them overtly toward the goal of remediation, and to serve as professional gatekeepers to protect the public in the event that the supervisee is unable or unwilling to make the necessary improvements in their professional behavior.

(p. 16)

Strategies to foster an integrative approach include the following. First, supervisees can be encouraged to link their behavior to the rules governing their profession (e.g., *ACA Ethics Guidelines*, state laws) and to their own personal overarching ethical theory (e.g., principle-based ethics, virtue ethics, a system based on their religious traditions). Evaluation of both standards can help them deliberate dilemmas in a more comprehensive way (Handelsman, Gottlieb, & Knapp, 2008). Second, supervisors can think aloud when confronted with situations that require ethical reasoning and show how they are linking their behaviors to the values of the profession. Supervisors can work to normalize and help supervisees accept that everyone has blind spots and will make mistakes, yet when errors are made, they should acknowledge and try to correct them.

The supervisor also needs to continually reflect on their own competence in the supervisory relationship. Falender and Shafranske (2021) discuss the prospect of 360-degree feedback, where multiple levels of personnel rate the supervisor on a set of scales like interpersonal factors and professionalism (p. 273). See Hitzeman et al. (2020) for a literature review of other techniques to foster reflective practice, and Neimeyer and Taylor (2019) for a review of instruments to incorporate in training and supervision experiences to measure continuing professional development and competence.

Maintain Competence through Ongoing Formal Education and Training

Ongoing education and training in supervision and group psychotherapy help ensure supervisors are aware of developments in evidence-based practice for supervision and the clinical work they supervise (Brabender & MacNair-Semands, 2022). While most psychology and counselor education programs offer a course in supervision at the doctoral level, training for supervisors at the master's level is lacking. When courses and training exist for either level of training, a focus on supervision of *group psychotherapy* is rare. The *APA Supervision Guidelines* (2015) state that, at minimum, education and training should include

models and theories of supervision; modalities; relationship formation, maintenance, rupture and repair; diversity and multiculturalism; feedback, evaluation; management of supervisee's emotional reactivity and interpersonal behavior; reflective practice; application of ethical and legal standards; decision making regarding gatekeeping; and considerations of developmental level of the trainee.

(p. 10)

Thus, considering the lack of training in this area, supervisors of psychotherapy groups are under an obligation to seek out specialty training to gain and maintain competency.

Creating a Strong Supervisory Relationship

Falender and Shafranske (2021) state, "All supervision hinges on the formation of the supervisory relationship as it serves as the foundation" (p. 35). Such a foundation helps ensure ethical dilemmas are detected and addressed promptly. The quality of the supervisory relationship is associated with self-disclosure including reactivity and countertransference (*APA Supervision Guidelines*, 2015; Riva, 2014). Unchecked reactivity can potentially interfere with clinical decision-making or even result in the therapist acting out in a way that could lead to unethical situations, such as attacking or colluding with scapegoating an individual in the group (Brabender & MacNair-Semands, 2022; Salvendy, 1993). Effectively providing difficult feedback to supervisees also requires a sound relational foundation. For example, some supervisees' style of leadership may have the potential for risk of harm that requires artful guidance from a supervisor to remediate (Roback, 2000).

Helping Supervisees Develop Competencies and Applied Skill in Ethics

Group psychotherapy supervisees will be faced with a multitude of challenging situations in their therapy groups, such as relational abuse, substance use, discrimination, multiple relationships, and boundary violations. Having a framework and foundation is necessary to navigate these situations in ways that are measured, informed, ethically sound, and fosters professional and personal growth. Several resources are available that provide guidance on handling challenging situations. Riva and Cornish (2018) outlined vignettes on four of the more common situations that group leaders face and how a supervisor can approach them ethically in supervision (i.e., confidentiality, dual and multiple relationships, voluntary participation, and group leader competence). Handelsman et al. (2005) advanced the EAM, which explains that contact and direct experiences help novice trainees integrate into the new culture and synthesize the values of this new profession with their own morals. Gottlieb et al. (2008) suggested that ethics education should be much more than didactic and include the supervisor modeling ethical values and behavior and defining the limits and expectations for ethical conduct.

Ethical Dilemmas in Group Therapy Supervision

Application of Ethical Decision-Making

To ensure supervisors act in a way that balances the multiple pulls of often conflicting ethical situations, many ethical decision-making models have been devised for when a dilemma presents itself, such as those described by Koocher and Keith-Spiegel (2008), Beauchamp and Childress (1979), Juntunen et al. (2023), Pope and Vasquez (2011), and Welfel (2022). Generally, these models guide consideration of ethical dilemmas by first encouraging identification of what ethical standards may be at odds with one another, considering the risks and benefits of various approaches, selecting a path of action, evaluating the outcome, and adjusting as needed. All these models routinely draw attention to individual psychotherapy dilemmas without mention of group psychotherapy or group psychotherapy supervision. However, most aspects apply to group psychotherapy as well such as identifying the dilemma, identifying the client, generating potential solutions, and seeking consultation. Given that group psychotherapy is multidimensional and more complex than individual therapy, each step of these models needs to be expanded when applying them to group psychotherapy and supervision. As the simplest example, the first step of identifying the client may involve several group members, or even potential group members, rather than only one established client.

When faced with an ethical dilemma, there are various processes that influence ethical decisions, such as value systems, the speed with which decisions are made, emotional reactions (with a negative or positive valence), fatigue, and knowledge. A lack of appreciation for these variables put the supervisor, supervisee, and patients at risk. There are various ways to help promote effective processes with decision-making. For example, in chapter 17, Koocher and Speigel (2008) provide a list of "Red Flags" in clinical work to promote self-awareness for when one is vulnerable for making a poor decision (e.g., believing you are the only therapist who can help a patient, dreading a certain patient's appointment, giving a client a gift). The use of ethical decision models is strongly encouraged in supervision and training so supervisees have a systematic and standardized framework to determine an acceptable and defensible outcome when confronted with an ethical dilemma. Each has several steps to help the decision maker identify the ethical dilemmas, and the options available. Most models include one and possibly two steps that highlight cultural implications. A more recent model is Juntunen et al. (2023) that centers equity, diversity, and inclusion in each of seven steps. For example, in Step 2 it encourages self-reflection on own biases and potentially racist beliefs and practices, Step 3 encourages consultation "with ethical standards and laws, including ethical minority psychology guidelines and commentaries" and Step 5 points to consulting with diverse peers and colleagues.

Diversity and multiculturalism go hand in hand with ethical practice requiring supervisors and supervisees to assess dilemmas using a cultural lens. Applying professional standards or decision-making models to members of diverse cultures without knowledge of issues like acculturation or power contexts could lead to negative outcomes. These may include imposition of Western values (e.g., encouraging a patient to forge independence over their cultural value of interdependence), therapeutic ruptures, or misdiagnosis (Frame & Williams, 2005; Davidson & Hauser, 2015). An emphasis on known causes of culturally based harm including Eurocentric therapeutic practices, microaggressions, and personal biases held by the therapist is key (Davidson & Hauser, 2015). Group therapists will want to seek out guidance for when patients from diverse backgrounds engage in behaviors that violate generally accepted Western standards of conduct (Knapp & Vandecreek, 2007). Frame and Williams (2005) provide such guidance with another ethical decision-making model that includes reflection on power, acculturation and racial identity development, and a universalist perspective. Finally, it is useful to have scripts of verbal prompts that can be utilized to broach the subject of cultural diversity in the supervisory relationship (Jones, 2019) and foundational principles that can enrich multicultural conversations and relationships in supervision and training (Hardy, 2017).

Teaching Supervisees How to Notice Ethical Dilemmas

An ethical dilemma exists when there are "good, but contradictory ethical reasons to take conflicting and incompatible courses of action" (Kitchener, 1984, p. 43). Brabender (2010) describes the felt sense of unease that emerges when an ethical dilemma becomes apparent and the therapist feels pulled in different incompatible directions. Trainees can be taught to apply slow, conscious thinking and ethical decision-making skills when one or more of the following circumstances are present: (1) when there is room for interpretation for an applicable ethical or legal standard that requires them to use their professional judgment in its implementation (e.g., when an ethics code uses phrases like, "reasonably," or "appropriately," or as an example, "psychologists inform clients/patients as early as feasible in the therapeutic relationship about therapeutic fees"), (2) when an ethics code or other legal standards are silent on a particular issue, and (3) when laws or organizational standards have conflicting ethics codes (Knapp et al., 2023). One method to facilitate this process is to identify typical critical incidents and ethical dilemmas *before* they occur, and for those that do occur, the supervisor will want to elucidate processes that a trainee has or has not recognized as a legal or ethical dilemma (de las Fuentes et al., 2005).

De las Fuentes et al. (2005) reported on a working group of trainers and regulators that brainstormed ethical competencies, concurring with an earlier quote by Vasquez (1992) that "the strongest weapon against professional misconduct may be the education of trainees" (p. 196). Focusing on early training, these authors suggested that ethical integrity can be embedded in every course throughout psychology training program with an eye on plagiarism, fabricating data, and misrepresenting one's work or amount of contribution in group projects. All of these areas are potential opportunities to provide early trainees with a foundation of honesty and an ethical stance prior to their work with clients.

Role plays and vignettes are considered an indispensable tool for supervisors so that a group leader can visualize and experience an active encounter of an ethical dilemma and have insight into the unpredictable nature of what and how ethical dilemmas may arise and ways to manage them (Drogin, 2019). Likewise, Corey et al. (2014) suggested trainees in group psychotherapy be given case vignettes of typical problems that occur in group situations and encourage discussion of ethical issues and pertinent guidelines. They point out that these experiences guide deeper learning on issues like confidentiality and dual relationships. These vignettes can be naturally occurring in groups that are brought up in a group supervision context. Experiential learning helps trainees learn to recognize and effectively manage countertransference reactions toward group members. Given the emotionally charged nature of group settings, the ability to do role plays that infuse experiential work with reflection and deliberate practice can be effective (Lefforge et al., 2020).

Ethical Dilemmas that Regularly Occur in Group Psychotherapy Supervision

One step in understanding ethical dilemmas is for supervisors to distinguish between ethical imperatives and ethical dilemmas. Some ethical imperative occurrences transpire in group psychotherapy around life-threatening situations which by law *require* a response, such as suicidal intent and behavior, homicidal concerns, and physical and sexual abuse of a minor, or physical intimacy between therapist and client. In many cases, confidentiality on the part of the group leader is also an ethical imperative and governed by law, meaning there is an obligation to respond. Ethical dilemmas, although often quite complicated, are ones where more than one direction may be taken and often require discretion by the supervisor and supervisee. As examples, dilemmas commonly emerge within dual and multiple relationships/roles, supervisor and group psychotherapist competence, confidentiality between group members outside of group, addressing microaggressions/conflict and scapegoating, evaluation of group psychotherapists by their supervisor, supervisor and supervisees coleading groups together, boundary crossings, and the use of technology and telehealth.

At the outset, supervisors will want to apprise their supervisees of the areas that will reduce ethical blunders such as being clear about informed consent, documentation of group process, setting clear norms and imparting information about confidentiality, and other aspects routinely covered in a thorough group agreement. Regarding ethics and legal requirements, the supervisor may need to take on the role of teacher by providing didactic information or assigning readings and educational videos so that the group supervisee appreciates the high stakes of being uninformed about ethical and legal mandates.

Supervisor and Supervisee Competence and Client Safety

Of prime concern for supervisors is the safety of the group members who are clients in group psychotherapy led by their supervisees. The point of credentialling and licensing is to provide safety and ensure the public of professionals' competency. One of the supervisor's roles is to be cognizant of any potential risk of self-harm or harming any other person. Groups that include clients with depression and other psychopathology need to be assessed for suicidal risk and whether a medical consultation is needed to determine if a client would benefit from medication or hospitalization. Another priority for the supervisor is to be aware of whether a group member is abusing a person who is a minor, elderly, or a vulnerable person. For all these dangerous and ethical situations, the supervisor will need to safeguard that all steps are taken to assess and treat any of these life-threatening situations occurring within or among members of the group.

An additional area of severe risk is when group members verbally attack or threaten another person in the group. These types of behaviors will likely cause the safety of the group to dissipate and may cause group members to deteriorate or drop out. Under this category is the importance of being attuned to microaggressions against any individual in the group regarding their identity status. An ethical dilemma can occur if a supervisor or supervisee are reticent to discuss cultural insults and microaggressions between members resulting in ruptures. Repairing ruptures requires a skillful supervisor who appreciates that open discussions and sensitivity is needed and that great harm can occur if not addressed (Miles et al., 2021).

With new group leaders who do not yet meet competency standards, the supervisor has a greater burden to make sure ethical standards of care are being delivered. Novice group leaders are often highly anxious and at times they do not know how to proceed or even start their first group session. It's normal for early group leaders-in-training to lack skills in group psychotherapy given that they may only have taken one course in group theory and facilitated one therapy group. This will often require the supervisor to be more didactic, direct, active, and supportive. It may also necessitate videotaping, or at least audio taping group sessions which imposes added ethical awareness of confidentiality concerns.

In many training settings a supervisor is in a position of monitoring group member composition. Here the supervisor needs to be vigilant about group members having high risk behaviors that may be beyond the competency of the group leader to handle on their own. It is incumbent on supervisors and supervisees to understand the ethical and legal requirements around suicidal, homicidal, and physical/sexual abuse behaviors including how to respond to members who hint about suicide ("that seems like an easy way out," or "I am not sure I could do it") or members who are more blatant ("I repeatedly think about killing myself," or "I have no reason to live"). In such cases the supervisor and group leader assess the client's intent, available means, and impulsivity. Added concern for group therapy is the client's effect on the group or other individuals in the group. Supervisory support and guidance are helpful in monitoring the group leader's anxiety and countertransference.

In agencies, group leaders often do not select their group members and rarely screen them as they are clients who are placed in a group based on a theme or because they need services, and a group is open and available (Riva et al., 2000). This becomes an ethical dilemma for the supervisor. The ACA Ethics Code clearly states that "counselors screen prospective group counseling/therapy participants" (A.9.a). It is not clear what constitutes a screening session, yet the mandate should be implemented to provide safety and reduce risk for group members. On the other side of the dilemma, Corey et al. (2014) point out:

> It is essential to consider including potentially difficult individuals as they may well be the very ones who could most benefit from a group experience. Sometimes leaders screen out individuals due to their own personal dislike or countertransference issues even though these individuals might be appropriate clients for the group ... The goal of screening is to prevent potential harm to clients, not to make the leader's job easier by setting up a group of homogeneous members.
>
> (p. 151)

Yet, heeding these comments from Corey et al. (2014), a supervisor will want to intervene with an early supervisee in the screening and selection of clients who are a fit for their therapy group experience. Much of the work of the group psychotherapist begins before the group gets under way (Yalom & Leszcz, 2020). A thorough screening/selection and preparing the members for group will go a long way to reduce ethical entanglements.

Dual and Multiple Relationships

APA Ethics Code (Standard 3.05) states that a "multiple relationship occurs when a psychologist is in the professional role with a person and at the same time is in another role with the same person." This ethics code focuses mostly on individual professional relationships, but group psychotherapy magnifies the potential ethical dilemmas that can occur. Dual and multiple relationships can occur in several different ways and even include the supervisor and supervisee relationships, between the group psychotherapist and their group members, and among the members of a psychotherapy group. The supervisor will want to monitor all three of these areas as boundary crossing and multiple relationships can inadvertently interfere with the supervisory relationship and consequently, the work of the group leader, and the clients. It is the work of the group leader and supervisor to ensure boundaries are intact even when group members invite and seem to benefit from boundary violations.

One consideration that can be knotty is the inclusion of members into a psychotherapy group that are also in individual therapy with the group leader(s) (combined therapy). It becomes even more problematic if some of the members are being seen individually with the group leader while others are not in individual therapy with the group psychotherapist. Several authors including Yalom and Leszcz (2020) recommend against this dual relationship of treating a client in group and in individual therapy simultaneously given that it may impede the development of group cohesion. Some members who are in both formats may perceive themselves as favorites while others may have a hard time sharing the session with others after having individual therapy time to themselves (Riva & Erickson Cornish, 2018). Other authors see advantages to "combined" individual and group therapy so that the therapist holds both views of the client; sometimes clients share different material in each modality (Alonso & Rutan, 1990). If the group and individual therapist are different, the therapists will likely want to exchange informed consent to speak to each other so that treatment goals and understanding of the client can be shared.

Other dual relationship quandaries with members in both group and individual with the same facilitator is when a client reveals material in individual sessions that they do not want disclosed in the group. Although difficult, remaining clear as to whether the group leader heard the therapeutic material in group or in individual treatment is paramount and not offering information to the group before the client is comfortable with it being shared. It is best if an issue is revealed in individual therapy that the group leader encourages the client to bring it up in group when they are ready.

For supervisors, it is necessary to help group leaders mitigate dual/multiple relationships from the beginning of their group and ideally prior to developing the group and member selection. An additional ethical concern that is specific to group psychotherapy is socialization of group members outside of the group sometimes to the extent of developing romantic relationships or friendships where secrets are divulged and kept from the group. With the extensive use of social media and the potential for socialization outside of the group, it seems prudent for supervisors to address the limits and norms for socialization in a group agreement. When romantic relationships do occur between group members it becomes a quandary for the therapist and supervisor to enforce it as a rule. The dilemma is whether one or both members need to leave the group, being careful not to abandon the members or is it more "grist for the mill" to be handled therapeutically by the leader and the group.

Boundary Violations

Boundary crossings are similar to dual relationships in their perils and dilemmas. They relate to the perimeters of professional behavior where the therapist crosses the line of acceptable therapeutic practice into the realm of unacceptable behavior that result in unethical transactions. Boundary violations, though in the moment may seem helpful, can be harmful to the client and to the therapeutic relationship. At all times the hierarchical relationship between supervisor and supervisee, and between supervisee and client must be held in mind. Despite egalitarian intentions, the power differential is consciously and unconsciously embedded in the relationship. There are some gray areas in what is considered a boundary violation and often relates to cultural or socially acceptable practices. For example, some friendly behavior may be therapeutically helpful, although sexual behavior is never acceptable. It is important for the supervisor to monitor their own feelings and behavior toward a supervisee. In addition, it is important to be open and frank in helping supervisees address their feelings toward their clients (e.g., sexual, anger, hate) and separate those feelings from behavior.

The issues related to boundary crossing, as with other ethical impropriety, are ones that the supervisor is encouraged to address directly and immediately. Examples of unethical behavior include any sexual involvement between the supervisee and their group members, potentially exploitive business relationships, assuming the role of friend with contacts outside the therapy, and inappropriate self-disclosure. Other involvement in clients' lives outside of the group sessions is more of a gray area as some participation such as attending a group member's family funeral or wedding is not specifically an ethical concern and depends on the clinical circumstances of the situation. Similarly, boundary crossing can occur between a supervisor and a supervisee. Sometimes supervisor–supervisee relationships can take on a more mentoring and friendship relationship than might be expected in the client–therapist relationship, but the supervisor is expected to continue to appreciate the boundaries and hierarchy of these relationships and the damage that can occur if boundary crossing such as sexual intimacy ensues.

Group Supervision of Group Therapy

Being competent in supervising a group leader at minimum requires the supervisor to be skillful in group psychotherapy and in the practice of supervision. Most supervisors are trained to supervise one supervisee who is conducting individual therapy. It quickly becomes a multilayered challenge if the supervisor provides supervision to a group of group thera- pists. Complicated dilemmas can occur in group supervision of group therapy. There can be challenging situations with supervisees such as those who monopolize the time, do not participate, overshare personal information, or are unable to hear feedback. The supervisor becomes a model for the group therapists on how to intervene between the group's negative interactions or encourage a positive group climate. In a group of colleagues, supervisees may hesitate to bring up questions about their own ethical conduct. The supervisor helps to hone the supervisees' skills by encouraging safety and trust among the group members. It is important to maintain an atmosphere in the group that allows the supervisee group to grap- ple with ethical dilemmas. It can also be a good learning tool about parallel process in that dilemmas in supervisee groups may mirror those in their own groups.

Confidentiality

The APA Ethics Code Principal E: Respect of Peoples Rights and Dignity states "psycholo- gists respect the dignity and worth of all people and the rights of individuals to privacy, confidentiality, and self-determination." Regarding confidentiality, group psychotherapy is dissimilar to that of individual therapy. The group leader cannot guarantee confidentiality among members in a group. The supervisor has at least two responsibilities here: (a) one is to train and supervise group leaders on addressing confidential communication with group members, and (b) to discuss the confidentiality of supervisee revelations during supervision. Standard 10.03 (Group Therapy) in the APA Ethics Code and B.4 in the ACA Ethics Code each specify addressing confidentiality in group formats. Also, the APA Ethics Code Standard 4.02 (Discussing the Limits of Confidentiality) mandates psychologists to clearly convey the limits of confidentiality. It should be noted that confidentiality is not a static component but rather addressed several times across the life of the group to ensure a sense of safety in the group. In supervision, it is acknowledged that "confidentiality" between members is a verbal agreement among group members and cannot necessarily be enforced. Group leaders, on the other hand, can promise confidentiality of group member conversations in the group. However, within agencies and hospital settings, it is typical for all staff to have availability to client notes, and therefore, clients need to know the extent of the limits of their confiden- tiality. Many therapists have a HIPAA compliant contract that is signed at the beginning of therapy. HIPAA laws came about when computer medical data could so easily be shared, so they mostly address the limits of shareability of such data. The laws are actually quite complicated and detailed so that many people have come to equate "HIPAA compliant" to mean enforcement of confidentiality in general.

The ubiquitous use of social media provides a risk to confidentiality in psychotherapy groups. Even inadvertently and when group members feel positive about their group, a member could talk about it online (e.g., "I am in a group with six other women and Angela is so brave in discussing her abuse history"). The ACA Code of Ethics (2014; H.6.b) includes an explicit statement that reads "counselors clearly explain to their clients, as part of the informed consent procedure, the benefits, limitations, and boundaries of the use of social media." An ethical dilemma occurs when a group member violates the confidentiality of another member. It is unethical to ban the member from the group (abandonment of treat- ment) or to publicly chastise a group member, yet it must be addressed in a therapeutic man- ner. Additionally, confidentiality is required by the group leader surrounding the material disclosed in the group, privacy of medical records and charting, communication with third parties, and managed care. To provide information to a family member or any other party requesting information, permission is required by the group member, or the group member's guardian if the member is unable to provide this permission. Those who receive insurance or Medicare reimbursement are required by the insurance company to have signed consent by the client/patient for their charts and treatment to be reviewed at will of the insurance company.

Multicultural and Diversity Considerations

Knowledge of relevant literature on diversity and multicultural practices and their application within supervision is essential and currently available. It is part of the guiding principle of professional ethics and supervision (i.e., Domain B: Multicultural Orientation; and Domain F: Ethical, Legal, and Regulatory Considerations of the *APA Supervision Guidelines*, 2025). Developing the ability to recognize and intervene ethically and effectively when marginalization and microaggressions occur in groups is considered a competency of group training (Group Specialty Guidelines, e.g., Barlow, 2012, 2013).

Several authors have asserted that all supervisory exchanges are fundamentally multicultural (e.g., Chin et al., 2014; Tohidian & Quek, 2017). Addressing diversity conversations in supervision and in group psychotherapy can be particularly overwhelming for trainees, as group members will hold multiple identities, along with each of their clients. Supervisors can frame this as an opportunity to experience members of diverse backgrounds. Within a supervisory group setting, supervisees can address their personal biases and prejudices, work to understand stuck points in their personal relationships, practice valuing and respecting differences in group members, and managing any conflict between group members in a constructive manner (Chang-Caffaro & Caffaro, 2018; Ribiero, 2021; Riva, 2014). Although rarely used, unhealthy power dynamics can be reduced through use of a written supervisory agreement that clearly outlines the responsibilities of the supervisor and the supervisee. In any case an open verbal acknowledgment of the power dynamics and how they might play out in supervision, especially giving consideration to the identities of the supervisor and supervisee(s) improves the opportunity for discussion of power dynamics both in the supervisory relationship and in the therapist's groups.

A supervisor might enhance awareness of multicultural and diversity concerns by having proactive dialogue surrounding multicultural topics in group work and in the supervisory relationship, by disclosing one's limits of multicultural knowledge, by self-disclosing one's cultural biases, cultural background, values, and/or experiences, and by encouraging discussions related to the impact of a trainee's cultural differences on client conceptualization (Ancis & Marshall, 2010), but mostly by being open to discussion of their impact within the supervisory relationship without defensiveness. When supervisors are capable of showing appreciation for cultural viewpoints, supervisees have higher levels of satisfaction with their supervision (Chin et al., 2014).

Ethical dilemmas go hand in hand with multicultural awareness. In a meta-analysis of multicultural competence and psychotherapy process and outcome, Tao et al. (2015) found that supervisees' views of their group supervisor's diversity competence were related to stronger therapeutic alliance and better results. Unfortunately, at times there is a misalignment between the supervisor's and supervisees' knowledge, awareness, and openness to have multicultural discussions. This gap may be closing as multicultural training is now an almost universal requirement of psychology and counseling graduate programs but supervisors who were trained earlier may be less skillful than their supervisee counterparts (Somerville et al., 2019). When supervisors are oblivious to or discount cultural affronts, the supervisees along with their clients can suffer (Burkard et al., 2006). When supervisors are underdeveloped in their cultural competence compared to their supervisees, they will want to gain training separate from their supervisees and outside of the supervisory relationship, instead of burdening the trainee with imparting that knowledge to them or ignoring its importance altogether. At the same time, neither supervisee nor supervisor will be aware of, or know all there is to know at any one time about multicultural areas, and open communication and feedback during supervision is beneficial for both the relationship and ethical treatment of clients. With the number of multiple identities and histories of group members, supervisees, and supervisors, it is highly likely that multicultural missteps will arise. Watkins et al. (2015) describes the need for genuine apologies in response to these multicultural blunders which can open an exchange with the psychotherapy group members or within the supervisory relationship that values the group process and appreciates the vast diversity of perspectives.

Welfare of the Client and of the Supervisee

In Domain G of the *APA Ethics Guidelines* (APA, 2010), the supervisor's central ethical and legal obligation is to the clients/patients being seen by the supervisee. It can be a delicate balance between the welfare of the clients and the professional growth of the supervisee. Guiding supervisees to self-reflect and to be candid in supervision about mistakes made or when they possess limited knowledge and competence will minimize the harmful risks to group members and facilitators of group psychotherapy (Corey et al., 2014; Falender & Shafranske, 2021). An ethical conflict can occur when the group therapist avoids responding to inferences from a group member of suicidal behavior because they think that it will cause a rupture in the relationship or the member will drop out of group. Revealing ethical and moral dilemmas can easily bring up shame or self-righteousness which can be explored in an open supervisory relationship.

Evaluation of Supervisees

Evaluation evokes the hierarchical relationship and can inhibit supervisee openness to authentic self-disclosure. The dilemma for the supervisor is to give detailed, clear, and specific feedback while not raising the supervisee's anxiety level and interfering with the relationship. Supervisees require accurate and well-timed feedback during their training in group psychotherapy. Research shows that providing positive feedback for supervisees is fairly easy for supervisors to deliver yet the reverse is not true concerning corrective feedback. Even then, negative information is easier for supervisors to impart when it is skill related but much tougher when it comes to focusing on trainee personal experiences (Burkard et al., 2014; Hoffman et al., 2005). "There is a well-documented tendency for people in evaluative roles to shy away from sharing negative judgements" (Riva & Smith, 2024, p. 166). This has been referred to as the MUM effect for staying *Mum about Unpleasant Messages* (Rosen & Tesser, 1970; Scarff et al., 2019).

The *APA Supervision Guidelines* state that "ideally, assessment, evaluation, and feedback occur within a collaborative supervisory relationship. Supervisors promote openness and transparency" and "provide feedback that is direct, clear, and timely … and mindful of the impact on the supervisory relationship" (APA, 2015, p. 39). Supervisors can convey to the supervisee feedback that is specific, concrete, behaviorally anchored, outlines positives on which to build, provides a developmental framework, encourages reflection, and provides relevant examples (Falender et al., 2014). Ethical feedback should also be provided in a timely manner that allows for remediation. The supervisee should not hear about a concern in their final evaluation that was never communicated to them earlier.

Given that supervisors are also responsible for the care of the clients/group members, a supervisee who demonstrates behavior that is dangerous to the psychotherapy group or a group member (e.g., missing or ignoring suicidal messages), or for that matter, may be in danger of ignoring or normalizing an ethical imperative, needs to have that information conveyed to them promptly. According to the *APA Supervision Guidelines*, Domain F: Problems of Professional Competence states that "supervisors strive to identify potential performance problems promptly (Guideline 1), communicate these to the supervisee, and take steps to address these in a timely manner allowing for opportunity to effect change" (Guideline 2), "supervisors are competent in developing and implementing plans to remediate performance problems" (Guideline3); and "supervisors strive to closely monitor and document the progress of supervisees who are taking steps to address problems of competence" (Guideline 4; APA, 2015, pp. 40–44). Guidance can also be found in the work of Forest and Elman (2014) who have studied performance problems for psychology trainees and how to grapple with them for over 20 years. There are many options to address performance problems. The remediation plan will be related to several variables including the risk of the supervisee's behavior, the supervisee's ability to hear and respond to the feedback, and the number of times the behavior or similar ethical lapses have occurred in the past, to name a few.

Conversely, it is also recommended that "supervisors seek feedback from their supervisees and others about the quality of the supervision they offer and incorporate that feedback to improve their supervisory competence" (*APA Supervision Guidelines*, 2015, p. 39). Due to the power differential between the supervisor and supervisee, gaining information after the supervisory relationship has ended may be one option. There are several surveys that look at skills and the supervisory relationship in Bernard and Goodyear's (2019) *Fundamentals of Clinical Supervision* that could provide important feedback. Some are self-report measures completed by the supervisor about their own behavior (e.g., "I help my supervisee stay on track during our meetings") such as the Supervisor Working Alliance, Supervisor Form (p. 333) and others are completed by the supervisee (e.g., Supervisor Working Alliance, Supervisee Form, p. 335). It is also suggested that supervisors gain information from supervisees as to their openness and respect for diversity.

Using these same comments on constructive feedback also are true for how group leaders can respond to their group members. Supervisors will want to provide training to group psychotherapists on how to provide respectful and effective feedback and how to intervene with group members if their feedback is experienced as harmful.

Ethical Management of Therapy Records

Management of therapy records is another area where different states, associations, insurance companies, and settings have varying requirements of what needs to be recorded so that the supervisor needs to be aware of what they are. The supervisor often has responsibility for monitoring that records are completed by the supervisee. The most standard requirements are diagnosis, treatment plan, when visits occurred and for how long, and session progress notes.

During supervision sessions, the supervisor may require the supervisee bring the client charts for review. Charts might include any signed contracts, permission to audio or videotape, summaries of all group sessions for each group member, and contact with any collateral communication. Likewise, it is prudent for supervisors to keep careful notes of the supervisory sessions that include date, time, session length, and summary of session content, and that each supervisee has an individual file. Any specific group member data should not appear in any other member's individual files given ethical codes concerning confidentiality.

Group therapist records are considered medical records and must conform to HIPAA regulations. The Health Insurance Portability and Accountability Act of 1996 (HIPAA) is a federal law that protects the privacy and security of health information, containing standard information about informing all individuals concerning their rights to understand and control how their health information will be used. Supervisors of group therapists will need to assure that group leaders inform their group members about HIPAA, letting them know they have access to their medical records, and that there are limits to their rights of confidentiality as in the case of a court subpoena or insurance review of case files. Having a signed standard HIPAA form that the group member can refer to can be helpful.

Informed consent is often required but always advisable. It is a process that involves clarifying with clients what the procedures of treatment will entail so that they can make informed and voluntary decisions. Supervisors need to ensure that informed consent has been attained by their supervisee and that it is easy to understand, voluntary, and allows the client to ask questions. Here it is important that the supervisee provides time for the client to read the informed consent materials, and the supervisees ask questions such as "What questions do you have?" Informed consent is often part of the initial contract for treatment. It is also used when there is contact with a third party to help manage the care of clients.

In the event that records are requested by outside sources, or the medical records are subpoenaed, medical records are required to be available but, in many cases, personal notes are not. A discussion of the distinction between medical records and the group psychotherapist's personal notes will be a critical aspect of supervision. Given that in some jurisdictions, personal notes can and have been subpoenaed, they should be used with caution and with the understanding that although they are intended to be separate from the official records, they can be used in a court order depending on the jurisdiction.

Ethical Use of Technology and Telehealth

Legal statutes and guidelines for ethical practice in telepsychology vary across states and countries. Though such guidelines are essential, providers should be aware that technology changes quickly and they must continually work to stay abreast of practices in tele-mental health services. It is important to note that even when a supervisor is authorized to provide services across state lines, the privilege to do so may not extended to their supervisees. An ethical dilemma can develop when group members move to a different state or jurisdiction with dissimilar ethics codes or when the group leader is reluctant to terminate a group member who is no longer under the same ethics guidelines. Supervisors will want to help the supervisee respond to these situations and consult with a telecommunication attorney if needed (Kaklauskas & Olsen, 2020).

Telehealth services became commonplace since the epidemic of Covid-19 when hospitals, schools, psychotherapy sessions, along with group psychotherapy and the supervision of therapeutic groups began or expanded their usage of this online format. Supervision of group psychotherapy delivered via telehealth requires the supervisor to understand ethics and best practices of this modality. Advances in technology and the increased use of telehealth services have resulted in the creation of professional guidelines and legal standards related to their use (e.g., *APA Guidelines for the Practice of Telepsychology*, 2013) and studies that compared telehealth with in-person mental healthcare. Findings from the group psycho-therapy literature indicate that online formats may be equally effective as those provided in person (Marton & Kanas, 2016; Trenoska Basile et al., 2022). Nevertheless, group therapists differ with their comfort and sense of effectiveness levels with teletherapy. Many prefer the immediacy of in-person where they can feel more engaged with the group, the group members with each other, and sense the group climate. Whereas others believe there is benefit from simultaneously viewing faces across the screen, and the technology regulation that only one person can talk at a time; and, the added benefit that group members, and group supervisee members can meet when they live a considerable distance apart. Brabender and MacNair-Semands (2022) discuss potential risks of synchronous group therapy (i.e., group therapy conducted on an online video platform) including risks to privacy, distractions (e.g., pets walking into room), less access to behavioral observations and physical information about the member, and some patients not having access to adequate technology to effect-ively join a group.

To support ethical application of telehealth, it is important for supervisors to gain com-petence in how to structure one's online groups in a way that is likely to facilitate the most effective treatment for group members. Helpful information is presented by Weinberg (2020) who provided research supported guidance on effective implementation of online group therapy, including a focus on fostering group cohesion in virtual settings. Weinberg recom-mended "being more active and increasing self-disclosure in online groups to compen-sate for the challenge of being present and the lack of body-to-body interaction" (p. 201). Other beneficial articles outline promises and challenges of technology innovations (Renfro-Michel et al., 2016, and Weinberg, 2023) who discuss online training for group therapists).

Many of the benefits and risks with a virtual format discussed above can be extended to telesupervision. Trainees and supervisors must be aware of the potential for inadvertent breaches of confidentiality. For example, with online platforms it is much easier for mis-steps regarding confidentiality and privacy to occur than for in-person sessions, and these blunders can be unintentionally broadcast to a large audience. Additionally, supervisees need to be reassured of the confidentiality. Supervisors will need to understand state laws surrounding telepsychology and supervision (e.g., whether supervisors and supervisees must be in the same state as the patients they are treating; Falender & Shafranske, 2021, p. 256) and whether they can adequately address training needs when the supervisor is off-site from their trainees (Renfro-Michel et al., 2016). To aid supervisors, Phillips et al. (2021) provided a useful overview of the limited research on telesupervision and proposed rapid training for both supervisees and supervisors. These authors point to research and best practice art-icles that underscore safety and confidentiality, trainee anxiety/comfort, difficulty with non-verbal communication, self-care and self-reflection, and the supervisory relationship, areas for supervisors to address in the ethical practice of telesupervision.

Closing Comments

The goal of this chapter is to consolidate the complex and vast domain of ethics in the supervision of group leaders and give structure for the application of ethics in supervi-sion. The work of the Group Specialty Counseling (e.g., Lefforge et al., 2020) and other professional organizations are examples of increased awareness of the unique ethical dilemmas that can arise in group psychotherapy training and the resources available to address them with confidence. Simultaneously, it is hoped that this chapter gives super-visors tools to be an ethical and competent supervisor that provides effective training to supervisees in group psychotherapy. Because it is necessary but not sufficient for group therapists and supervisors to be aware of their professions' codes of ethics and federal and state statutes and case law, this chapter integrates ways to effectively apply these codes and includes resources and methods for group psychotherapy supervisors to help supervisees develop an ethical stance through awareness of competencies and applied skills in ethics. Supervision of group psychotherapy is multidimensional and can be emotionally difficult, yet with competency-based knowledge and frameworks, supervisors can feel confident and skillful in their ability to be a proficient supervisor who is capable of positively impacting their supervisees.

References

Alonso, A. & Rutan, J. S. (1990). Common dilemmas in combined individual and group treatment. *Group,* 14, 5–12.

*Altfeld, D. A. & Bernard, H. S. (1999). Experiential group psychotherapy supervision. *Group, 23,* 1–17. https://doi.org/10.1023/A:1023088328341

American Counseling Association. (2014). *2014 ACA code of ethics.* www.counseling.org/docs/defa ult-source/default-document-library/ethics/2014-aca-code-of-ethics.pdf

American Group Psychotherapy Association (AGPA) & International Board for Certification of Group Psychotherapists (IBCGP). (2002). *AGPA and IBCGP guidelines for ethics.* American Group Psychotherapy Association and International Board of Certification of Group Psychotherapists.

American Psychological Association. (2017). *Ethical principles of psychologists and code of conduct* (2002, amended effective June 1, 2010, and January 1, 2017). https://www.apa.org/ethics/code/

American Psychological Association. (2025). Guidelines for clinical supervision in health service psychology, APA Guidelines for Clinical Supervision in Health Service Psychology.

American Psychological Association. (2015). Guidelines for clinical supervision in health service psychology. *American Psychologist, 70*(1), 33–46. https://doi.org/10.1037/a0038112

American School Counseling Association. (2022). ASCA ethics standards for school counselors. www. schoolcounselor.org/About-School-Counseling/Ethical-Responsibilities/ASCA-Ethical-Standards-for-School-Counselors-(1)

Ancis, J. R. & Marshall, D. S. (2010). Using a multicultural framework to assess supervisees' perceptions of culturally competent supervision. *Journal of Counseling and Development, 88,* 277–284. https://doi.org/10.1002/j.1556-6678.2010.tb00023.x

Association for the Advancement of Social Work with Groups. (2005). *Standards for social work practice with groups* (2nd ed.). Association for the Advancement of Social Work with Groups.

*Association for Specialists in Group Work. (2000). Association for specialists in group work professional standards for training group workers (2000). *Journal for Specialists in Group Work, 25,* 327–342.

*Association for Specialists in Group Work. (2007). ASGW best practice. *Journal for Specialists in Group Work, 33,* 111–117.

Barlow, S. H. (2012). An application of the competency model to group-specialty practice. *Professional Psychology, Research and Practice, 43*(5), 442–451.

Barlow, S. H. (2013). *Specialty competencies in group psychotherapy.* Oxford University Press. https:// doi.org/10.1521/ijgp.2014.64.2.277

Beauchamp, T. L. & Childress, J. F. (1979). *Principles of biomedical ethics.* Oxford University Press.

Bernard, J. M. & Goodyear, R. K. (2019). *Fundamentals of clinical supervision* (6th ed.). Pearson.

Best Practices in Clinical Supervision. (2011). Association for Counselor Education and Supervision (1–17) online. ACES Best Practices in Clinical Supervision Task Force. http://digitalcommons.george fox.edu/gsc/7

Brabender, V. (2010). The developmental path to expertise in group psychotherapy. *Journal of Contemporary. Psychotherapy, 40*(3), 163–173.

*Brabender, V. & MacNair-Semands, R. (2022). *The ethics of group psychotherapy: Principles and practical strategies*. Routledge.

Brown, N. & Lefforge, N. L. (2023). Education and training guidelines of group psychology and group psychotherapy. *Training and Education in Professional Psychology, 17*(2), 126–132. https://doi.org/10.1037/tep0000417

Burkard, A. W., Johnson, A. J., Madson, M. B., Pruitt, N. T., Contreras-Tadych, D. A., Kozlowski, J. M., Hess, S. A., & Knox, S. (2006). Supervisor cultural responsiveness and unresponsiveness in cross-cultural supervision. *Journal of Counseling Psychology, 53*(3), 288–301. https://doi.org/10.1037/0022-0167.53.3.288

Burkard, A. W., Knox, S., Clarke, R. D., Phelps, D. L., & Inman, A. G. (2014). Supervisors' experiences of providing difficult feedback in cross-ethnic/racial supervision. *Counseling Psychologist, 42*(3), 314–344. https://doi.org/10.1177/0011000012461157

Chang-Caffaro, S. & Caffaro, J. (2018). Differences that make a difference: Diversity and the process group leader. *International Journal of Group Psychotherapy, 68*(4), 483–497. https://doi.org/10.1080/00207284.2018.1469958

Chin, J. L., Petersen, K., Nan, H. M., & Nicholls, L. (2014). Group supervision as a multicultural experience: The intersection of race, gender, and ethnicity. In C. A. Falender, E. P. Shafranske, & C. J. Falicov (Eds.), *Multiculturalism and diversity in clinical supervision: A competency-based approach* (pp. 255–272). American Psychological Association. https://doi.org/10.1037/14370-011

Corey, M. S., Corey, G., & Corey, C. C. (2014). *Groups: Process and practice* (9th ed.). Cengage Learning.

*Cundiff, J. L. (2023). Understanding and Interrupting Bias. *BioScience, 73* (11), pp. 781–784. https://doi.org/10.1093/biosci/biad086

Davidson, M. M. & Hauser, C. T. (2015). Multicultural counseling meets potentially harmful therapy: The complexity of bridging two discourses. *Counseling Psychologist, 43*(3), 370–379. https://doi.org/10.1177/0011000014565714

de las Fuentes, C., Willmuth, M. E., & Yarrow, C. (2005). Competency training in ethics education and practice. *Professional Psychology: Research and Practice, 36*(4), 362–366. https://doi.org/10.1037/0735-7028.36.4.362

*DeLucia-Waack, J. L. (2002). A written guide for planning and processing group sessions in anticipation of supervision. *Journal for Specialists in Group Work, 27*(4), 341–357. https://doi.org/10.1080/714860198

*DeLucia-Waack J. L. & Fauth, J. (2004). The effective supervision of group leaders: Current theory, research, and implications for practice. In J. L. DeLucia-Waack, C. R. Kalodner, & M. T. Riva (Eds.), *Handbook of group counseling and psychotherapy* (pp. 136–150). Sage.

Drogin, E. Y. (2019). *Ethical conflicts in psychology* (5th ed.). American Psychological Association.

Falender, C. A. & Lee, E. (2015). New guidelines and best supervision practices. *Psychotherapy Bulletin, 50*(4), 35–39.

Falender, C. A. & Shafranske, E. P. (2014). Clinical supervision and the era of competence. In W. B. Johnson & N. J. Kaslow (Eds.), *The Oxford handbook of education and training in professional psychology* (pp. 291–313). Oxford University Press.

Falender, C. A. & Shafranske, E. P. (2021). *Clinical supervision: A competency-based approach* (2nd ed.). American Psychological Association. https://doi.org/10.1037/0000243-000

Falender, C. A., Shafranske, E. P., & Ofek, A. (2014). Competent clinical supervision: Emerging effective practices. *Counselling Psychology Quarterly, 27*(4), 393–408. https://doi.org/10.1080/09515070.2014.934785

Falender, C. A., & Shafranske, E. P. (2021). *Clinical supervision: A competency-based approach* (2nd ed.). American Psychological Association. https://doi.org/10.1037/0000243-000 27(4), 393–408. https://doi.org/10.1080/09515070.2014 .934785

*Fernando, D. M. & Herlihy, B. R. (2010). Supervision of group work: Infusing the spirit of social justice. *Journal for Specialists in Group Work, 35*(3), 281–289. https://doi.org/10.1080/01933922.2010.492905

Forest, L. & Elman, N. (2014). Trainees with problems of professional competence. In W. B. Johnson & N. J. Kaslow (Eds.), *The Oxford handbook of education and training in professional psychology* (pp. 314–334). Oxford University Press.

Frame, M. W. & Williams, C. B. (2005). A model of ethical decision making from a multicultural perspective. *Counseling and Values, 49*, 165–179.

Gottlieb, M. C., Handelsman, M. M., & Knapp (2008). Some principles for ethics education: Implementing the acculturation model. *Training and Education in Professional Psychology, 2*(3), 123–128. https://doi.org/10.1037/1931-3918.2.3.123

*Granello, D. H. & Underfer-Babalis, J. (2004). Supervision of group work: A model to increase supervisee cognitive complexity. *Journal for Specialists in Group Work, 29*(2), 159–173. https://doi.org/10.1080/01933920490439310

Handelsman, M. M., Gottlieb, M. C., & Knapp, S. (2005). Training ethical psychologists: An acculturation model. *Professional Psychology: Research and Practice, 36*(1), 59–65. https://doi.org/10.1037/0735-7028.36.1.59

Handelsman, M. M., Gottlieb, M. C., & Knapp, S. (2008). Training ethical psychologists: An acculturation model. In D. N. Bersoff (Ed.), *Ethical conflicts in psychology* (4th ed., pp. 122–127). American Psychological Association.

Hardy, K. V. (2017). Toward the development of a multicultural relational perspective in training and supervision. In K. V. Hardy and T. Bobes (Eds.). *Culturally sensitive supervision and training: Diverse perspectives and practical applications.* (pp. 3–10) Routledge.

Hitzeman, C., Gonsalvez, C. J., Britt, E., & Moses, K. (2020). Clinical psychology trainees' self versus supervisor assessments of practitioner competencies. *Clinical Psychologist, 24*(1), 18–29. https://doi.org/10.1111/cp.12183

Hoffman, M. A., Hill, C. E., Holmes, S. E., & Freitas, G. F. (2005). Supervisor perspective on the process and outcome of giving easy, difficult, or no feedback to supervisees. *Journal of Counseling Psychology, 52*, 3–13.

Jones, K. M. L. (2019). "Just because you can doesn't mean you should": Practitioner perceptions of learning analytics ethics. *portal: Libraries and the Academy, 19*(3), 407–428. https://dx.doi.org/10.1353/pla.2019.0025

Juntunen, C. L., Crepaeau-Hobson, F., Riva, M. T., Baker, J., Wan, S., Davis III, C., & Caballero, A. M. (2023). Centering equity, diversity, and inclusion in ethical decision-making. *Professional Psychology: Research and Practice, 54*, 17–27.

Kaklauskas, F. J. & Olson, E. A. (2020). History and contemporary developments. In F. J. Kaklauskas & L. R. Greene (Eds.), *Core principles of group psychotherapy: An integrated theory, research, and practice training manual* (pp. 3–24). Routledge.

Kaslow, N. J., Grus, C. L., Campbell, L. F., Fouad, N. A., Hatcher, R. L., & Rodolfo, E. R. (2009). Competency assessment toolkit for professional psychology. *Training and Education in Professional Psychology, 3*(4, Suppl), S27–S45.

Kaslow, N. J., Rubin, N. J., Forrest, L., Elman, N. S., Van Horne, B. A., Jacobs, S. C., Huprich, S. K., Benton, S. A., Pantesco, V. F., Dollinger, S. J., Grus, C. L., Behnke, S. H., Miller, D. S. S., Shealy, C. N., Mintz, L. B., Schwartz-Mette, R., Van Sickle, K., & Thorn, B. E. (2007). Recognizing, assessing, and intervening with problems of professional competence. *Professional Psychology: Research and Practice, 38*(5), 479–492. https://doi.org/10.1037/0735-7028.38.5.479

Kitchener, K. S. (1984). Intuition, critical evaluation and ethical principles: The foundation for ethical decisions in counseling psychology. *Counseling Psychologist, 12*(3–4), 43–55. https://doi.org/10.1177/0011000084123005

Knapp, S., Handelsman, M. M., Gottlieb, M. C., & VandeCreek, L. D. (2013). The dark side of professional ethics. *Professional Psychology: Research and*

Knapp, S., & VandeCreek, L. (2007). When values of different cultures conflict: Ethical decision making in a multicultural context. *Professional Psychology: Research and Practice, 38*(6), 660–666. https://doi.org/10.1037/0735-7028.38.6.660

Knapp, S. J., VandeCreek, L. D., & Fingerhut, R. (2023). *Practical ethics for psychologists: A positive approach* (4th ed.). American Psychological Association.

Koocher, G. O. & Keith-Spiegel, P. (2008). *Ethics in psychology and the mental health professions: Standards and cases* (3rd ed.). Oxford University Press.

Lefforge, N. L., McLaughlin, S., Jones, M., & Mejia, C. (2020). A training model for addressing microaggressions in group psychotherapy. *International Journal of Group Psychotherapy, 70*(1), 1–28. https://doi.org/10.1080/00207284.2019.1680989

*Luke, M. & Goodrich, K. M. (2013). Investigating the LGBTQ responsive model for 71 Tessmer & Storlie supervision of group work. *Journal for Specialists in Group Work, 38*(2), 121–145. https://doi.org/10.1080/01933922.2013.775207

Marton, K. & Kanas, N. (2016). Telehealth modalities for group therapy: Comparisons to in-person group therapy. *International Journal of Group Psychotherapy, 66*(1), 145–150. https://doi.org/10.1080/00207284.2015.1096109

Miles, J. R., Anders, C., Kivlighan III, D. M., & Belcher Platt, A. A. (2021). Cultural ruptures: Addressing microaggressions in group therapy. *Group Dynamics: Theory, Research, and Practice, 25*(1), 74–88. https://doi.org/10.1037/gdn0000149

Neimeyer, G. J. & Taylor, J. M. (2019). Advancing the assessment of professional learning, self-care, and competence. *Professional Psychology: Research and Practice, 50*(2), 95–105. https://doi.org/10.1037/pro0000225

*Okech, J. E. & Rubel, D. (2007). Diversity competent group work supervision: An application of the supervision of group work model (SGW). *Journal for Specialists in Group Work, 32*(2), 245–266. https://doi.org/10.1080/01933920701431651

Phillips, L. A., Logan, J. N., & Mather, D. B. (2021). Covid-19 and beyond: Telesupervision training within the supervision competency. *Training and Education in Professional Psychology, 15*(4), 284–289.

Pope, K. S. & Vasquez, M. J. T. (2011). *Ethics in psychotherapy and counseling: A practical guide* (4th ed.). Wiley. https://doi.org/10.1002/9781118001875

Rapin, L. (2014). Guidelines for ethical and legal practice in counseling and psychotherapy groups. In J. L. DeLucia-Waack, C. R. Kalodner, & M. T. Riva (Eds.), *Handbook of group counseling & psychotherapy* (2nd ed.., pp. 71–83). Sage.

Renfro-Michel, E., Rousmaniere, T., & Spinella, L. (2016). Technological innovations in clinical supervision: Promises and challenges. In T. Rousmaniere & E. Renfro-Michel (Eds.), *Using technology to enhance clinical supervision* (pp. 3–18). American Counseling Association. https://doi.org/10.1037/tep0000417

Ribiero, M. D. (2021). Intentional call to action: Mindfully discussing race in group psychotherapy. *American Journal of Psychotherapy, 74*(2), 889–896. https://doi.org/10.1176/appi.psychotherapy.20200041

*Riva, M. T. (2014). Supervision of group leaders. In J. L. DeLucia-Waack, C. R. Kalodner, & M. T. Riva (Eds.), *Handbook of group counseling and psychotherapy* (2nd ed., pp. 146–158). Sage.

*Riva, M. T. & Erickson Cornish, J. A. (2018). Ethical considerations in group psychotherapy. In M. M. Leach & E. R. Welfel (Eds.), *The Cambridge handbook of applied psychological ethics* (pp. 218–238). Cambridge.

Riva, M. T., Lippert, L., & Tackett, J. (2000). Selection practices of group leaders: A national survey. *Journal for Specialists in Group Work, 25*(2), 157–169. https://doi.org/10.1080/01933920008411459

Riva, M. T. & Smith, R. D. (2024). Beyond the dyad: Broadening the APA supervision guidelines to include group supervision. *Psychotherapy, 61*(2), 161–172. https://doi.org/10.1037/pst0000525

Roback, H. B. (2000). Adverse outcomes in group psychotherapy: Risk factors, prevention and research directions. *Journal of Psychotherapy Practice and Research, 9*(3), 113–122.

Rosen, S. & Tesser, A. (1970). On reluctance to communicate undesirable information: The MUM Effect. *Sociometry, 33*(3), 253–263. https://doi.org/10.2307/2786156

*Rubel, D. & Atieno Okech, J. E. (2009). The expert group work supervision process: Apperception, actions, and interactions. *Journal for Specialists in Group Work, 34*(3), 227–250. https://doi.org/10.1080/01933920903032596

Salvendy, J. T. (1993). Control and power in supervision. *International Journal of Group Psychotherapy, 43*(3), 363–376. https://doi.org/10.1080/00207284.1993.11732599

Scarff, C. E., Bearman, M., Chiavaroli, N., & Trumble, S. (2019). Keeping mum in clinical supervision: Private thoughts and public judgments. *Medical Education, 53*(2), 133–142. https://doi.org/10.1111/medu.13728

Shen-Miller, D. S., Schwartz-Mette, R., Van Sickle, K. S., Jacobs, S. C., Grus, C. L., Hunter, E. A., & Forrest, L. (2015). Professional competence problems in training: A qualitative investigation of trainee perspectives. *Training and Education in Professional Psychology, 9*(2), 161–169. https://doi.org/10.1037/tep0000072

Singh, A. A., Merchant, N., Skudrzyk, B., & Ingene, D. (2012). Association for specialists in group work: Multicultural and social justice competence principles for group workers. *Journal for Specialists in Group Work, 37*, 312–325. https://doi.org/10.1080/01933922.2012.721482

Somerville, W., Marcus, S., & Chang, D. F. (2019). Multicultural competence-focused peer supervision: A multiple case study of clinical and counseling psychology trainees. *Journal of Multicultural Counseling and Development, 47*(4), 274–294. https://doi.org/10.1002/jmcd.12158

*Stockton, R., Morran, K., & Chang, S. (2014). An overview of current research and best practices for training beginning group leaders. In J. L. DeLucia-Waack, C. R. Kalodner, & M. T. Riva (Eds.), *Handbook of group counseling & psychotherapy* (2nd ed., pp. 133–145). Sage.

Tao, K. W., Owen, J., Pace, B. T., & Imel, Z. E. (2015). A meta-analysis of multicultural competencies and psychotherapy process and outcome. *Journal of Counseling Psychology, 62*(3), 337–350. https://doi.org/10.1037/cou0000086

*Tessmer, S. S. & Storle, C. A. (2021). Clinical supervision of group work: A conceptual review. *Journal of Counselor Practice, 12*(1), 48–72. https://doi.org/10.22229/sta1212021.

Tohidian, N. B. & Quek, K. (2017). Processes that inform multicultural supervision: A qualitative meta-analysis. *Journal of Marital and Family Therapy, 43*(4), 573–590. https://doi.org/10.1111/jmft.12219

Trenoska Basile, V., Newton-John, T., & Wootton, B. M. (2022). Remote cognitive-behavioral therapy for generalized anxiety disorder: A preliminary meta-analysis. *Journal of Clinical Psychology, 78*(12), 2381–2395. https://doi.org/10.1002/jclp.23360

Vasquez, M. J. T. (1992). Psychologist as clinical supervisor: Promoting ethical practice. *Professional Psychology: Research and Practice, 23*, 196 –202.

Watkins Jr., C. E., Reyna, S. H., Ramos, M., & Hook, J.N. (2015). The ruptured supervisory relationship alliance and its repair. On supervisor apology as a reparative intervention. *Clinical Supervisor, 34*(1), 98–114. https://doi.org/10.1080/07325223.2015.1015194

Weinberg, H. (2020). Online group psychotherapy: Challenges and possibilities during Covid-19: A practice review. *Group Dynamics: Theory, Research, and Practice, 24*(3), 201–211. http://dx.doi.org/10.1037/gdn0000140

Weinberg, H. (2023). Online training process groups for therapist: A proposed model, *International Journal of Group Psychotherapy, 73*(2), 141–165. https://doi.org/10.1080/00207284.2023.2170236

Welfel, E. R. (2022). *Ethics in counseling and psychotherapy* (6th ed.). Cengage.

Yalom, I. & Leszcz, M. (2020). *The theory and practice of group psychotherapy* (6th ed.). Basic Books.

Chapter 7

The Research–Supervision Relationship

Michelle A. Collins-Greene and Les R. Greene

Two of the core domains required for competency in leading a psychotherapy group are becoming an effective supervisor and gaining familiarity with the research literature on group therapy (Barlow 2012, 2013b). These two domains have a bidirectional and reciprocal relationship to each other. On the one hand, inviting supervisees to learn about research findings, operationally defined variables, methodologies and measures within the supervisory relationship can enhance both clinical and leadership skills which, in turn, can positively affect treatment outcomes. On the other hand, supervisory competence can be enhanced by means of scientific studies that explore (1) what factors make supervision effective, (2) how supervision affects patient outcome (Watkins, 2011), and (3) how the supervision alliance can be strengthened (Watkins, 2014).

How Group Therapists and Supervisors Can Be Informed by Research

Familiarity and comfort with research findings, methods, and instruments are useful for clinical work in groups, particularly those scientific works investigating group processes. Educating supervisees about process measures can provide understanding of the ways that group therapy processes have been conceptualized and operationally defined by researchers and can serve as a means of sharpening clinical-conceptual awareness of what is occurring in the moment (Pascual-Leone & Andreescu, 2013). As Greene (2019) proposed, "Reading sophisticated process-outcome research can help clinicians think more analytically and with greater cognitive complexity. It … can help them further develop a scientific attitude toward the work, providing fruitful constructs and constructions that can help bring coherency and meaningfulness to the, at times, overwhelming and uncontained stream of data, and thus keep the group afloat" (p. 358).

Another avenue for the group therapist and supervisor to use research is learning about routine outcome monitoring (ROM), through either sharpening clinical observation skills or training in formal assessment instruments. Most recently, Westra and Di Bartolomeo (2024) have posited ways to train therapists to track real-time changes in clinical processes, particularly negative process markers of ruptures and resistances that are found to adversely affect outcomes. They propose that training in tracking of the subtleties of change within the therapy session can help supervisees enhance observational and conceptualization skills while also giving them the opportunity to address ruptures before they lead to dropouts or negative effects on the group climate. These researchers are exploring how to provide

DOI: 10.4324/9781003410621-8

supervisees knowledge about process variables that can enhance therapists' capacities to explore, see, and understand what is going on in the here-and-now clinical arena. Other researchers offer ways of familiarizing supervisees with the administration of validated process measures within the session to enhance their capacity to sensitively "take the pulse of the group" and alert them to those group members who may be experiencing negative reactions to the treatment (Jensen et al., 2012; Svien et al., 2021). However, supervisees need to appreciate that the findings from such measures are not replacements for clinical observation and judgment but rather enhancements to them (Greene et al., 2020; MacNair-Semands & Whittingham, 2023).

Integrating formal measures organically and seamlessly into the clinical arena is no easy feat. The mindful group therapist needs to explore and be open to hearing group members' concerns and anxieties about the deploying of such measures and how the data are to be used. In addition, the group therapist's own concerns about how to introduce the measures into the group with the least amount of disruption to the group process, as well as concerns about what the measures may say about the members' engagement with the therapist, would be good fodder for supervision.

As regards the usefulness of assessment measures of client experience in group, the therapist can feel affirmed when their clinical judgment aligns with findings from empirical measures; however, when there are divergences in these two sources of data, the therapist has the opportunity to explore the meaning of such discrepancies with group members and the supervisor. Discrepancies could stem from the clinician's biases, blindspots, and resistances to awareness that something might be awry in the group. As well, there is the possibility that members may feel it is safer (or, conversely, riskier) to express their genuine feelings and reactions about the group, themselves, and the therapist privately via paper-and-pencil inventories than in the public arena of the therapy group. It is important for the supervisee to appreciate that neither source of data—subjective meaning making of the therapist's clinical observations or "objective" results from paper-and-pencil measures—is absolutely foolproof. They both contribute to a fuller understanding of the group process. This is where the third eye of a supervisor may be particularly valuable in assisting the supervisee's interpretation and understanding.

It is worth emphasizing that in introducing a research agenda into clinical supervision, the studies of most clinical relevance are those that explore the process, the interior of the psychotherapy situation, the emergent processes (sometimes referred to as small "o") arising in the session that ultimately affect outcome (or big "O"). This kind of process-oriented research lags far behind the current prototypical psychotherapy study, the randomized control outcome trial, that contrasts the researcher's favored treatment with a control or comparison treatment. For studies on group therapy, the control condition has typically been individual therapy, no treatment (or wait list), or treatment as usual (Burlingame & Strauss, 2021). Such outcome studies do provide important empirical support and accountability for various therapy treatments, and in this case, group therapy (cf. Burlingame et al., 2024; Evidence-based Group Treatment, n.d.; Leszcz, 2024). They have provided the basis for the "three E's" that legitimize group therapy as an "evidence-based" practice; group therapy is now recognized as "efficient," "effective," and "equivalent" to individual therapy and other combined treatments. These amassing outcome studies contribute to the group therapist's confidence that group therapy is indeed a healing modality. However, the design employed in these well-constructed randomized control studies shed little light on the intricacies of what actually happens in the room between patients and therapists and how the therapist might intervene at any specific moment and thus, as many have critiqued, hold only limited value to the practitioner.

The very features that lend scientific legitimacy to the typical outcome study, including meta-analyses that aggregate data generated from several studies of relatively homogeneous individuals, fail to address what is of primary interest to the therapist, namely a consideration of what specific interventions at a particular moment in a particular clinical situation with a particular therapist and particular patient or group of patients will be most beneficial. Often what the outcome researcher considers as "noise" in the data is the bread-and-butter focus of the therapist who wants to explore and understand the vagaries and complexities of here-and-now dynamics (Greene, 2017). As Corey (2023) recently concluded: "Researchers know little about how group processes mediate change in participants, how members influence group processes, and what dimensions of psychological functioning are most amenable to change in small groups. Quite simply, although researchers know that group treatments can be effective, they do not know much about why this is so" (p. 31). Similarly, Burlingame and Strauss (2021) conclude: "Interestingly, as the rigor of the group treatment outcome research increases (e.g., manualized protocols, powered studies, fidelity checks, random assignment, etc.), we know less about group dynamics and processes" (p. 584).

Recently Greene (2017) catalogued the kinds of research designs that are much more clinician-friendly precisely because they address the kinds of questions that practitioners raise, such as the identification of mediators (i.e., the underlying change mechanisms operating in this group), moderators (i.e., those variables that enhance or diminish therapeutic outcome), and core group therapy processes. Take as an example of a question about a mediator that a group therapist might raise in a situation where the therapist complements a member in the group and then observes that the group-as-a-whole becomes more engaged and the members report enhanced self-esteem on the outcome measure of the group that day. How can this sequence of events be understood? Perhaps a shared identification by the group with the one member who was complemented led to the positive reactions throughout the group. Or was it a result of a shift to a more positive perception of the group therapist? Such hypotheses reflect the therapist's efforts to understand the underlying mechanisms that lead to positive observable change. The therapist further notes that not all of the group members showed increased engagement and enhanced self-esteem to the same degree and discovers that those members with longer tenure in the group were more positively affected than the newer ones, thus hypothesizing about a moderating variable (tenure in the group) that might account for the differential responsiveness.

All of this is to emphasize that the goal of incorporating a research focus into supervision is to support the clinician in seeing and understanding what is occurring in the here-and-now of the group. Further, incorporating a scientific attitude into the work of supervision can facilitate an openness to exploring one's own subjectivities, countertransference reactions, and blindspots for the developing, or even seasoned, therapist. However, the supervisory consult with the group leader, that includes their observations and interpretations, along with consideration of relevant research, ultimately is the best practice in providing informed group therapy.

Practitioner-Relevant Process Research

Therapeutic Factors

Many process variables have been scientifically studied that are relevant to the practicing group psychotherapist and supervisor. Yalom and Leszcz's (2020) conceptual-clinical analysis of the group processes that promote therapeutic change in groups was seminal in this regard. They postulated 11 curative factors that seemed to benefit patients, clients, and participants in almost all types of groups: Altruism, Catharsis, Corrective recapitulation of the primary family group, Development of socializing techniques, Existential factors, Group cohesiveness, Imitative behavior, Imparting information, Instillation of hope, Interpersonal learning, and Universality. These were to become what are now called "common variables," "curative factors," "process variables," or "therapeutic factors" (Kivlighan et al., 2010). They figured that if the group therapist could capitalize on these variables, and even more if they could figure out the most important ones, there would be better outcomes. Soon a number of studies appeared in the literature that reported how group members in a variety of groups perceived the therapeutic importance of these factors. Taken together, the studies revealed that there was not one universal pattern of rankings but rather considerable variability based on many factors such as therapeutic orientation of the group and the setting in which the group was conducted. Yalom's factors are still universally considered when understanding process variables and can be usefully kept in mind by the clinician to assess which factors are in play at any moment in the group.

Following this work, more recent efforts have attempted to quantify and operationally define these factors to make them more amenable to more rigorous scientific investigation. The development of the Therapeutic Factors Inventory (TFI) (MacNair-Semands, et al. (2010) was constructed as a 99-item self-report measure designed to formally assess group members' perceptions of Yalom's 11 factors operating in their groups (Lese & MacNair-Semands, 2000). Still more recently, efforts have been directed at reducing the number of items of the TFI to facilitate the administration of the measure and at identifying a fewer number of more abstract dimensions underlying the 11 curative factors. A 19-item Therapeutic Factors Inventory-19 (TFI-19) (Joyce et al., 2011) was designed to assess the perceived presence or absence of four higher order therapeutic factors derived from the original 11: Instillation of Hope, Secure Emotional Expression, Awareness of Relational Impact, and Social Learning.

Alliance and Cohesion

Currently, two process variables have been identified as having a significant positive relationship to outcome: (1) the therapeutic alliance, adapted from the individual psychotherapy literature and reflecting the degree to which patients and therapists share a sense of goals and tasks and experience a positive bond with each other (Bordin, 1983); and (2) cohesion, tapping the experience of connection, communion, and comradery among the group participants (Marmarosh & Van Horn, 2010). These variables reflect core elements of the quality of the interpersonal relationships in the group and they have received considerable empirical validation, and are thus considered evidence-based process variables (Alldredge et al., 2021; Burlingame et al., 2018; Burlingame & McClendon et al., 2018).

Despite significant findings that "alliance" and "cohesion" are positively correlated with outcome, both variables have been critiqued in terms of conceptual ambiguity and inconsistency. For example, the cohesion construct has been defined in numerous ways and, to date, there have been no efforts to compare and contrast these differences (Burlingame et al., 2018; Greene, 2017). More importantly, while the relationship between cohesion and outcome is statistically significant, meta-analysis that have collected correlations of 55 studies reveal that the variance accounted for is only about 6% of the total variance. A similar story holds for the alliance–outcome relationship. Taken together, these findings suggest that focusing on isolated variables, divorced from other theoretically derived concepts, may be limited and even misleading. So, for example, the notion that greater cohesion always leads to better outcomes may be simplistic and reductionistic. Such a conclusion fails to take into account, for example, those group members who value self-definition and autonomy over relationship and connection and who may find too much cohesion toxic and threatening. As Barlow (2013a) advises, competent therapists should promote "good" cohesion, that which explicitly addresses group members' needs to belong while still maintaining a sense of self and differentiate it from "bad" cohesion which capitalizes on coercive pressures on members to stay in line and that often leads to scapegoating. Group life is complex, and trying to comprehend it by means of a few univariate equations, such as the linear association between cohesion and outcome, may unintendedly limit the supervisee's appreciation of the complexity of dynamic life within groups.

Despite such methodological problems in definition, Barlow (2013a) offers that given the centrality of the cohesion construct, it needs to be an essential focus in the work of supervising the developing group therapist, including appreciating those interventions that promote constructive cohesion as well as those which can interfere with its development such as those empathic failures of misunderstandings, miscommunications, and microaggressions. The complexity of group treatment requires that interventions that promote cohesion consider interactions between group members, as well as those between the group therapist and the group-as-a-whole and with members. Barlow further posits that the exploration of cohesion needs to occur in all phases of the group: In pregroup preparation and selection of group members by assessing how a new member will fit into the existing group, particularly in terms of expectations and attachment and interpersonal styles; in the initial phases of the group, where a significant aspect of the therapeutic work is to promote safety and connection, and in later stages of the group where dysfunctional subgrouping and scapegoating dynamics could erode a sense of communion and shared group identity. The limitations of the cohesion research, particularly the multiplicity of operational definitions, could be viewed as an opportunity for growth and development of the group therapist by using supervision for reviewing the extant operational definitions and exploring and examining which ones best resonate with the understandings of the concept by both supervisor and supervisee(s).

Supervisory work could fruitfully engage not only in the exploration of such well-established and well-researched process variables as cohesion and alliance, but also be open to new ideas about change processes in group as they are introduced into the clinical-theoretical literature and about the construction of new measures to formally assess them. Case in point are recent methodologies to explore rupture and repair sequences in groups (Burlingame et al., 2018; Garceau et al., 2021; Greene & Kaklauskas, 2020; Gullo et al., 2021) and the multicultural orientation (Kivlighan & Chapman, 2018) of group leadership and group-as-a-whole, two newer foci of group processes reflecting an enhanced appreciation of how empathic failures, cultural blindspots and implicit biases can unknowingly get enacted and lead to withdrawal or premature termination. Learning about such measures in supervision and/or introducing them into the clinical work can enhance the therapist's attunement to present or potential problems in maintaining a cohesive and task-oriented group.

Sets of Variables

Other prominent developments in research on group process have moved beyond single variables to empirically derived sets of variables, allowing researchers and clinicians to explore the relationships among several group process dimensions and thus develop more nuanced and complex formulations about individual group members and the group-as-a-whole. Two of the most well-known systems are the Group Climate Questionnaire (MacKenzie, 1983) and the Group Questionnaire (Krogel et al., 2013). As described in detail by Miles et al. (2023), these measures share two essential features: (1) both assess members' perception of the emotional quality of the group along three dimensions that were extracted from larger item data sets and (2) both measures tap positive and negative aspects of emotional life in groups. The subscales of the Group Climate Questionnaire consist of Engagement (experiencing the group members as liking and caring for each other), Avoidance (tapping the experience of group members' resistance to the exploratory work of the group and to therapeutic change, and Conflict (reflecting a climate of hostility and mistrust). The later GQ similarly taps three dimensions of quality of therapeutic interactions—(1) positive bonding, (2) positive working, and (3) negative relationships—and, importantly, assesses these experiences across the three primary relationship structures in the group—member to member, member to group, member to leader. Noteworthy for supervision is that the recent literature nicely illustrates how the GQ can be used clinically to gain an alternative perspective, beyond clinical observation and interpretation, about the goings on in the group (Burlingame et al., 2021; Griner et al., 2018). In particular, process measures such as the GQ can aid the therapist in spotting potentially problematic issues in order to repair and redress them before they become destructive of therapeutic goals and aims and, in that regard should be a useful part of the supervisory work.

Beyond Process Research: Assessment Instruments for Intake and Outcome

Beyond the value of familiarizing the trainee with process research as a means to sharpen and deepen one's conceptualizations of what is occurring in the group at any moment, other research questions and methods can be incorporated into the work of supervision, including assessment issues pertaining to patient selection and preparation before a patient enters a group, on the one hand, and to treatment outcomes as a patient leaves a group, on the other hand.

Intake Assessment

The work of intake is to explore two primary and interrelated questions: (1) will the group be helpful to this patient and (2) will this patient fit into the group, whether it is an ongoing group or one that is currently being constructed. In essence, these are two sides of the same coin that reflect matters of accommodation and assimilation, the suitability of the group for the patient and the fitting in of the patient to the group. To assess these questions, the group therapist needs a formulation of the group, as it currently exists, or as it is being planned in the mind of the therapist and also needs to develop a case formulation of the prospective patient.

While the process measures described above are useful in helping the therapist conceptualize the group experience, in terms of norms, process, culture, task and work, the literature also contains a number of validated instruments that can aid the therapist in assessing the readiness and suitability of a prospective member for a particular group. Using the supervision to gain familiarity with these research instruments, whether or not they are actually administered in the intake process, can help the therapist consider the range of issues that should be addressed. The two most utilized measures are the Group Therapy Questionnaire (MacNair-Semands, 2002) and the Group Readiness Questionnaire (Baker et al., 2013), conceptually similar measures (Joyce & Marmarosh, 2023) that are designed to explore a range of affective and motivational issues shown to affect participation and outcome, including expectations about and fears of the group. They also tap personality features and interpersonal style dimensions such as hostility and likeability that have been found to relate to a patient's fate in the group. As such, these measures can be used by novice and experienced group therapists alike as a springboard for more personalized questions and explorations designed to aid in decisions about the goodness of fit between a prospective client and a particular group, even if the actual questionnaire is not administered.

There are also a number of measures in the clinical research literature that aim at assessing what alternatively have been called scripts, transferences, internal object relations, social cognitive schemas, cyclical relational patterns, and attachment styles all reflecting deeply entrenched views of the self in the world acquired early in life that tend to get reenacted in all contemporary social contexts. In essence these self-schemas serve as templates or guideposts, rendering the current social field as familiar and predictable and consist of the usual fears and desires one holds about others, the expectations about how others will treat self, and the effects of these anticipated and perceived interpersonal dynamics upon the sense of self. Included here are the Core Conflictual Relationship Theme (Siefert, 2019; Tallberg et al., 2020), Structural Analysis of Social Behavior (Critchfield & Benjamin, 2024), Cyclical Maladaptive Interpersonal Patterns (Hewitt et al., 2018; Tasca et al., 2021), and the interpersonal Circumplex (Whittingham, 2018). All of these methodologies offer a means to construct an interpersonal narrative of the prospective member's life and, as Tasca et al. (2021) posit, "the fundamental building block of a [pregroup] assessment is the therapist's ability to help the patient provide an interpersonal narrative that includes aspects of self-concept … The end goal is to predict as accurately as possible the patient's interpersonal approach to the group, their expectations of the group, how the group might respond, and how these interactions may affect the individual's sense of self" (p. 82). "The formulation is used to collaborate with the prospective patient in specifying treatment goals and also to identify the kinds of interpersonal patterns that are likely to be manifested in the group and the challenges and maladaptive reactions that could arise as a result" (Hewitt et al., 2018, p. 181). Learning these methods takes considerable training and the supervisory work is not necessarily to have the supervisee gain expertise in administering these instruments but rather to acquire understanding and appreciation of the underlying theoretical formulations about these engrained interpersonal patterns of needs, wishes, fears, anticipations and defenses that get externalized and relived in the immediate social field, including the therapy group. As such, this work can help the developing group therapist not only in skills needed to select and prepare prospective patients for a group but in appreciating in deeper, more articulated and more nuanced ways the dynamic interplay between the internal world and the social field.

Outcome Assessment

In terms of treatment outcome, some researchers distinguish between "progress monitoring" (where the same measures are administered intermittently throughout the course of treatment to note individual and group trends that might signal needs for the therapist's attention) and "outcome monitoring" that entail examining changes between pretreatment and posttreatment (cf. Kivlighan & Tasca, 2023). The latter method is important in establishing the effectiveness of the treatment, for the individual and the group-as-whole, vital in establishing accountability, though less helpful in illuminating why observed changes occurred. In general, group therapy researchers suggest using both traditional outcome measures as well as the kinds of process measures described earlier to explore not only what changes occur but what factors might be contributing to those changes (cf. Burlingame et al., 2018).

Supervision can be useful in helping the group therapist explore what measures might be most meaningfully employed. This work is important, regardless of whether the therapist actually administers the measures, by helping the clinician keep in mind the various kinds of changes that treatment is aimed at attaining and staying focused on the rational goals for which the work of the group is directed. The research informed supervisor can assist in the exploration of measures based on the therapist's specific goals, their underlying theory of therapy, and the type of the group being led. The best measures are clinically useful, offer learning opportunities for both therapist and members, are culturally applicative, and appealing to the clients (Whittingham et al., 2023). More than that, if measures are to be administered, the choices need to be dictated by considerations of how readily they will be assimilated into the overall work of the group without stirring a sense of intrusiveness or disruption or arousing behavioral resistance.

As reviewed by Greene et al. (2020), therapeutic change can be viewed and assessed along a variety of dimensions including (1) symptomatic relief, (2) increased insight and self-awareness, (3) shift to more adaptive interpersonal behavioral patterns, (4) enhanced ego functions such as greater empathy and capacities for reflection and mindfulness, (5) enhanced emotional regulation and stress tolerance, (6) satisfaction with treatment, and (7) improved sense of well-being and of quality of life. Some measures, notably the OQ-45 (Burlingame et al., 2018; Lambert et al., 2013; Whittingham et al., 2023), assess multiple dimensions of outcome like Symptom Distress (or subjective discomfort, particularly experiences of depression and anxiety), Interpersonal Relations (loneliness and conflict with others), and Social Role (difficulties in the workplace, school or home duties). The recommended and most frequently used measure of outcome for group therapists wanting to measure outcome in their own groups is the OQ 45.2.

In contrast to these instruments which measure what the therapist ultimately deems important, the Target Complaint Form (cf. Battle et al., 1966; Joyce & Marmarosh, 2023; Kealy et al., 2019), guides the therapist and prospective patient in collaborating on defining three idiographic and measurable goals that the patient wants to achieve in treatment. Such a measure is appealing because it is essentially just a formalization of what would typically be asked in the course of a clinical intake and empowers the client in determining what the desired outcomes should be (cf. Cuijpers, 2019a, b). When administered either pre–post treatment or routinely over the course of therapy, it provides a useful assessment of the patient's view of goal attainment. Supervision can serve a vital role in helping the supervisee clearly conceptualize what the goals of therapy are for the individual members and the group-as-a-whole and what work is needed to achieve those ends.

Researching Supervision

In the following section we shift from the question of how supervision can help the developing group therapist gain expertise of the research literature in the service of clinical work to the question of how research can help explore whether and in what ways the supervision of group therapy is effective. Unfortunately, little outcome research on the supervisory process has been conducted to date (cf. Falender, 2018; Simpson-Southward et al., 2017; Watkins, 2021). Barlow (2013b) asserts: "Supervision and consultation are two of the least researched areas in professional psychology" (p. 166). While there is general agreement about the relative scarcity of research on clinical supervision compared to other psycho-therapy research domains, the deficit is even more pronounced in terms of research on the supervision of group psychotherapy, and research is virtually nonexistent regarding the group-based supervision of group therapy. The good news is that as models of clinical super-vision (Watkins, 2017), in general, and of the supervision of group therapy (Barlow, 2013b; Rubel & Atieno Okech, 2006; Tessmer & Storlie, 2021), in particular, become increasingly articulated, the greater the opportunities emerge to generate hypotheses and study specific components within these complex models, as well as the supervisory model as a whole.

The most obvious and straightforward question that can be raised has to do with the effectiveness of supervision on the development of the group therapist. What effects does supervision have on the professional growth of the supervisee and along what dimensions does change occur? Weaving together the extant models of clinical supervision, the lim-ited but promising empirical studies on supervision outcome (although most pertaining to the supervision of individual psychotherapy), and the delineation of competencies to be acquired by the group psychotherapist, a number of group-specific and more general clinical/professional dependent variables can be identified. The following are some of the measurable dimensions along which growth and development of the supervisee is expected to occur:

1. the supervisee's enhanced sense of confidence and therapeutic presence (cf. Gans, 2015);
2. decreased anxiety, self-doubt and shame, including fears about being the center of attention in the group, the public nature of one's actions and interventions in the group, the fear of losing control or being swept away by overpowering forces in the group or losing one's sense of self due to the multiple projections and transferences directed at the therapist (cf. Riva, 2014);
3. more salient identity as an effective group psychotherapist and greater allegiance to one's theories of therapy;
4. greater access to one's own inner world, including acknowledgment and management of countertransference reactions, and a deeper appreciation of the role of unconscious needs, motivations and defenses in self and others;
5. acquisition of deeper, more nuanced and more cognitively complex conceptualiza-tions about group members' dynamics (Kivlighan Jr. et al., 2007), group-as-a-whole dynamics (Li et al., 2015), and leader interventions (Kivlighan Jr. & Kivlighan III, 2009);
6. acquisition of group-specific technical and relational skills to provide a sense of caring and safety which include offering empathic understandings about what is happening within the group, effectively maintaining boundaries and reinforce norms, maintaining a therapeutic emotional climate (Barnes et al., 2020; Chapman et al., 2010) and facili-tating exploration of cultural differences in the group (cf. Grimes & Kivlighan III, 2022);
7. greater tolerance for ambiguity, not knowing, uncertainty and loss of control;
8. greater sensitivity and attunement to patients' reactance and resistance and the know-ledge about how to respond effectively to them;
9. increased foundational and functional knowledge specific to group dynamics (cf. Barlow, 2012);
10. knowledge of some of the newer ideas and trends in the group therapy literature, including appreciation of the rupture–repair sequence (cf. Marmarosh, 2021; Miles et al., 2021), the impact of attachment styles (cf. Marmarosh & Magenheimer, 2018), and the need for multicultural openness and competence (cf. Miles et al., 2021).

Beyond assessing the overall effects of supervision on the multitudinous ways that the group therapist can develop greater competence, research can also be usefully directed at studying the components of the supervision process as postulated in various models. Arguably the component that has received the most research investment, albeit with a comparatively small number of empirical studies of limited methodology and exclusive focus on individual therapy, is the supervisory working alliance (Atieno Okech & Rubel, 2009; Bordin, 1983; Kleinberg, 1999; Rubel & Atieno Okech, 2009; Watkins, 2014). This component, analogous to the working alliance between therapist and patient, explores the degree of collaboration between supervisor and supervisee on the tasks and goals of supervision and the affective bond toward each other and is rather straightforwardly measured by two widely accepted instruments: The Supervisory Working Alliance Inventory (SWAI; Efstation et al., 1990) and an adaptation of the Working Alliance Inventory (WAI; Horvath & Greenberg, 1989). And because the study of the alliance is an exploration of a two-person dynamic relationship, it seems reasonable to assume that the results of the extant studies of supervisory alliance from individual therapy hold promise for future studies on the alliance in group therapy supervision, if nothing more than to stimulate much needed empirical work in this area. Given the core underlying assumption that it is through the alliance that the professional development of the supervisee occurs, a range of theory and practice-informed questions can be raised about how the alliance can be optimized (cf. Watkins, 2017), on the one hand, and how differences, tensions, rifts and ruptures that arise within the supervisory relationship can be successfully negotiated, contained, bridged and repaired, on the other.

The supervisory alliance can be studied both in terms of its inputs, especially the personalities, psychological resources and interpersonal styles of supervisor and supervisee and also in terms of downstream effects, that is, the degree to which and how it influences and shapes the development of the supervisee. In his recent review, Watkins (2014) reports positive associations between the supervisory alliance in psychological treatments and

> higher supervisee self-efficacy and well-being, greater willingness to self-disclose during supervision, more satisfaction with supervision, more job satisfaction, greater perceived effectiveness of supervision, more availability of coping resources, secure attachment style, more supportively-perceived gender events during supervision, an attractive, interpersonally sensitive supervisor style, higher interactional complementarity between supervisee and supervisor, higher supervisee and supervisor racial identity statuses, more discussions of culture in supervision, more favorable perceptions of supervisor ethical behaviors, greater supervisor relational ability, and more frequent yet appropriate supervisor self-disclosures. A weak or unfavorably rated supervisory alliance was found to be related to such variables as: Supervisee avoidant attachment style, higher degree of perceived stress, more exhaustion and burnout, greater amount of role conflict and role ambiguity, and more frequently perceived occurrences of negative supervision events.
>
> (p. 41)

Another intriguing hypothesis regarding the supervisory alliance has been proposed in the literature but has not yet been put to rigorous test, namely the association, or more precisely parallel process, between the alliance in supervision and the alliance in therapy. Gerstenblith et al. (2022) are the most recent of clinical researchers who have proposed that the interpersonal dynamics in the supervisory arena could be mirrored, either via conscious modeling or unconscious identification, in the psychotherapy arena, a phenomenon known as the triadic effect, because "clients, trainees, and supervisors unconsciously reenact interactions up and down the chain (from client to trainee to supervisor, as well as from supervisor to trainee to client)" (p. 200). For example, a supervisee who is struggling with an anxious, agitated and intrusive member of a therapy group might, through identification with that patient, enact that same dynamic vis-à-vis the supervisor. To the extent that the supervisor can hold and contain the supervisee's emotional distress with support, compassion and empathy, the supervisee has an opportunity to internalize that salutary interaction and bring it back into the clinical situation, thus benefiting the group process.

As this example implies, the supervisory alliance, and indeed the supervision process as a whole, could be studied in terms of patient outcomes. But, as Watkins (2011) has pointed out, "it is a most difficult endeavor to trace triadic impact—the effect of the supervisor/supervision experience as processed through the supervisee upon the patient. Yet the importance of this type of outcome research cannot be overemphasized; it was identified as a significant press or need for 21st-century psychotherapy supervision well over a decade ago and continues to be referred to as the real 'acid test' or 'gold standard' of supervision efficacy" (pp. 236–237). And the call for investigations of supervisor effects on patient outcomes remains an important, although as yet unanswered, need (cf. Hill & Castonguay, 2023).

Going Forward

The myths that any clinician can run a psychotherapy group and that no unique skills are needed have long been shattered. Within the past two decades, group psychotherapy has achieved remarkable recognition as a distinct and validated form of treatment requiring group therapists to master a range of foundational and functional competencies. More than this, the supervision of group therapy is no longer considered "the quiet" profession (cf. Alonso, 1985). Learning how to be an effective group therapy supervisor is itself a required competency for the group therapist, and sophisticated analyses and models of group therapy supervising are flourishing. Supervision is now regarded as a core requirement for the development of the group therapist (Hahn et al., 2022). And the research–supervision relationship—both helping the supervisee acquire a scientific attitude and gain familiarity with research methods and measures to enhance practice, on the one hand, and the empirical study of the processes that optimize and/or impede supervision, on the other hand—seems primed to be the next arena for development. Ultimately, group therapy supervision will need to demonstrate, in a more compelling way, its effects and effectiveness on the development of the group therapy supervisee as well as in group patient outcomes.

References

Alldredge, C. T., Burlingame, G. M., Yang, C., & Rosendahl, J. (2021). Alliance in group therapy: A meta-analysis. *Group Dynamics: Theory, Research, and Practice, 25*, 13–28. http://dx.doi.org/10.1037/gdn0000135

Alonso, A. (1985). *The quiet profession: Supervisors of psychotherapy*. Macmillan.

Atieno Okech, J. E. & Rubel, D. (2009). The experiences of expert group work supervisors: An exploratory study. *Journal for Specialists in Group Work, 34*(1), 68–89. https://doi.org/10.1080/01933920802578087

Baker, E., Burlingame, G. M., Cox, J. C., Beecher, M. E., & Gleave, R. L. (2013). The Group Readiness Questionnaire: A convergent validity analysis. *Group Dynamics: Theory, Research, and Practice, 17*, 299–314. https://psycnet.apa.org/doi/10.1037/a0034477

Barlow, S. H. (2012). An application of the competency model to group-specialty practice. *Professional Psychology: Research and Practice, 43*, 442–451. http://dx.doi.org/10.1037/a0029090.

Barlow, S. H. (2013a). Cohesion, interpersonal relationships and attachment. In S. H. Barlow (Ed.), *Specialty competencies in group psychology* (pp. 91–111). Oxford University Press.

Barlow, S. H. (2013b). *Specialty competencies in group psychology*. Oxford University Press.

Barnes, M. A., Schwartzberg, S. L, Bedell, G., Counselman, E., & Marfeo, E. (2020). The Group-Leader Self-Assessment (GLSA) tool: Preliminary study of reliability and validity. *Journal for Specialists in Group Work, 45*, 277–291. https://doi.org/10.1080/01933922.2020.1799466

Battle, C. C., Imber, S. D., Hoehn-Saric, R., Stone, A. R., Nash, E. R., & Frank, J. D. (1966). Target complaints as criteria of improvement. *American Journal of Psychotherapy, 20*, 184–192. https://doi.org/10.1176/appi.psychotherapy.1966.20.1.184

Bordin, E. S. (1983). A working alliance model of supervision. *Counseling Psychologist, 11*, 35–42.

Burlingame, G. M., Alldredge, C. T., & Arnold, R. A. (2021). Alliance rupture detection and repair in group therapy: Using the Group Questionnaire. *International Journal of Group Psychotherapy, 71*, 338–370. https://doi.org/10.1080/00207284.2020.1844010.

Burlingame, G. M., McClendon, D. T., & Yang, C. (2018). Cohesion in group therapy: A meta-analysis. *Psychotherapy, 55*(4), 384–398. https://doi.org/10.1037/pst0000173

Burlingame, G. M. & Strauss, B. (2021). Efficacy of small group treatments: Foundation for evidence-based practice. In M. Barkham, W. Lutz, & L. G. Castonguay (Eds.), *Bergin and Garfield's handbook of psychotherapy and behavior change: 50th anniversary edition* (7th ed., pp. 583–624). John Wiley & Sons.

Burlingame, G. M., Strauss, B. M., & Clayton, D. (2024). The complexity of becoming an evidence-based group clinician: Introducing an evidence-based group treatment website. *Group Dynamics: Theory, Research, and Practice, 28*(3), 121–131. https://doi.org/10.1037/gdn0000228

Burlingame, G. M., Whitcomb, K. E., Woodland, S. C., Olsen, J. A., Beecher, M. E., & Gleave, R. L. (2018). The effects of relationship and progress feedback in group psychotherapy using the Group Questionnaire and Outcome Questionnaire-45: A randomized clinical trial. *Psychotherapy, 55*, 116–131. https://doi.org/10.1037/pst0000133

Chapman, C. L., Baker, E. L., Porter, G., Thayer, S. D., & Burlingame, G. M. (2010). Rating group therapist interventions: The validation of the Group Psychotherapy Intervention Rating Scale. *Group Dynamics: Theory, Research, and Practice, 14*(1), 15–31. https://doi.org/10.1037/a0016628

Corey, G. (2023). *Theory and practice of group counseling* (10th ed.). Cengage Learning.

Critchfield, K. L. & Benjamin, L. S. (2024). *Structural analysis of social behavior (SASB): A primer for clinical use*. American Psychological Association.

Cuijpers, P. (2019a). Measuring success in the treatment of depression: What is most important to patients? *Expert Review of Neurotherapeutics, 20*, 123–125. http://dx.doi.org/10.1080/14737175.2020.1712807.

Cuijpers, P. (2019b). Targets and outcomes of psychotherapies for mental disorders: An overview. *World Psychiatry, 18*, 276–285.

Efstation, J. F., Patton, M. J., & Kardash, C. M. (1990). Measuring the working alliance in counselor supervision. *Journal of Counseling Psychology, 37*(3), 322–329. https://doi.org/10.1037/0022-0167.37.3.322.

Evidence-based Group Treatment. (n.d.). https://evidencebasedgrouptherapy.org

Falender, C. A. (2018). Clinical supervision: The missing ingredient. *American Psychologist, 73*(9), 1240–1250. https://doi.org/10.1037/amp0000385

Gans, J. S. (2015). The insufficiency of theory: Gaining one's voice as a group therapist. *International Journal of Group Psychotherapy, 65*(2) 317–325. https://doi.org/10.1521/ijgp.2015.65.2.317

Garceau, C., Chyurlia, L., Baldwin, D., Boritz, T., Hewitt, P. L., Kealy, D., Sochting, I., Mikail, S. F., & Tasca, G. A. (2021). Applying the rupture resolution rating system (3RS) to group therapy: An evidence-based case study. *Group Dynamics: Theory, Research, and Practice, 25*(1), 89–105.

Gerstenblith, J. A., Kline, K. V., Hill, C. E., & Kivlighan Jr., D. M. (2022). The triadic effect: Associations among the supervisory working alliance, therapeutic working alliance, and therapy session evaluation. *Journal of Counseling Psychology, 69*(2), 199–210. https://doi.org/10.1037/cou0000567

Greene, L. R. (2017). Group psychotherapy research studies that therapists might actually read: My top 10 list. *International Journal of Group Psychotherapy, 67*, 1–26. https://doi.org/10.1080/00207284.2016.1202678

Greene, L. R. (2019). A part of and apart from: Recent studies on the relationships of connection and disconnection to treatment outcome in the psychotherapy group. *International Journal of Group Psychotherapy, 69*, 354–360. https://doi.org/10.1080/00207284.2019.1614450

Greene, L. R. & Kaklauskas, F. J. (2020). Anti-therapeutic, defensive, regressive, and challenging group processes and dynamics. In F. J. Kaklauskas & L. R. Greene (Eds.), *Group principles of group psychotherapy: An integrated theory, research, and practice training manual* (pp. 71–86). Routledge.

Greene, L. R., Kaklauskas, F. J., & Rutan, J. S. (2020). Advanced skills. In F. J. Kaklauskas & L. R. Greene (Eds.), *Group principles of group psychotherapy: An integrated theory, research, and practice training manual* (pp. 122–140). Routledge.

Grimes, J. L & Kivlighan III, D. M. (2022). Whose multicultural orientation matters most? Examining additive and compensatory effects of the group's and leader's multicultural orientation in group therapy. *Group Dynamics: Theory, Research, and Practice, 26*(1), 58–70. https://doi.org/10.1037/gdn0000153

Griner, D., Beecher, M. E., Brown, L. B., Millet, A. J., Worthen, V., Boardman, R. D., Hansen, K., Cox, J. C., & Gleave, R. L. (2018). Practice-based evidence can help! Using the Group Questionnaire to enhance clinical practice. *Psychotherapy, 55*, 196–202. https://psycnet.apa.org/doi/10.1037/pst0000136

Gullo, S., Kivlighan Jr., D. M., Giordano, C., Di Blasi, M., Giannone, F., & Lo Coco, G. (2021). Bond and work ruptures in group counseling. *Group Dynamics: Theory, Research, and Practice, 25*(1), 29–44.

Hahn, A., Paquin, J. D., Glean, E., McQuillan, K., & Hamilton, D. (2022). Developing into a group therapist: An empirical investigation of expert group therapists' training experiences. *American Psychologist, 77*, 691–709. https://doi.org/10.1037/amp000095

Hewitt, P. L., Mikail, S. F., Flett, G. L. & Dang, S. S. (2018). Specific formulation feedback in dynamic-relational group psychotherapy of perfectionism. *Psychotherapy, 55*(2), 179–185. https://doi.org/10.1037/pst0000137

Hill, C. E. & Castonguay, L. G. (2023). Clinical, research, and policy implications for psychotherapy training and supervision in the 21st century. In L. G. Castonguay & C. E. Hill (Eds.), *Becoming better psychotherapists: Advancing training and supervision* (pp. 381–399). American Psychological Association. https://doi.org/10.1037/0000364-018.

Horvath, A. O., & Greenberg, L. S. (1989). Development and validation of the Working Alliance Inventory. *Counseling Psychology, 36*(2), 223–233. https://doi.org/10.1037/0022-0167.36.2.223

Jensen, D. R., Abbott, M. K., Beecher, M. E., Griner, D., Golightly, T. R., & Cannon, J. A. N. (2012). Taking the pulse of the group: The utilization of practice-based evidence in group psychotherapy. *Professional Psychology: Research and Practice, 43*, 388–394. http://dx.doi.org/10.1037/a0029033.

Joyce, A. S., MacNair-Semands, R., Tasca, G. A., & Ogrodniczuk, J. S. (2011). Factor structure and validity of the Therapeutic Factors Inventory-Short Form. *Group Dynamics Theory, Research, and Practice, 15*, 201–219. https://psycnet.apa.org/doi/10.1037/a0024677

Joyce, A. S. & Marmarosh, C. L. (2023). Group selection, group composition, and pre-group preparation. In R. MacNair-Semands & M. Whittingham (Eds.), *Group psychotherapy assessment and practice: A measurement-based care approach* (pp. 31–82). Routledge.

Kealy, D., Joyce, A. S., Weber, R., Ehrenthal, J. C., & Ogrodniczuk, J. S. (2019). What the patient wants: Addressing patients' treatment targets in an integrative group psychotherapy programme. *Psychology and Psychotherapy: Theory, Research and Practice, 92*, 20–38. https://doi.org/10.1111/papt.12174

Kivlighan Jr., D. M. & Kivlighan III, D. M. (2009). Training related changes in the ways that group trainees structure their knowledge of group counseling leader interventions. *Group Dynamics: Theory, Research, and Practice, 13*, 190–204. http://dx.doi.org/10.1037/a0015357

Kivlighan Jr., D. M., Markin, R. D., Stahl, J. V., & Salahuddin, N. M. (2007). Changes in the ways that group trainees structure their knowledge of group members with training. *Group Dynamics: Theory, Research, and Practice, 11*(3), 176–186. https://doi.org/10.1037/1089-2699.11.3.176

Kivlighan Jr., D. M., Miles, J. R., & Paquin, J. D. (2010). Therapeutic factors in group-counseling: Asking new questions. In R. K. Conyne (Ed.), *The Oxford handbook of group counseling* (pp. 121–136). Oxford University Press.

Kivlighan III, D. M. & Chapman, N. A. (2018). Extending the multicultural orientation (MCO) framework to group psychotherapy: A clinical illustration. *Psychotherapy.* http://dx.doi.org/10.1037/pst0000142

Kivlighan III, D. M. & Tasca, G. A. (2023). Assessing outcomes in group psychotherapy. In R. MacNair-Semands & M. Whittingham (Eds.), *Group psychotherapy assessment and practice: A measurement-based care approach* (pp. 120–161). Routledge.

Kleinberg, J. L. (1999). The supervisory alliance and the training of psychodynamic group psycho-therapists. *International Journal of Group Psychotherapy, 49*(2), 159–179. http://dx.doi.org/10.1080/00207284.1999.11491579.

Krogel, J., Burlingame, G., Chapman, C., Renshaw, T., Gleave, R., Beecher, M., & MacNair-Semands, R. (2013). The Group Questionnaire: A clinical and empirically derived measure of group relation-ship. *Psychotherapy Research, 23*, 344–354.

Lambert, M. J., Eggett, D. L., Goates, M. K., Vermeersch, D. A., & Hatch, A. L. (2013). The Outcome Questionnaire-45.2 (OQ-45.2): A comprehensive review of its use and applications. *Psychotherapy Research, 23*(2), 154–170.

Li, X., Kivlighan Jr., D. M., & Gold, P. B. (2015). Errors of commission and omission in novice group counseling trainees' knowledge structures of group counseling situations. *Journal of Counseling Psychology, 62*, 159–172. http://dx.doi.org/10.1037/cou0000070

Lese, K. P. & MacNair-Semands, R. R. (2000). The Therapeutic Factors Inventory: Development of a scale. *Group, 24*, 303–317. https://doi.org/10.1023/A:1026616626780

Leszcz, M. (2024). The evidence-based group therapy website: A commentary on opportunities, chal-lenges, and next steps. *Group Dynamics: Theory, Research, and Practice, 28*(3), 254–265. https://doi.org/10.1037/gdn0000229

MacKenzie, K. R. (1983). The clinical application of a group climate measure. In R. R. Dies & K. R. MacKenzie (Eds.), *Advances in group psychotherapy: Integrating research and practice* (pp. 159–170). International Universities Press.

MacNair-Semands, R. R. (2002). Predicting attendance and expectations for group therapy. *Group Dynamics: Theory, Research, and Practice, 6*(3), 219–228. https://doi.org/10.1037/1089-2699.6.3.219

MacNair-Semands, R. R., Ogrodniczuk, J. S., & Joyce, A. S. (2010). Structure and initial validation of a short form of the Therapeutic Factors Inventory. *International Journal of Group Psychotherapy, 60*(2), 245–281. https://doi.org/10.1521/ijgp.2010.60.2.245

MacNair-Semands, R. & Whittingham, M. (Eds). (2023). *Group psychotherapy assessment and prac-tice: A measurement-based care approach*. Routledge. https://doi.org/10.4324/9781003255482

Marmarosh, C. L. (2021). Ruptures and repairs in group psychotherapy: From theory to practice. *International Journal of Group Psychotherapy, 71*, 205–223. http://dx.doi.org/10.1080/00207284.2020.1855893.

Marmarosh, C. L. & Magenheimer, M. (2018). Applications of attachment research: Evidence you can apply to your group. *International Journal of Group Psychotherapy, 68*, 459–464. http://dx.doi.org/10.1080/00207284.2018.1456801.

Marmarosh, C. L. & Van Horn, S. M. (2010). Cohesion in counseling and psychotherapy groups. In R. K. Conyne (Ed.), *The Oxford handbook of group counseling* (pp. 137–163). Oxford University Press.

Miles, J. R., Anders, C., Kivlighan III, D. M., & Belcher Platt, A. A. (2021). Cultural ruptures: Addressing microaggressions in group therapy. *Group Dynamics: Theory, Research, and Practice, 25*, 74–88. https://doi.org/10.1037/gdn0000149

Miles, J. R., Strauss, B. M. & Greene, L. R. (2023). Process measures. In R. MacNair-Semands & M. Whittingham (Eds.), *Group psychotherapy assessment and practice* (pp. 83–119). Routledge.

Pascual-Leone, A. & Andreescu, C. (2013). Repurposing process measures to train psychotherapists: Training outcomes using a new approach. *Counselling and Psychotherapy Research, 13*, 210–219. http://dx.doi.org/10.1080/14733145.2012.739633

Riva, M. T. (2014). Supervision of group leaders. In J. L. DeLucia-Waack, C. R. Kalodner, & M. T. Riva (Eds.), *Handbook of group counseling and psychotherapy* (2nd ed., pp. 146–158). Sage Publications

Rubel, D. & Atieno Okech, J. E. (2006). The supervision of Group Work Model: Adapting the Discrimination Model for supervision of group workers. *Journal for Specialists in Group Work, 31*(2), 113–134. https://doi.org/10.1080/01933920500493597.

Rubel, D. & Atieno Okech, J. E. (2009). The expert group work supervision process: Apperception, actions, and interactions. *Journal for Specialists in Group Work, 34*, 227–250. http://dx.doi.org/10.1080/01933920903032596.

Siefert, C. J. (2019). Exploring relational episodes with the core conflictual relationship theme method to develop treatment goals, build alliance, and set client expectations in brief psychodynamic psychotherapy. *Psychotherapy, 56*(1), 28–34. https://doi.org/10.1037/pst0000212

Simpson-Southward, C., Waller, G., & Hardy, G. E. (2017). How do we know what makes for "best practice" in clinical supervision for psychological therapists? A content analysis of supervisory models and approaches. *Clinical Psychology and Psychotherapy, 24*, 1228–1245. https://doi.org/10.1002/cpp.2084

Svien, H., Burlingame, G. M., Griner, D., Beecher, M. E., & Alldredge, C. T (2021). Group therapeutic relationship change: Using routine outcome monitoring to detect the effect of single versus multiple ruptures. *Group Dynamics: Theory, Research, and Practice, 25*, 45–58. https://doi.org /10.1037/gdn0000148.

Tallberg P., Ulberg R., Johnsen Dahl, H.-S., & Hoglend P. A. (2020). Core conflictual relationship theme: The reliability of a simplified scoring procedure. *BMC Psychiatry, 20*(1), 150. https://dx.doi.org/10.1186/s12888-020-02558-4

Tasca, G. A., Mikail, S. F., & Hewitt, P. L. (2021). Assessment and case formulation. In G. A. Tasca, S. F. Mikail, & P. L. Hewitt (Eds.), *Group psychodynamic-interpersonal psychotherapy* (pp. 51–88). American Psychological Association.

Tessmer, S. S. & Storlie, C. A. (2021). Clinical supervision of group work: A conceptual review. *Journal of Counselor Practice, 12*(1), 48–72. http://dx.doi.org/10.22229/sta1212021

Watkins Jr., C. E. (2011). Does psychotherapy supervision contribute to patient outcomes? Considering thirty years of research. *Clinical Supervisor, 30*(2), 235–256. http://dx.doi.org/10.1080/07325223.2011.619417

Watkins Jr., C. E. (2014). The supervisory alliance: A half century of theory, practice, and research in critical perspective. *American Journal of Psychotherapy, 68*, 19–55. http://dx.doi.org/10.1176/appi.psychotherapy.2014.68.1.19.

Watkins Jr., C. E. (2017). How does psychotherapy supervision work? Contributions of connection, conception, allegiance, alignment, and action. *Journal of Psychotherapy Integration, 27*, 201–217. http://dx.doi.org/10.1037/int0000058

Watkins Jr., C. E., Vîşcu, L. I., & Cadariu, I.-E. (2021). Psychotherapy supervision research: On roadblocks, remedies, and recommendations. *European Journal of Psychotherapy & Counselling, 23*, 8–25. http://dx.doi.org/10.1080/13642537.2021.1881139.

Westra, H. A. & Di Bartolomeo, A. A. (2024). Developing expertise in psychotherapy: The case for process coding as clinical training. *American Psychologist, 79*(2), 163–174. https://doi.org/10.1037/amp0001139

Whittingham, M. (2018). Innovations in group assessment: How focused brief group therapy integrates formal measures to enhance treatment preparation, process, and outcomes. *Psychotherapy, 55*(2), 186–190. https://doi.org/10.1037/pst0000153

Whittingham, M., Arnold, R., & Burlingame, G. (2023). Assessment in group therapy: An introduction and overview. In R. MacNair-Semands & M. Whittingham (Eds.), *Group psychotherapy assessment and practice: A measurement-based care approach* (pp. 1–30). Routledge.

Yalom, I. D. & Leszcz, M. (2020). *The theory and practice of group psychotherapy* (6th ed.). Basic Books.

Reflections and Final Comments

Maria T. Riva, Michelle A. Collins-Greene, and Noelle L. Lefforge

Almost 20 years have passed since the *Training in Group Psychotherapy Supervision* by Bernard and Spitz (2006) was published, and 40 years since Alonso's *Silent Profession*. We can say with certainty that the supervision of group psychotherapy has continued to develop and mature. Our knowledge and understanding of this discipline have grown throughout the writing of this Manual, and we are excited to see the advances that will come in the future.

It was our goal to add to the practice and research of group psychotherapy supervision in a way that supervisors and supervisees could benefit from these pages. After reading the seven chapters in this Manual, we hope that you will find a wealth of knowledge on supervision of groups on the history, the parameters of group therapy supervision, the supervisory relationship, multicultural and diversity applications, ethics, and research. Additionally, the chapter on contemporary approaches demonstrates vignettes and highlights the many ways that supervision is and can be practiced.

We wrote chapters intending to provide readers with information on how to practice supervision, what some of the pitfalls are in the supervisory process, and directed the readers to additional sources in each chapter. In the future, we hope this Manual serves to stimulate practitioners and researchers alike in supervision of group psychotherapy and to increase the focus on the supervision component of training group psychotherapists.

Supervision of group psychotherapy is complex and multilayered, and it requires the supervisor to have competence in both supervision *and* group processes. Although the *practice* of group psychotherapy supervision and the *research* on group psychotherapy supervision often are seen as two distinct threads, actually what is needed for the field is a strong connection between research and practice so that these two complimentary prongs inform each other.

Here are some of our reflections. Research on group psychotherapy supervision is currently quite limited, and future directions need to target methodologies and content that are useful for the practice of supervision of groups. Salient topics for future research include emphases on the effective processes within the supervisory relationship, such as the type of feedback (especially corrective feedback given by the supervisor and the supervisee's response to it), the rupture and repair cycle, the supervisor's modeling of skills and how and whether those skills generalize to the supervisee's group leadership, the quality of the supervisory relationship and its relationship to the supervisee's group facilitation, and whether and how supervision connects to group psychotherapy outcomes.

Research methodologies such as case studies of supervisors and supervisees that use repeated observations of supervision across several sessions will benefit group supervisors since this method is similar to how supervision is practiced. An emphasis on supervisory constructs for clarity will also be a rich avenue of study such as defining competency,

DOI: 10.4324/9781003410621-9

supervisory alliance, and the necessary components of a skillful supervisor– supervisee relationship. Additionally, studies need to consider the nuances within the supervisor relationship and appreciate that supervision is intricate and multidimensional, such as those studies that look at investigating moderator effects. It is likely that multiple variables are interrelated to create effective supervision and not a singular or one-variable pursuit.

We appreciate that the field of group psychotherapy supervision is somewhat early in its development, although it also has come a long way in the past decade. We look to the future with much eagerness as we learn more about the advancements of group psychotherapy supervision practice and research.

Index

For Product Safety Concerns and Information please contact our EU
representative GPSR@taylorandfrancis.com
Taylor & Francis Verlag GmbH, Kaufingerstraße 24, 80331 München, Germany

www.ingramcontent.com/pod-product-compliance
Lightning Source LLC
Chambersburg PA
CBHW080554270326
41929CB00019B/3299